"It is a pleasure to commend this [...] Testament urban legends. No doub[...] ers, including some pastors and eve[...] careful analysis of each urban legend, the relevant texts, contexts, and array of significant scholarly insights. But perhaps even more important than correcting these urban legends is the careful reading of Scripture that the book models. Let us not blindly accept handed-down beliefs about the New Testament; rather, examine the text carefully for the truth of God's Word. This compelling and engaging book helps us all to do just that."

Constantine R. Campbell, associate professor of New Testament,
Trinity Evangelical Divinity School

"We live in an age of biblical illiteracy; that much is undeniable. But as someone once noted, it's not just what you don't know, it's also what you *do* know that just ain't so! David Croteau does a great job in *Urban Legends* of winsomely, kindly, and carefully correcting misconceptions about the Bible. Here is a book that will not just interest, but inform!"

Greg Gilbert, senior pastor,
Third Avenue Baptist Church, Louisville, Kentucky

"Evangelicals rightly insist that 'Scripture only' is our source of truth. Yet our interpretations of Scripture sometimes owe more to tradition than to the Bible itself. David Croteau unmasks some common interpretations that have only dubious biblical support. But he does more than debunk these 'myths' of interpretation: he also helps us understand what these passages really are saying and why they matter. Perhaps just as importantly, he encourages all of us to be more careful and attentive readers of Scripture."

Douglas Moo, Kenneth T. Wessner Professor of New Testament,
Wheaton College

"As evangelicals who believe that Scripture is inspired and authoritative, we want to preach and teach what the Bible truly teaches. Croteau takes on a number of 'urban legends' and unpacks for us the meaning of a number of texts by paying attention to context and to historical background. Even if one were to disagree with Croteau here or there, one will be challenged to support alternative interpretations. This is a valuable resource full of wise advice and persuasive exegesis, and I hope it is read widely."

Thomas R. Schreiner, James Buchanan Harrison Professor of
New Testament Interpretation and professor of biblical theology
and associate dean of the School of Theology,
The Southern Baptist Theological Seminary

"Although we prefer not to acknowledge it, all of us hold fervently to certain beliefs about what the Bible teaches that, on closer inspection, turn out to be false. No one has done a better job of demonstrating this than David Croteau in this excellent and informative book. Not everyone will enjoy reading it, as human nature typically recoils from admitting error and being forced to give up long-held and deeply cherished interpretations. But there is no virtue in error, and no Christian can be edified by it. Read this book closely and humbly. Even though you may not agree with everything Croteau asserts, your grasp of God's Word will undoubtedly increase."

Sam Storms, lead pastor for preaching and vision,
Bridgeway Church, Oklahoma City, Oklahoma

Urban Legends
of the New Testament

David A. Croteau

Leo Percer, Consulting Editor

ACADEMIC

Nashville, Tennessee

Contents

Acknowledgments vii
List of Abbreviations ix
Foreword xi
Prologue xiii

Part I
Urban Legends in the Gospels

1. There Was No Room at the Inn 3
2. We Three Kings of Orient Are 9
3. Shepherds Were Societal Outcasts 15
4. Jesus Was a Carpenter 21
5. Jesus Died When He Was Thirty-Three 27
6. All Giving Must Be Done in Secret 33
7. Do Not Judge Others 37
8. Jesus' Most Famous Quote Is John 3:16 43
9. Hell Referred to a First-Century Garbage Dump near Jerusalem 49
10. The Gospel of John Never Refers to Repentance 55
11. The "Eye of a Needle" Was a Gate in Jerusalem 61
12. When Two Are Gathered in Prayer, God Will Be There 67
13. Jesus Sweat Drops of Blood 73
14. Jesus Was Flogged Once 79
15. *Agapē* Is a Superior Love to *Phileō* 85
16. "Go" Is Not a Command in the Great Commission 91

Part II
Urban Legends in The Acts of the Apostles, the Epistles, and Revelation

17. *Repent* Means "to Change Your Mind" 99
18. The Philippian Jailer "Just Believed" and Was Saved. 105
19. Paul Was a Tent Maker. 111
20. Jews (and Jesus) Primarily Spoke Hebrew in Jesus' Day 117
21. The Gospel Is Dynamite 125
22. Just Say You Believe in Jesus and You Will Be Saved. 129
23. Synagogues Had Men and Women Seated Separately. 135
24. Grace Is Unmerited Favor 139
25. Good Works Are Optional for Christians 145
26. Pastors Are Required to Do the Ministry of the Church 151
27. Jesus Emptied Himself of the Glory of Heaven 157
28. We Can Do Anything Through Christ Who Gives Us Strength. 163
29. Abstain from All Appearance of Evil 167
30. Hell Is the Absence of God. 175
31. A Divorced Man Cannot Be a Pastor 181
32. Money Is Evil 189
33. A Pastor's Children Must Be Saved 195
34. Christians Are Commanded to Tithe 201
35. Christians Are Commanded to Go to Church 205
36. Women Should Not Wear Jewelry 211
37. First John 1:9 Is a Formula for Salvation 217
38. Christians Should Not Allow Cults into Their Homes 223
39. God Would Rather You Be Cold Toward Him than Lukewarm 227
40. Accept Jesus into Your Heart to Be Saved 233

Epilogue. 239
Name Index 243
Subject Index 247
Scripture Index 249

Acknowledgments

This book is the culmination of so many conversations with friends, so many articles and books read, and so many classroom dialogues that thanking everyone is beyond my ability. Several students have assisted in research for this volume: Rory Chapman, Mark Dickson, Scott Holcombe, James Mac-Donald, Zack Melder, Eric Mitchell, Jordan Steffaniak, and Phil Thompson. Shane Kraeger's help in researching many of the bibliographies was invaluable. Many of the students in courses I taught at Liberty University, particularly New Testament Backgrounds, were helpful dialogue partners.

The opportunity afforded by the pastors at Heritage Baptist Church in Lynchburg, Virginia, to teach a Bible study class covering twenty-six of these topics was extremely helpful. The feedback gained throughout the course by the members (and some pastors) was priceless.

Leo Percer, the managing editor, has been helpful in reading through the entire manuscript and making many fruitful comments along the way. Others who have provided helpful feedback include Larry Dixon, John Harvey, Rob Stansberry, Tom Medeiros, Jeff Philpott, Mike Naylor, and Gaylen Leverett. Kerry Poulton has earned my gratitude for her assistance as well.

As always, my family (Ann, Danielle, and D. J.) has been understanding as I worked through the manuscript. May the Lord bless this effort to accurately interpret his Word.

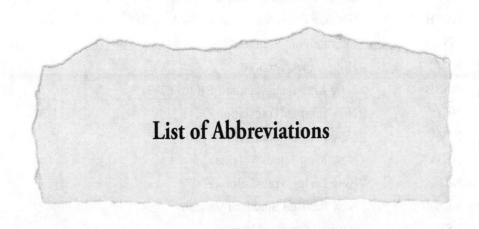

List of Abbreviations

BDAG · Bauer, Walter. *A Greek-English Lexicon of the New Testament and Other Early Christian Literature*. 3rd ed. Revised and edited by F. W. Danker, W. F. Arndt, and F. W. Gingrich. Chicago: University of Chicago Press, 2000.

BECNT Baker Exegetical Commentary on the New Testament

Louw and Nida Louw, Johannes P., and Eugene A. Nida, eds. *Greek-English Lexicon of the New Testament Based on Semantic Domains*. 2 vols. New York: United Bible Societies, 1988, 1989.

EBC Expositor's Bible Commentary

HNTC Holman New Testament Commentary

ICC International Critical Commentary

NAC New American Commentary

NICNT New International Commentary on the New Testament

NIGTC New International Greek Testament Commentary

PNTC Pelican New Testament Commentaries

WBC Word Biblical Commentary

Bible Translations

ASV American Standard Version

ESV   English Standard Version (2011)

HCSB   Holman Christian Standard Bible (2009)

ISV   International Standard Version

KJV   King James Version

NASB   New American Standard Bible (1995)

NET   New English Translation

NIV   New International Version (2011)

NKJV   New King James Version

NLT   New Living Translation (2007)

NRSV   New Revised Standard Version

RSV   Revised Standard Version

YLT   Young's Literal Translation

All Scripture quotations are from the HCSB unless otherwise noted.

Foreword

For almost a decade I have had the joy of teaching hermeneutics in a college and seminary setting. Often we define this discipline as the art and science of biblical interpretation. The class is, in a real sense, foundational to the rest of the program of study our students will engage. That is why we encourage our students to take it in their first semester of study if at all possible. The primary goal is to help them "rightly [divide] the word of truth" (2 Tim 2:15 NKJV), the Bible. Because we operate from the presuppositional conviction that the Bible is the inerrant and infallible Word of God, we believe we have a moral and spiritual obligation to honor the authorially intended meaning of the text. After all, the Holy Spirit of God is the ultimate author of Scripture. Bible interpreters have a holy assignment that must be undertaken with gravity and seriousness. Eternal truth is before us. Human souls and their destiny hang in the balance.

As we "do hermeneutics," we teach our students to follow several tried and proven principles. These include: (1) Observation: what do I see? (2) Interpretation: what does it mean? (3) Application: how does it work? Further, I encourage my students to ask five theological/practical questions that have a definite ordering and, in a sense, follow what we call The Grand Redemptive (or Narrative) Story Line of the Bible:

Creation-Fall-Redemption-New Creation (or Restoration)

Those five questions are: (1) What does this text teach us about God? (2) What does this text teach us about fallen humanity? (3) How does this text point to Christ? (4) What does God want us to know? (5) What does God want us to do? We encourage them to take a good hard look at the text before consulting resources like commentaries, Bible dictionaries, encyclopedias, etc. We urge them to learn the biblical languages, if at all possible, and to read a text in multiple translations like the HCSB, ESV, NASB, NIV, and NLT.

As they are putting all of this together, we remind them over and over of a vitally important principle: context is king. You must know both the immediate (what goes right before and after the text you are studying) and the far (chapters, book, testament) contexts. And this is so crucial: what is the genre or type of literature you are examining?

All of this may, at first, sound like a daunting task. However, it is much like riding a bicycle. The more you do it, the better you get, and the faster you can go! The key to developing the skills of a good Bible interpreter is practice, practice, and more practice.

I share all of this because what I have described above is masterfully displayed in this book by David Croteau. *Urban Legends of the New Testament* is a model of biblical scholarship and hermeneutics. Each of the forty legends David tackles is addressed with care and respect for the authority of Scripture. His practice of careful and humble hermeneutics is a model worthy of emulation. You will not have to agree with every conclusion he reaches. However, you will have to do your homework to swim against the tide of the interpretation he reaches.

David recognizes that while we do have an inerrant Bible, we do not have inerrant interpreters! However, when we approach the Word of God with good interpretive tools, we can quickly narrow the options and, more often than not, make a compelling case the majority of Bible students will agree on. Further, we can put to rest "urban legends" that are inaccurate understandings of God's Word, misunderstandings that sometimes bring significant hurt to the bride of Christ.

Dr. Croteau is a graduate of Southeastern Baptist Theological Seminary. I am proud of that fact. This superb treatment has only increased my gratitude to our God for how he is using this fine servant for his glory and the good of his people.

Daniel L. Akin
President
Southeastern Baptist Theological Seminary
Wake Forest, North Carolina

Prologue

What's an Urban Legend?

In 1876 a whaling ship named *Velocity* was sailing off the coast of Australia near New Caledonia. Those on board saw some rough water and thought they saw something sandy. They marked the area on their map charts and named the island Sandy Island.[1] After that other map makers saw *Velocity's* map, and Sandy Island started making its way into maps. In 2012, if you had looked at the midpoint between Australia and New Caledonia on Google Maps, you would have found the island. A scientist in Australia thought the water was too deep at that location for an island to be present. So he decided to search for the island. But when he arrived at the location, *there was no island*. The whaling boat in 1876 made a mistake, and everyone afterward has copied the mistake for over 130 years. No one had double-checked *Velocity's* map for *130 years*. We don't know how they made the error. Perhaps they were mistaken about their location. Regardless, the island's existence has become an urban legend. An urban legend is a commonly circulated myth, repeated throughout the culture as common knowledge, but which isn't true.

Interpretations of certain passages in the New Testament have fallen victim to this. Somehow something false is stated, and it gets heard and passed down without someone checking all the facts. Was there really a gate in Jerusalem

---

[1] Some accounts refer to it as Sable Island.

called the "Needle Gate" (cf. Mark 10:15)? I've heard this preached numerous times. But what is the evidence for this supposed gate?

The New Testament commands us to be "approved to God, a worker who doesn't need to be ashamed, correctly teaching the word of truth" (2 Tim 2:15). The question we will be asking is not whether you have heard some of the supposed legends I will be unraveling, because you might have heard the questionable interpretation repeated five, ten, or twenty times! The real question is this: can the interpretation be justified? Is there a good reason this interpretation has been passed down and taught this way?

You may find that I disagree with an interpretation you have heard from your pastor or favorite preacher. This does not, of course, mean they are bad preachers. I am simply disagreeing with their interpretation of a specific passage. In fact, many of the people who have promulgated these legends (and I won't necessarily tell you who they are) are pastors and scholars I highly appreciate and love. Let's focus on the correct interpretation of each passage and not on who has taught a legendary interpretation.

The Structure of Each Chapter

The title of each chapter is actually the legend itself, not the correct interpretation of the text(s) at hand. If a certain passage has more than one legend connected to it, only one will be included in the chapter title. Each chapter will begin with a presentation of the legend. I am going to present the legend *as if* I believe it. Then I will try to prove to you that it is an invalid interpretation of the passage. I will explain some problems I see with that particular interpretation and then tell you what I believe the text means.

Cocaine and Coca-Cola: Types of Urban Legends

There are different types of legends. The legend of Sandy Island is one without any solid evidence. We can trace its historical origins, but we are not sure why the legend began. Another type of legend is one that is part truth but doesn't tell the whole story.

For example, take the following legend: Coca-Cola contained cocaine from 1885 to 1929. Is that true? Yes and no. Yes, in that while Coca-Cola technically did have derivatives of the coca leaf in it (which is what cocaine is made from),[2] that isn't the entire story. In fact, the amount of coca leaf derivative in Coca-Cola was so miniscule by the late 1920s, about twenty-five million gallons of Coca-Cola syrup might have six-hundreths of an ounce of coca leaf

---

[2] That's the "Coca" part in the name, from "cocaine." The "Cola" part of the name comes from kola nuts.

derivative.[3] In other words, simply saying "Coca-Cola originally contained cocaine" has an element of truth but is misleading because the amount was ridiculously small. So while the Sandy Island legend relates to mistaken legends, the Coca-Cola legend refers to misleading legends. Which is which in the following chapters? You'll have to read to find out!

Addressing Legends

Let me offer a warning. Some readers might be tempted to use the information in this book as a sledgehammer upon hearing someone preach one of these legendary interpretations. In the epilogue I will provide some advice about how to address legends when you hear them.

I was honored to be able to teach through some of these chapters at Heritage Baptist Church in Lynchburg, Virginia, in the Spring of 2013. You will notice ten QR codes placed throughout this book. By scanning the code with your mobile device, you can view a short video clip summarizing the content of that chapter. If you do not have a mobile device, the videos clips are also available at http://www.bhpublishinggroup.com/.

---

[3] Cf. Mark Pendergast, *For God, Country, and Coca-Cola: The Definitive History of the Great American Soft Drink and the Company That Makes It*, 3rd ed. (New York: Basic Books, 2013), 149–50; James Hamblin, "Why We Took Cocaine Out of Soda," *The Atlantic* (January 31, 2013), accessed May 20, 2014, www.theatlantic.com/health/archive/2013/01/why-we-took-cocaine-out-of-soda/272694, and Barbara Mikkelson, "Cocaine-Cola," *Snopes* (May 19, 2011), accessed May 20, 2014, www.snopes.com/cokelore/cocaine.asp.

PART I

Urban Legends in the Gospels

CHAPTER 1

There Was No Room at the Inn

Luke 2:1–7

The Legendary Teaching on Luke 2:1–7

Joseph was required to take his betrothed wife, Mary, to Bethlehem, the city of his ancestors. It was a long journey, probably three or four days' travel, and Mary was already far along in her pregnancy. They traveled south through Israel, and as they approached Bethlehem, Mary started to feel the baby pressing. Joseph began to panic, and as they entered the town of Bethlehem, he went from house to house looking for a place for them to stay. Everyone was turning them away, door after door, house after house.

Carrying Mary, he finally received permission to use someone's stable, a place where only animals should be kept. Joseph took Mary inside, and she gave birth to Jesus. Jesus should have been placed on a throne, but he was rejected from the beginning, being placed in a feeding trough for animals. There was no place for him at the inn, and there was no place for him in many of their hearts.

Introduction: Unraveling the Legend

I love the movie *The Nativity*, but the history behind some of the details in the movie and the legendary teaching above do not come from Scripture. Some of it comes from the *Protoevangelium of James*, a short book written around AD 200. It was not written by James the brother of Jesus or James son of Zebedee. They had died long before AD 200. It contains a fanciful and fascinating retelling of the birth of Jesus. It appears to be the earliest document that portrays the birth of Jesus as an emergency upon approaching Bethlehem. In fact, the way the story reads in the *Protoevangelium of James*, they are about three miles from the town when Joseph found a cave for Mary to give birth in, not ever reaching Bethlehem. There are several problems with this depiction of the birth of Jesus. For example, if it is true, then Jesus was not born in Bethlehem and the prophecy about that did not get fulfilled (cf. Matt 2:6 and Mic 5:2). Regardless, there are two problems with the traditional understanding of the birth story about Jesus, particularly the idea (1) that there was no room at the inn, and (2) that they had a hard time finding a place to stay.

The Historical Setting

The traditional portrayal has Joseph, a descendant of the famous King David, going back to Bethlehem, the city of David, and having a hard time finding a place to stay. On the surface that seems hard to believe. Even with the census taking place, it's difficult to believe he arrived in Bethlehem and was rejected. Also, Mary had relatives nearby. Luke 1:39–40 mentions Mary staying with Zechariah and Elizabeth, who lived in the hill country of Judea. Bethlehem was a small town in the region of Judea. Zechariah and Elizabeth were probably fairly nearby. But *if* Mary went into labor suddenly as they were approaching Bethlehem, her relatives being nearby wouldn't help much.

Hospitality was greatly important in that culture. It would have been unthinkable for a pregnant Jewish woman to arrive in a city and have people turn a blind eye to her. That might not be unthinkable today, but we are not as hospitable as first-century Israel. Many verses in the Old Testament talk about the importance of hospitality.[1] If someone knocked on the door of a house and the person said, "Go away," the inhospitable person would be shunned by that community. That is how seriously hospitality was taken back then.

Urgency, the Manger, and the Inn

Was there an urgency upon approaching or entering Bethlehem? Luke 2:6 says, "*While they were there*, the time came for her to give birth" (emphasis added), not "as they were approaching." He doesn't mention whether they were there for five minutes or five weeks, but it could allow for both. Luke does not portray that her time for giving birth came as she was approaching the city, so there was no reason for panic or urgency. There is no evidence that the baby was pressing as they arrived. But if they got to Bethlehem and Mary was fine, why couldn't Joseph find adequate housing? Zechariah and Elizabeth were nearby, they were in a hospitable culture, and he was from the line of David. Why did he put his pregnant wife into a stable filled with animals?

---

[1] For example, see Genesis 18–19; Exod 23:9; Lev 19:33–34; Deut 10:19; Isa 58:6–10; Ezek 16:49.

The HCSB says they "laid Him in a feeding trough" (Luke 2:7). When you read "feeding trough," images of a stable probably come to mind. However, there are three options for the location of the feeding trough. First, feeding troughs were placed outside homes in a stable. This is the traditional understanding: wealthy homes in first-century Israel would have a stable. Countering the traditional view are two other options. Understanding how houses were typically constructed will help comprehend the other options.

A first-century house in Israel would have a large family room where the family would eat, cook, sleep, and do general living. At the end of the room there would be some steps down to a lower level, going down only a couple of feet. That lower level would be the "animal room" of the house. There was no wall separating the rooms, just one room with two parts: the family room and the animal room. They would construct it so it slanted slightly toward the animal area for easy cleaning because the exterior door would be in the animal area. On the raised surface in the family room would be a feeding trough for the larger animals carved out of the floor. The larger animals in the animal area, like a cow or a donkey, could walk over and eat out of this trough. The smaller animals, like sheep, would have a smaller manger that would be carved out of the floor in the animal room, or the family might have a wooden trough that could be brought inside.

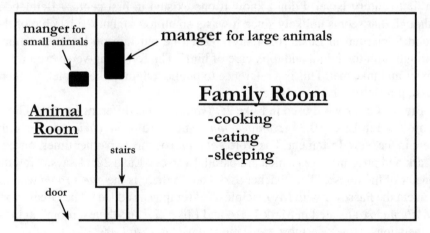

Scripture offers no explicit description of this design, but archeological evidence and implicit evidence from Scripture suggest that this was the general design of houses. Animals are mentioned being inside houses in a few biblical stories. First Samuel 28:24 describes Saul going to the witch of Endor. As they were talking, she decided to slaughter the "fattened calf *in* the house" (ESV, emphasis added). Judges 11 tells the story of Jephthah making a vow. He asked the Lord to help him win the battle. Then, if the Lord helped him, he promised to sacrifice the first thing that came out of his house (Judg 11:31). When he arrived home, the first thing out of his house was his daughter. Since animals were kept in the house, he probably expected a calf or sheep to come out.

The design of one-room houses can be seen in verses like Matthew 5:15, where Jesus mentions a light on a lampstand giving light to all who are in the house. If there were multiple stories, multiple rooms, hallways, and bathrooms, that would be impossible. But when the house has one big room with one section being a little lower for the entrance and animals, it becomes clear how a light on a lampstand would give light to the whole house.

The larger manger is in the family room, and the smaller manger is in the animal room. These are the other two options for its location. The most likely location for Jesus' manger is the one in the family room. But the traditional understanding of the story doesn't say Jesus was born in a house. It says the family was turned away from the inn so they went to a stable. Why am I describing a house?

Notice how the HCSB translates Luke 2:7: "And laid Him in a feeding trough—because there was no room for them at the lodging place." Most translations use the word "inn" rather than "lodging place." The word "inn" or the phrase "lodging place" bring to mind the idea of a hotel, which did exist in first-century Israel. I don't know if one existed in first-century Bethlehem (though that seems unlikely since it was a small town), but the parable of the good Samaritan in Luke 10:34 says, "Then he put him on his own animal, brought him to an inn, and took care of him." The following verse even references an innkeeper. This is a reference to public lodging, like a hotel. So there were inns in first-century Israel.

But the Greek word used in Luke 2:7 (*kataluma*) is different from the Greek word used in Luke 10:34 (*pandocheion*). The word *pandocheion* occurs only here in the New Testament. The word *kataluma* occurs two other times, once in Mark and once in Luke (which are parallel verses). Luke 22:11 says, "Tell the owner of the house, 'The Teacher asks you, "Where is the *guest room* where I can eat the Passover with My disciples?"'" (emphasis added). The Greek word *kataluma* is translated in Mark 14:14 and Luke 22:11 as "guest room" in most translations. However, most translations have "inn" in Luke 2:7.

A Closer Look at Luke 2:7

The NIV says, "Because there was no *guest room* available for them" (Luke 2:7, emphasis added). This is probably the most accurate translation of Luke 2:7. It was the only translation I examined that had *kataluma* translated the same way in all three places. The guest room in Luke 2:7 most likely referred to a room added on to a single-story house. The guest room (*kataluma*) would have its own exterior entrance.

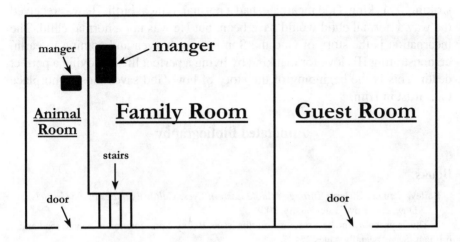

Another piece of evidence implies that Joseph and Mary had attained adequate accommodations when they got to Bethlehem and were not in a stable. The shepherds were told by an angel that they would see a baby lying in a feeding trough (Luke 2:12). After the shepherds saw this, Luke says, "The shepherds returned, glorifying and praising God for all they had seen and heard, just as they had been told" (Luke 2:20). In a culture that prized hospitality so highly, it would have been unimaginable that the shepherds would have walked away and left the family with a newborn baby in a stable. The more you understand Middle Eastern hospitality, the more powerful that verse becomes.

Joseph took Mary to Bethlehem for the census ordered by Caesar Augustus. He was not rushed to find a place. When he arrived, the guest room was already full, so he and Mary had to stay in the family room with everyone else. When it came time for Mary to give birth, she did so in the family room. They placed the baby Jesus into the feeding trough for animals located in the floor of the family room. There was no cave, no stable, and probably no wooden trough.

Application

If we tell the story of Jesus' birth with an inaccurately reconstructed historical backdrop, skeptics to Christianity will find out. When they point out the unbiblical and unhistorical picture being painted, it can cause panic and doubt for the believer. I've seen this happen with some of the legends in this book. Let's dedicate ourselves to being precise and accurate about the way we portray the birth of the Savior.

The story of Jesus' birth is not a story of rejection, a harsh innkeeper, or an incompetent husband. It is the story of a normal birth in humble surroundings. There was no palace and no throne. The absolute "normalness" of the birth is striking. This king, God incarnate, had a normal, typical birth. He was received the way a normal child would have been, but He was not a normal child. The incarnation is the story of God the Son leaving heaven and coming to earth, demonstrating His love for mankind by living a perfect life and dying a perfect death. This is the beginning of the story of how God saves those who place their trust in Him.

Annotated Bibliography

Books

Bailey, Kenneth E. *Jesus Through Middle Eastern Eyes: Cultural Studies in the Gospels.* Downers Grove: InterVarsity, 2008.

This is probably the best resource on this issue. Bailey's presentation is easy to read and brilliant. See especially pages 25–37.

Journals

Bailey, Kenneth E. "The Manger and the Inn: The Cultural Background of Luke 2:7." *Theological Review* 2, no. 2 (1979): 33–44.

This immensely helpful article is available online at www.tinyurl.com/MangerInn.

Carlson, Stephen C. "The Accommodations of Joseph and Mary in Bethlehem: κατάλυμα in Luke 2.7." *New Testament Studies* 56, no. 3 (2010): 326–42.

Carlson's study demonstrates the unlikelihood of Jesus being born in a stable, though his conclusion slightly differs from the one above.

Websites

MacPhail, Bryn. "From a Throne to a Feeding Trough." *MacPhail's Manuscripts.* Accessed July 14, 2014. www.reformedtheology.ca/luke2a.htm.

A helpful summary of the issue at hand.

Sprinkle, Preston. "Was Jesus Born at an Inn?" *Theology for Real Life.* December 15, 2011. Accessed July 12, 2014. www.facultyblog.eternitybiblecollege.com/2011/12/was-jesus-born-at-an-inn.

Sprinkle's discussion on the inn is well done, though I disagree with his (admittedly) speculative conclusion.

CHAPTER 2

We Three Kings of Orient Are

Matthew 2:1

The Legendary Teaching on Matthew 2:1

"We three kings of Orient are, bearing gifts we traverse afar. Field and fountain, moor and mountain, following yonder star." Probably written in 1857, but not appearing in print until 1863, this famous Christmas carol was written by John Henry Hopkins, who became a priest in the Episcopal Church. It was the featured song in a Christmas pageant he organized. Reverend Hopkins was able to write lyrics and a tune that has captured the text of Scripture so well. What a wonderful carol!

Introduction: Unraveling the Legend

The opening line of this hymn brings to mind three questions.

1. "We three"—Were there three?
2. "kings"—Were they kings?
3. "from Orient are"—Were they from the Orient?

When I was in college, I was listening to J. Vernon McGee on the radio while driving to a friend's house. While teaching on Matthew 2, he mentioned that there were not three wise men. My car swerved on the road as I exclaimed out loud: "Not three wise men?!" Every manger scene I had ever seen had three wise men. I wondered if he was denying the Bible. Then he read the verse, and I thought, *Why did I think there were three wise men?* I was simply stunned, shaken in my faith.

I want to investigate the opening line of this Christmas carol and compare it to what is stated in Scripture. Matthew 2:1 says, "After Jesus was born in

Bethlehem of Judea in the days of King Herod, wise men from the east arrived unexpectedly in Jerusalem." Verse 7 says, "Then Herod secretly summoned the wise men and asked them the exact time the star appeared." Verse 16 mentions the wise men two more times, for a total of four times in this passage. What can we glean about the "three kings from the Orient" in Matthew 2:1? The word translated "wise men" is plural, so there was more than one. But some translations have "magi," the plural of "magus," referring to priests in ancient Media and Persia. No translation used "king." Also, the text says they came "from the east." No translation says "Orient." That's what Scripture says.

Background Texts on the Wise Men

Most scholars believe the mention of *three gifts* has caused many people in church history to assume there were three wise men. In fact, the "three wise men" have been given names: Melchior (supposedly King of Arabia), Balthazar (supposedly King of Persia), and Caspar or Gaspar (supposedly King of India). Three ancient documents mention some details about these "three kings." The *Armenian Infancy Gospel*, which was written around AD 600, mentions the three names. The second document was a Greek text written in Alexandria, Egypt, around AD 500. The translation into Latin (titled *Excerpta Latina Barbari*) includes these names as well. Some people have proposed that these are legitimate texts on which to base this conclusion, but there is another document many people aren't as familiar with: *Revelation of the Magi*. This document was written in the eighth century in Syriac. It was kept in the Vatican library for many years and was recently translated into English.[1] The translator believes the text goes back to a mid-second century document (I remain unconvinced). It was written as if the wise men themselves were writing it. While it is not a reliable source for interpreting Scripture, it has some interesting details regarding the wise men. First, what characterizes the magi is that they pray in silence, which was abnormal during that time period. Second, there were twelve or more wise men, maybe even forty or fifty in the group. Third, they were from Shir, possibly a reference to China. Fourth, they were descendants of Seth, Adam and Eve's third son. Being descendants of Seth, they had knowledge of an old prophecy passed down by word of mouth about a star that would appear proclaiming that God would come in human form. Those are some salient points from the *Revelation of the Magi*, an unreliable source for interpreting the New Testament text.

---

[1] Brent Landau, *Revelation of the Magi: The Lost Tale of the Wise Men's Journey to Bethlehem* (New York: HarperOne, 2010).

All the theories and traditions advocating there being *three* wise men are late and unreliable documents. An alternate tradition states there were at least twelve, but there wasn't a uniform tradition throughout church history.

I believe it is unlikely that there were only three wise men. While I don't have proof, I think there is some compelling evidence. There is no compelling reason to believe there were three wise men. On the one hand, if three men were traveling hundreds of miles with expensive gifts, it would seem to be *unwise* for them to go in a group of only three. On the other hand, they could have had an entourage go with them. While, theoretically, there could have been three, there could also have been thirty. We simply do not know the precise number.

Who Were They, and Where Were They From?

Were these men kings, magi, or wise men? They are known as kings because of the Christmas carol, but church father Tertullian (died AD 225) referred to them as kings as well. We don't know for certain why he believed that. Regardless, in Daniel 2 the Greek word for *magi* is used to translate a Hebrew term that meant "astrologer" (Dan 2:2, 10). Several hundred years before the New Testament, *magi* referred to astrologers, but words can change in meaning through time. By the time of the New Testament, magi were most likely non-Jewish, religious, and (possibly) priestly. They were skilled in several areas including astronomy, astrology, dream interpretation, fortune telling, and magic or divination. This is what characterized the magi.

The magi in Matthew 2 are likely not Jewish since they were ignorant of Old Testament Scriptures. They asked Herod to inform them about the birthplace of the Messiah. They appear to be religious scholars skilled in astronomy. They had some dreams while they were visiting Jesus, so they were apparently skilled in dream interpretation. They probably interpreted the stars to indicate that a great Jewish king was about to be born. New Testament scholar Craig Blomberg says, "They combined astronomical observation with astrological speculation."[2]

Were the wise men from the Orient? The answer could depend on what you mean by the word *Orient*. Years ago that word referred to any where east of the Mediterranean. Now it typically refers to East Asia, near China. If the latter definition is meant, then the answer is probably no. However, they were from an area east of Israel. Given that astronomy was prevalent in Persia, and that it seems to have played a role in leading the wise men to Israel, perhaps a case can be made that wise men did come from Persia. However, the three gifts

---

[2] Craig Blomberg, *Matthew*, NAC (Nashville: B&H, 1992), 62.

they brought (gold, frankincense, and myrrh) connect them to Arabia. Since they appear to know something about Judaism, maybe there was a community of Jews in their homeland who supplied them with Old Testament passages (like Num 24:17) that led them to read the stars as pointing to the birth of a Jewish king.[3] That would point to Babylon as their origin. In the end we can't be certain, but I think Babylon and Arabia are most likely. This journey would probably have taken several months from deciding they wanted to go, getting the supplies together, and making the long journey.

There may have been three wise men, or there may have been thirty. They weren't kings, but astronomers, astrologers, and dream interpreters. They were from the east, but the term *Orient* is misleading.

The Main Point of Matthew 2: Worshipping the King

Matthew's focus is not the number, origin, or identity of the wise men, and that is probably why he is so ambiguous about some of the details we want to know. His main point is communicating that these non-Jewish men came to *worship* Jesus the king. Matthew 2:2 says, "Where is He who has been born King of the Jews? For we saw His star in the east and have come to worship Him." They are seeking to worship a king.

Jesus' receiving worship is a minor motif in Matthew's Gospel. It is mentioned at least six times, including this passage: Matthew 2:2, 8, 11; 14:33; 28:9, 17. Near the beginning of Matthew's Gospel, in 2:2, he mentions the wise men coming from outside the land of Israel to worship Jesus as king. Herod refused to worship Jesus, but the wise men seek to worship him. Then at the end of the Gospel, in Matthew 28:17, Matthew mentions that the disciples worshipped Jesus. That is followed by a command for the disciples to go outside the land of Israel to teach others about Jesus. The themes in 2:2 and 28:17 are overlapping: people outside the land of Israel and worshipping Jesus connect these two passages.

Another motif in the Gospel of Matthew is Jesus as king. In Matthew 2, two kings are discussed. In 2:1 Matthew mentions that Herod was the king. In 2:2 Jesus is referred to as "King of the Jews." The next verse and 2:9 mention Herod as king. Matthew 2 has four references to "king," and only one of those refers to Jesus. Matthew is preparing the stage for the conflict Herod is going to have with Jesus and the slaying of the boys two years and younger in Bethlehem and its vicinity (Matt 2:16).

---

[3] Allen C. Myers, ed. "Wise Men," in *The Eerdmans Bible Dictionary* (Grand Rapids: Eerdmans, 1987), 1,061. See also Chad Brand, Charles Draper, Archie England, et al., eds., "Magi," in *Holman Illustrated Bible Dictionary* (Nashville: B&H, 2003), 1066.

The Old Testament has a prophecy foretelling the coming of a king in the line of David. Matthew presents Jesus as the fulfillment of these prophecies, particularly in three places. Matthew 1:6 provides a genealogy declaring Jesus as a descendant of "David the king" (ESV). Matthew 21:5 cites a prophecy from Zechariah 9:9 ("your King is coming to you"), which is fulfilled by Jesus. Matthew explicitly connects Jesus to the Old Testament prophecy about a coming king. Matthew's portrayal of Jesus' crucifixion includes several references to the theme of Jesus as king. In 27:11, Pilate asks Jesus if he is "King of the Jews." In 27:29, Jesus is mocked as king. In 27:37, the charge for the crucifixion put on the sign on the cross says, "THIS IS JESUS THE KING OF THE JEWS." A few verses later (27:42) Jesus is mocked as "King of Israel." The entire crucifixion scene is filled with this theme of mocking Jesus as King. Matthew 2 and the visit of the magi serves to reinforce the Matthean motif of Jesus as king.

Application

Jesus is our King. As King, he rules over everything, including our lives. Therefore, we are to live in submission to our ruling King.

Also, Jesus deserves our worship. While worship should be reserved for God alone, Jesus deserves our worship because he is God. We should worship him with all of our lives, thoughts, decisions, relationships, attitudes, and emotions. Whether we are at work or at play, all of life should be considered an act of worship.

Annotated Bibliography

Commentaries

Blomberg, Craig. *Matthew*. NAC. Nashville: B&H, 1992.
   Blomberg's readable commentary on Matthew is good on textual and historical issues. See especially pages 61–66.

Books

Bailey, Kenneth E. *Jesus through Middle Eastern Eyes: Cultural Studies in the Gospels*. Downers Grove: InterVarsity, 2008.
   Bailey succinctly summarizes the issue at hand, deciding that the men came from Arabia. See especially pages 51–53.

Dictionary Articles

Witherington, Ben, III. "Birth of Jesus." Pages 60–74 in *Dictionary of Jesus and the Gospels*. Edited by J. B. Green and S. McKnight. Downers Grove: InterVarsity, 1992.

Witherington masterfully summarizes all pertinent issues involved. See especially pages 72–73.

Journals

Maalouf, Tony T. "Were the Magi from Persia or Arabia?" *Bibliotheca Sacra* 156 (1999): 423–42.

In trying to decipher the origin of the wise men, Maalouf touches on many of the issues discussed here in a nontechnical manner. He believes the origin is Arabia.

CHAPTER 3

Shepherds Were Societal Outcasts

Luke 2:8–12

The Legendary Teaching on Luke 2:8–12

The Christmas story is familiar to most American Christians, including a manger, a baby, three wise men, animals, and shepherds. It's so familiar to us that nothing seems out of place. Luke 2:8–12 says, "In the same region, shepherds were staying out in the fields and keeping watch at night over their flock. Then an angel of the Lord stood before them, and the glory of the Lord shone around them,  and they were terrified. But the angel said to them, 'Don't be afraid, for look, I proclaim to you good news of great joy that will be for all the people. Today a Savior, who is Messiah the Lord, was born for you in the city of David. This will be the sign for you: You will find a baby wrapped snugly in cloth and lying in a feeding trough.'" The original readers of Luke's Gospel had a different perspective on this scene. From their perspective it would be scandalous to think God could possibly give shepherds a birth announcement heralding the birth of the Christ as a newborn baby. Why would God invite shepherds when he could have invited Herod the Great, the high priest, or Caesar? Who were shepherds?

Shepherds were societal outcasts with no money, no education, and no culture. They were to be avoided socially. If you were walking down the street and a shepherd was walking toward you, you would cross to the other side of the street. You wouldn't want to be near a shepherd. In fact, they couldn't be judges, and their testimony was invalid in court.

They were also religious outcasts. Their work made them ceremonially unclean so they were not allowed in the temple. They were even considered to be as low and dirty as prostitutes. These men had been the outcasts of Jewish society their whole lives, and God invited them to the most important birth in the history of the world. He didn't invite Caesar, Herod the Great, or the Jewish leaders; he invited shepherds. And this is a theme in Luke's Gospel: God reaching out to societal outcasts—the poor, women, and slaves. God seeks those who live their lives on the fringe of society. Look at the men Jesus chose to be his disciples. Many of them were untrained and uneducated fishermen. Another was a Jewish traitor: a tax collector. Jesus lifted up those on the fringe and made them leaders of his ministry on earth. Realizing this should give us hope. If God reaches out to those on the fringe, certainly he can reach out to you and me.

Introduction: Sources for the Legend

The conclusion that shepherds were societal outcasts has been reached by many scholars, and they have repeated this concept over and over again. For example, Farrar said in 1893, "Shepherds at this time were a despised class." Strack and Billerbeck (1924) said, "The shepherds were despised people." Stein (1992) said, "In general, shepherds were dishonest and unclean according to the standards of the law. They represent the outcasts and sinners for whom Jesus came." Butler (2000) said, "Shepherding had changed from a family business as in David's time to a despised occupation." Finally, Utley (2004) said, "The rabbis considered them to be religious outcasts and their testimony was not admissible in court." Those are just a few quotes from scholars throughout the last 100 plus years.[1]

Three main sources are used to reach this conclusion. First, Aristotle was cited as saying that among people, "the laziest are shepherds, who lead an idle life, and get their subsistence without trouble from tame animals; their flocks wandering from place to place in search of pasture, they are compelled to follow them, cultivating a sort of living farm."[2] Aristotle declared that shepherding is easy because of the animals involved.

---

[1] F. W. Farrar, *The Gospel According to St Luke*, Cambridge Greek Testament for Schools and Colleges (Cambridge: Cambridge University Press, 1893), 112; Herman L. Strack and Paul Billerbeck, *Kommentar zum Neuen Testament aus Talmud und Midrasch*, 6 vols. (München, Germany: Beck, 1924), 2:113 (author's translation); Robert H. Stein, *Luke*, NAC (Nashville: B&H, 1992), 108; Trent C. Butler, *Luke*, HNTC (Nashville: B&H, 2000), 29; Robert James Utley, *The Gospel According to Luke* (Marshall, TX: Bible Lessons International, 2004), Luke 2:8.

[2] Aristotle, *Politics*, 1.8; cited in James S. Jeffers, *The Greco-Roman World of the New Testament Era: Exploring the Background of Early Christianity* (Downers Grove: InterVarsity, 1999), 21; Matthew Montonini, "Shepherd," in *The Lexham Bible Dictionary*, ed. John D. Barry and Lazarus Wentz (Bellingham, WA: Logos Bible Software, 2012). This is possibly why Philo, *On Husbandry*, 61, refers to "the care of goats or sheep" as "inglorious."

Using Aristotle as background information for understanding Luke 2 has two main problems. First, Aristotle was not a Jew and did not live in Israel; he was a Greek and lived in Greece. His views on shepherding are virtually irrelevant for first-century Judaism. Second, he lived more than 300 years before the birth of Christ. This also makes his view unhelpful for understanding the New Testament. He lived in a different culture, in a different society, during a different time period.

Scholars go to several sources for culling Jewish background material for the New Testament. The two main sources used for understanding shepherds in first-century Israel are the Mishnah and the Babylonian Talmud.[3] The Mishnah is a collection of rabbinic sayings. Rabbis would debate issues pertaining to the Old Testament and Mosaic Law. This collection of rabbinic traditions was from the time period before Christ started his public ministry up until around the year AD 200. It was written between AD 200 and 250. These traditions contained in the Mishnah can sometimes be useful for understanding the New Testament, depending on several factors (like the date of the rabbi being cited).[4]

The second source is the Babylonian Talmud. The Babylonian Talmud, compiled around the year AD 500, contains rabbinic interpretations of the Old Testament and interpretations based on the Mishnah. The Mishnah contains rabbinic debates over the correct interpretation and application of Old Testament Law, and the Talmud contains rabbis debating the content of the Mishnah. In general the information in the Talmud is not helpful for interpreting the New Testament. Many of the quotations are simply too late to be reliably useful because the rabbis are so far removed from the first-century context.

Besides Aristotle, a comment by Philo, and one statement in the Mishnah, the bulk of the quotes used to demonstrate that shepherds were despised were taken from the Babylonian Talmud. I was unable to find even one source from first-century Israel used to support the view that shepherds were societal outcasts. Therefore, this viewpoint is dated after the events being studied in Luke 2. It is unreliable information and should be discarded when interpreting the Gospels.

---

[3] Scholars also use Philo of Alexandria (first-century Hellenistic Jew), Josephus (first-century Jew), and intertestamental apocryphal and pseudepigraphal works.

[4] Though I didn't find any sources citing the Mishnah, *Qidduchin* 4.14 could be cited as evidence of a negative view toward shepherds. This view was given by Rabbi Abba Gurion of Sidon, who is dated around AD 165–200. Evidence to the contrary in the Mishnah would include *Bekhorot* 5:4: "Israelite shepherds are believed [to testify that the blemishes came about unintentionally]." This means the statement in the NET Bible footnote (on Luke 2:8) implying that there is no evidence before the fifth century is an overstatement.

Contextual Clues

One clue in the context, a subtle hint, supports the opposite view of the legend. Luke 2:18 says, "And all who heard it were amazed at what the shepherds said to them." They weren't amazed that *shepherds* were telling them; they were amazed at the content of what the shepherds said. If shepherds were viewed as societal outcasts, they would have been shocked that the shepherds were involved in the process. Instead, they were amazed at the story itself. This is a contextual clue that shepherds were not considered societal outcasts.

A Brief Biblical Portrayal of Shepherds

There is better evidence for the idea that shepherds were not viewed as societal outcasts: the overarching biblical portrayal of shepherds. The description of shepherds in the Old and New Testaments would be formative for the minds of first-century Jews and Christians.

Beginning in the Old Testament, Abraham was a shepherd. Genesis 13 describes him as having much livestock, herds, and flocks of sheep. Exodus 3:1 says Moses was a shepherd: "Meanwhile, Moses was shepherding the flock of his father-in-law Jethro." David was a shepherd (according to 1 Samuel 17) who took care of his father's flocks. These three men are pillars of the Old Testament. Abraham, Moses, and David were all connected to shepherding, and all three were greatly esteemed in Jewish society.

God is also pictured as a shepherd in the Old Testament. One of the most famous verses in all of Scripture proclaims this: "The LORD is my shepherd" (Ps 23:1). Genesis 49:24 says, "Yet his bow remained steady, and his strong arms were made agile by the hands of the Mighty One of Jacob, by the name of the Shepherd, the Rock of Israel." Psalm 80:1 says, "Listen, Shepherd of Israel." The Lord speaks in Ezekiel 34:12, saying, "As a shepherd looks for his sheep on the day he is among his scattered flock, so I will look for My flock. I will rescue them from all the places where they have been scattered on a cloudy and dark day." Many more could be quoted, but these should suffice. A Jew in the first century would connect shepherding to Abraham, Moses, David, and God himself.

In the New Testament, Jesus is tightly connected to the shepherd motif. Matthew 2:6 describes Jesus as a shepherd: "And you, Bethlehem, in the land of Judah, are by no means least among the leaders of Judah: because out of you will come a leader who will shepherd My people Israel." If shepherds were viewed as societal outcasts, it is highly doubtful that Matthew would connect shepherding terminology to Jesus. He does it again in Matthew 26:31: "For it is written: I will strike the shepherd, and the sheep of the flock will be scattered." The most powerful passage connecting Jesus to the shepherd motif is

John 10. Jesus discusses shepherding, and he places himself in the role of shepherd, calling himself "the good shepherd" (John 10:11). This would be an oxymoron if shepherds were viewed like prostitutes. Jesus is even referred to as a shepherd outside of the Gospels (see Heb 13:20; 1 Pet 2:25; 5:4). There is no hesitation in the New Testament to refer to Jesus as a shepherd.

Finally, church leaders are referred to as shepherds. In Acts 20:28, Paul explains that the overseers are "to shepherd the church of God." Peter says to church leaders, "Shepherd God's flock among you" (1 Pet 5:2). The title "pastor" refers to a shepherd. There is no evidence of embarrassment over referring to church leaders as shepherds.

Many scholars have taught that shepherds were societal outcasts in first-century Israel. Their sources are generally many years after the New Testament time period, plus Aristotle who was from a different culture and 300 years before Jesus. Luke 2:18 appears to lean against the view of shepherds as societal outcasts. The biblical portrayal of a shepherd is extremely positive in the Old and New Testaments.

Application

While shepherds weren't societal outcasts, they were in the lower class, and they do represent the poor and humble.[5] God chose to use to the poor and humble components of society to share his wonderful announcement of the birth of his Son. Jesus is not only for the rich.

Also, Luke 2 is telling the story of a pivotal event in the history of humankind. God and his angels are excited and want to rejoice over what is happening. This is the beginning of a life that will be lived in total submission and obedience to God. The second Adam has come, and Jesus will provide forgiveness for sin and reconciliation to God. That is why God and his angels are so excited, because that story is now beginning. We should be excited and passionately tell others about what Jesus came and did.

Annotated Bibliography

Commentaries

Bock, Darrell L. *Luke 1:1–9:50*. BECNT. Grand Rapids: Baker, 1994.

Bock's comments are not technical and summarize the issue well. See especially comments on pages 213–14.

---

[5] While this application might sound similar to the legendary teaching, saying someone is "poor and humble" is radically different from comparing them to a prostitute. Getting the right application using the wrong data is still not an appropriate hermeneutical path.

Strauss, Mark. "Luke." In *Zondervan Illustrated Bible Backgrounds Commentary: Matthew, Mark, Luke*. Grand Rapids: Zondervan, 2002.
This nontechnical commentary corrects many background mistakes that have worked their way into popular Christian culture. See comments on Luke 2:8.

Dictionary Articles

Vancil, Jack W. "Sheep, Shepherd." Pages 1187–90 in *The Anchor Bible Dictionary*. Edited by David Noel Freedman. New York: Doubleday, 1992.
This article gives a great biblical overview of the theme of sheep/shepherd.

Books

Laniak, Timothy S. *Shepherds After My Own Heart: Pastoral Traditions and Leadership in the Bible*. NSBT. Downers Grove: InterVarsity, 2006.
Laniak provides a balanced, cautious view on the shepherds. See especially 197–98.

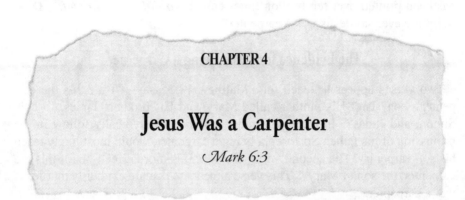

CHAPTER 4

Jesus Was a Carpenter

Mark 6:3

The Legendary Teaching on Mark 6:3

Have you ever wondered why Jesus was a carpenter? Mark 6:3 says, "'Isn't this the carpenter, the son of Mary, and the brother of James, Joses, Judas, and Simon? And aren't His sisters here with us?' So they were offended by him." The reasoning for this might be found in what carpenters do. A carpenter is someone who builds or repairs items made out of wood. Think about an old wooden door. The door has been on a certain house for many years. When a carpenter does some work on that door, he has to take the door off its hinges and bring it to his workbench. Then he has to carefully strip off the layers upon layers of cheap paint that have been used to cover up all the door's imperfections. Once he has the paint off the door, he can now see the door for what it truly is. But the brilliance of a carpenter is one who can see the door not for what it is but for what he can make it into. So the sanding begins, smoothing out all the imperfections in the door. He carefully, lovingly gets the door in just the right shape for the task he has for it. Jesus wasn't just a carpenter of wood, but he is the carpenter of our souls. He peels away the cheap paint we have used to cover up our imperfections. He sands away our rough spots, and he finishes us off with a beautiful coat of righteousness that brings glory to the carpenter himself.

Introduction: Unraveling the Legend

Challenging the idea that Jesus was a carpenter could seem sacrilegious to some people because it is so ingrained into American Christianity. Johnny Cash even wrote a song called "Jesus Was a Carpenter." Apparently Cash thought Jesus was a good carpenter because he sings, "His hands could form a

table true enough to stand forever." Josh McDowell wrote a book in 1977 that
has been printed over ten million times called *More than a Carpenter*. Does
Scripture ever say Jesus was a carpenter?

The Evidence for Jesus Being a Carpenter

Two verses appear to teach this. Matthew 13:55 says, "Isn't this the carpenter's son? Isn't His mother called Mary, and His brothers James, Joseph,
Simon, and Judas?" In the first century a son would typically follow in the
profession of his father. So Joseph, being a carpenter, would most likely teach
his son carpentry. The second verse, Mark 6:3, is more direct: "Isn't this the
carpenter, the son of Mary?" This verse appears to declare explicitly that Jesus
was a carpenter.

Let's examine some Bible translations. The HCSB, ESV, NASB, NIV, KJV,
NKJV, NLT, and NET all say Jesus was a carpenter. All major modern translations agree. What about some ancient translations? The Latin Vulgate, completed about AD 400, refers to Jesus as a *faber*, meaning a craftsman or an
artisan. This is a more general term incorporating many different disciplines,
not just carpentry. The Wessex Gospels are old English translations completed
before the year 1000, and they said Jesus was a "smith," meaning one who
works with metal. The Tyndale New Testament (completed in 1526) said Jesus
was a carpenter. These are some of the translations before the KJV (1611). In
AD 400 Jesus was described as a "craftsman" or an "artisan," near 1000 he was
described as a "worker with metal," and in 1526 he was called a "carpenter."
While probably every major translation after Tyndale has followed his translation of "carpenter," there was disagreement before that.

Studying the Greek Word: *Tektōn*

The Greek word used in both Matthew 13 and Mark 6 is *tektōn*. Greek dictionaries have some interesting insights into this word. The table on the next
page summarizes their thoughts.

Greek Dictionaries on *Tektōn*

While Thayer exclusively references the idea of carpentry, the rest include
that idea but add more. The evidence below will show that the definition provided by Louw and Nida is the most accurate. The Greek word *tektōn* refers to
someone who builds using whatever material necessary, be it wood (carpentry), stone (masonry), or metal (smithery). The more recent dictionaries tend
to emphasize *tektōn* as someone who builds things. The dictionary by Louw
and Nida adds an interesting sentence at the bottom of their entry: "There is

Year	Dictionary	Definition
1886	Thayer	"a worker in wood, a carpenter"
1957	Bauer, Arndt, & Gingrich	"carpenter, woodworker, builder"
1986	Packer	"craftsman or builder in wood, stone, or metal"
1989	Louw & Nida	"one who uses various material (wood, stone, and metal) in building—'builder, carpenter'"
1994	Friberg	"carpenter, builder, craftsman"
1996	Liddell, Scott, & Jones	"worker in wood, carpenter, joiner," "a smith," "a mason," "any craftsman or workman," including "metal-workers" or a "sculptor"
2000	Bauer, Danker, Arndt, & Gingrich	"one who constructs, builder, carpenter"*

* Joseph Henry Thayer, *A Greek-English Lexicon of the New Testament* (New York: American Book Company, 1886), 618; W. F. Arndt and F. W. Gingrich, eds., *A Greek-English Lexicon of the New Testament and Other Early Christian Literature*, 2nd ed. (Chicago: University of Chicago Press, 1957), 816; J. I. Packer, "Carpenter, Builder, Workman, Craftsman, Trade," in *The New International Dictionary of New Testament Theology*, ed. Colin Brown, 2 vols. (Grand Rapids: Zondervan, 1975), 1:279; Louw and Nida, 45.9; Timothy Friberg, Barbara Friberg, and Neva F. Miller, *Analytical Lexicon of the Greek New Testament* (Victoria, BC, Canada: Trafford, 2005), 377; Henry George Liddell and Robert Scott, *A Greek-English Lexicon*, ed. Henry Stuart Jones and Roderick McKenzie (Oxford: Clarendon Press, 1996), 1769; BDAG, 995.

every reason to believe that in biblical times, one who was regarded as a *tektōn* would be skilled in the use of wood and stone and possibly even metal."[1] They are trying to make clear that this word is not limited to the idea of a carpenter. The best way to study this word, which only occurs a few times in the New Testament, is to go back and look at the way that people used it near the first century. Did they describe a *tektōn* as someone who worked only with wood, or did they describe it as someone who worked with several different materials?

The ancient uses of *tektōn* reveal several instances where this word is used to describe someone working only with wood. Epictetus (died in AD 135) said, "This man is a carpenter? Why? Because he uses an axe."[2] Epictetus indicated that the *tektōn* was a carpenter because he used an axe.

Other uses of *tektōn* don't fit the idea that it refers exclusively to a carpenter. Plutarch (died about AD 120) said, "And so a *tektōn* would regard the

---

[1] Louw and Nida, 45.9.

[2] George Long, *The Discourses of Epictetus with the Encheiridion and Fragments* (London: George Bell and Sons, 1890), 352.

welding of iron or the tempering of an axe."[3] So *tektōn* in this writing referred to a smith, someone who worked with metal. Philo, a first-century Hellenistic Jewish man living in Alexandria, used the word in a manner consistent with the idea of a carpenter, but none of the examples are so specific that it demands that the word refer only to carpentry.

Josephus, a Jewish historian who died around the year AD 100, wrote two famous works: *The Antiquities of the Jews* and *The Wars of the Jews*. Every use of the word *tektōn* in *The Antiquities of the Jews* is consistent with the idea of a carpenter and describes someone involved with building the temple, the tabernacle, or the palace. However, he was describing people building a long time before his writing. The word occurs four times in *The Wars of the Jews*, and all of them refer to a builder in general and not specifically a carpenter. For example, Josephus says, "[They] summoned the *tektōn* and directed them to increase the height of the wall." If a *tektōn* was someone who worked only with wood and these walls were constructed not only of wood but mainly of stone, no one would order a *tektōn* to come and increase the height of the wall. They would summon a mason. But they summoned the *tektōn* because they were people skilled at building with various materials. All of the uses in *The Wars of the Jews* seem to describe the job of a mason rather than the job of a carpenter.

The Old Testament Background for Builders

Some helpful information from the Old Testament comes from the idea that builders did not typically specialize in a certain area, like wood, metal, or stone. For example, Exodus 35:30–35 describes Bezalel as a generalist who worked with several different materials. Bible scholar Ken Campbell has analyzed the Old Testament data and concluded that the Israelite builder "did not limit himself to working with only one material. He could move from stone to metal to wood as the need or opportunity arose (Neh 3:8, 31), and while he could probably specialize in one material if that was advantageous, he did not normally restrict himself in this way, as many modern tradesmen do."[4] Campbell says those who were builders in the Old Testament time period did not specialize; they were general contractors. They kept their job description as broad as possible so they could work wherever there was need in order to find employment.

---

[3] Plutarch, *Moralia*, ed. and trans. Frank Cole Babbitt, Loeb Classical Library 2 (Cambridge, MA: Harvard University Press, 1928), 405.

[4] Ken M. Campbell, "What Was Jesus' Occupation?," *Journal of the Evangelical Theological Society* 48, no. 3 (2005): 508.

Conclusion to the Meaning of *Tektōn*

A *tektōn* was someone who worked with stone, wood, and metal. Jesus did carpentry, but he was also a mason and a smith. The phrase used today for an ancient *tektōn* is a general contractor or a builder. When ancient sources wanted to specify that someone was a mason, they would say he was a builder in stone. When they wanted to say someone was a smith, they would say he was a builder in metal. When they wanted to say someone was a carpenter, they would say he was a builder with wood. But neither Matthew nor Mark mention that Jesus specialized in one material, so we should not add any specialization either.

The majority of references to building in Israel reference work in stone because of the material culture of Israel in the time of Jesus. To think that Jesus would have only worked in wood would be difficult to prove based on the materials people were working with in the culture of Israel in the first century. Joseph and Jesus were probably builders in the general sense and not specifically carpenters. So this legend is not a *mistaken* legend but a *misleading* legend. Jesus was *more than a carpenter*.

Application

The opening presentation of the legend was allegorizing Scripture, something to be avoided. Be careful when interpreting a passage that you are seeking the meaning the author intended for that passage. Stick to the main points the author was trying to make. When Mark 6:3 was written, Mark was not hoping we would compare what a carpenter does to wood with what Jesus does to our souls.

Second, accuracy is important in the face of critics. Christianity has many skeptics. We want to be precise and accurate in describing things that relate to Scripture. Don't give them an opportunity to showcase possible ignorance.

Third, we can learn about patience and vocation from Jesus' model. For five and a half years while in seminary, I worked as a security officer. For the first four years at that job, I was constantly trying to get a job in full-time ministry. I was desperate to get out of doing security; it was a fairly demeaning job. Sometimes in our lives we need to have patience with the vocation God has placed us in. God wanted to teach me many lessons during the time I spent as a security officer, and some of those lessons have been extremely helpful as I have been in full-time ministry as a Christian educator. Think about the job you have right now. Are you bringing glory to God in your attitude and work ethic? Recognize that God might have a change in store for you, but he might not. He could want you to stay where you are until you retire. But he might be preparing you for something totally different. The lessons he is teaching you right now will probably make you more prepared for what he has in store for you. Think about all the ways Jesus used his knowledge of construction and business sense in his teaching. He used references to construction, finances, and stewardship for illustrations while he was teaching. Those illustrations came from what he was doing all those years preceding His public ministry. God may be molding you for some ministry, some task, as well. So be patient and glorify God in the vocation you have right now.

Annotated Bibliography

Commentaries

Brooks, James A. *Mark*. NAC. Nashville: B&H, 1991.
  Very accessible commentary and summarizes these conclusions wonderfully.
Luz, Ulrich. *Matthew 8–20*. Hermeneia. Minneapolis: Fortress, 2001.
  A technical commentary, difficult to read for those without knowledge of Greek.

Journals

Campbell, Ken. "What Was Jesus' Occupation?" *Journal of the Evangelical Theological Society* 48, no. 3 (2005): 501–19.
  The go-to article for this topic. Campbell provides much evidence from the content of the New Testament itself.

Websites

Sprinkle, Preston. "Was Jesus a Carpenter?" *Theology for Real Life*. December 19, 2011. Accessed July 12, 2014. www.facultyblog.eternitybiblecollege.com/2011/12/was-jesus-a-carpenter.
  Sprinkle provides a great summary of the issue at hand.

CHAPTER 5

Jesus Died When He Was Thirty-Three

Luke 3:23

The Legendary Teaching on Luke 3:23

The Gospel of Luke declares that Jesus was thirty years old when he began his public ministry. All of Jesus' ministry in Matthew, Mark, and Luke could have taken place within one calendar year, though they never state this. However, John's Gospel paints a clearer picture of the chronology of Jesus' ministry. After John's version of the calling of the disciples (John 1:35–51), Jesus performs his first sign at the wedding at Cana in Galilee: turning water into wine (2:1–12). Then John says, "The Jewish Passover was near, so Jesus went up to Jerusalem" (v. 13). This is the first Passover to occur during Jesus' public ministry. Right before John's account of Jesus' feeding the multitudes (John 6:5–15), John says, "Now the Passover, a Jewish festival, was near" (v. 4). This is the second Passover during Jesus' public ministry. Finally, John 11:55; 12:1; and 13:1 declare that a third Passover was approaching. Therefore, Jesus' public ministry must have been about three years long. Since he began his ministry at the age of thirty, Jesus died when he was only thirty-three years old.

Introduction: Unraveling the Legend

There is much to be said about the above historical reconstruction. John's Gospel does explicitly reference three Passover festivals. While some believe the ambiguous Jewish festival in John 5:1 refers to a fourth Passover during Jesus' public ministry, it's more likely a reference to the Feast of Tabernacles.[1]

---

[1] See Andreas J. Köstenberger, *John*, BECNT (Grand Rapids: Baker, 2004), 195.

Therefore, it's likely that Jesus' public ministry was about three years long. However, how old was Jesus when his ministry began?

Luke 3:23 actually says, "As He began His ministry, Jesus was *about* 30 years old" (emphasis added). Luke doesn't actually say Jesus was thirty, only that he was *about* thirty. The Greek word translated *about* communicates approximation not precision. Luke uses this Greek word several times to refer to an approximate number (see Luke 9:14; 9:28; 22:59; 23:44; Acts 1:15; 2:41; 19:7). If Luke were trying to say Jesus was exactly thirty, he easily could have communicated that. Instead he chose to use the word *about* to communicate an approximate age for Jesus. How old was he?

The year of His birth must be calculated first. Jesus was born before Herod died (see Matt 2:1; Luke 1:5). Josephus said there was a lunar eclipse shortly before Herod's death; the eclipse took place on March 12 or 13, 4 BC.[2] He also mentioned that Herod died before Passover (April 11, 4 BC). When Herod was growing ill,[3] and before appointing a new ruler over the region, Caesar Augustus ordered a census be taken shortly before Herod died (Luke 2:1). Luke 2:2 says, regarding this census, "This first registration took place while Quirinius was governing Syria." Since there is no solid evidence that Quirinius became governor before AD 6, some scholars have concluded that Luke made a mistake. However, three major translations have footnotes at this point with alternate translations: HCSB ("This registration was before"), ESV ("This was the registration before"), and NIV ("This census took place before"). All of these indicate it is possible that Luke was claiming the census ordered by Caesar Augustus was *before* Quirinius was governor, not *while*.[4] Therefore, Jesus was probably born in late 5 BC or early 4 BC,[5] with September or October of 5 BC being most likely.

Three pieces of evidence will be useful in deciding between the two most likely years of the crucifixion (AD 30 and 33):[6] Tiberias's reign, the building of the temple in John 2:19–20, and the Passovers in John's Gospel. Those who argue for an AD 30 crucifixion date (the slight majority of New Testament scholars) claim that even though Luke 3:1–3 says John the Baptist's ministry

---

[2] Josephus, *Antiquities* 17.6.4 §167.

[3] H. W. Hoehner, "Herodian Dynasty," in *Dictionary of Jesus and the Gospels*, eds. Joel B. Green and Scot McKnight (Downers Grove: InterVarsity, 1992), 321.

[4] The Greek word under discussion is most naturally understood as "the first in a sequence," but it can mean "earlier" or "before" (see uses in John 1:15, 30). The "before" view is defended by F. F. Bruce, *New Testament History* (New York: Doubleday, 1971), 32, n. 1, and Harold W. Hoehner, *Chronological Aspects of the Life of Christ* (Grand Rapids: Zondervan, 1978), 21–22.

[5] See Hoehner, *Chronological Aspects*, 25.

[6] The following analysis is taken from Andreas J. Köstenberger, "When Was Jesus Born, and When Did He Die?" *Biblical Foundations* (December 23, 2010), accessed July 16, 2014, www.biblicalfoundations.org/when-was-jesus-born-and-when-did-he-die.

began in the fifteenth year of Tiberias's reign (which began in AD 14), Tiberias may have been co-emperor with Caesar Augustus beginning in AD 11/12. However, the evidence for Tiberias being co-emperor is lacking in reliability. Therefore, it is more likely that Luke is referring to AD 29 for the start of John the Baptist's ministry.

Those scholars claiming an AD 30 crucifixion date point out that the Jews stated it had taken forty-six years to build the temple in John 2 and Herod the Great began this restoration in 20/19 BC. This means Jesus' first Passover took place in AD 27/28. However, there are two Greek words for *temple*, and the word in John 2:20 (*naos*) refers to the sanctuary, not the temple complex (*hieron*). Josephus actually referred to the completion of the renovation of the temple sanctuary in 18/17 BC. The Jewish leaders cannot be claiming it is still ongoing when it was completed forty-six years prior. Forty-six years after 18/17 BC arrives at an AD 29/30 date for the beginning of Jesus' ministry.

Finally, some scholars have postulated that John references two, not three, Passovers, because the one mentioned in 2:13 actually occurred at the end of Jesus' ministry, paralleling the accounts in Matthew (21:12), Mark (11:15), and Luke (19:45). They believe John rearranged the temple clearing for thematic reasons. Therefore, Jesus only had a two-year ministry. However, Leon Morris convincingly argues that the wording and setting of the two accounts favors the idea of two separate clearings, not one.[7]

	Evidence	Evidence	Conclusion
1	Tiberias's reign began in AD 14.	John the Baptist's ministry began in fifteenth year of reign.	Jesus' ministry began in AD 29.
2	John 2:20 says forty-six years since sanctuary completed.	Josephus says sanctuary completed in 18/17 BC.	Jesus' ministry began in AD 29/30.
3	Jesus cleared the temple twice.	John's Gospel mentions three Passovers.	Jesus crucified in AD 33.

Therefore, the date of Jesus' crucifixion can be fixed at April 3, AD 33. Since Jesus was likely born in the fall of 5 BC and died in April AD 33, He was thirty-seven years old when he was crucified. Jesus began his public ministry when he was about thirty-three or thirty-four years old, adequately accounted for by Luke's use of "about" in 3:23.

---

[7] Leon Morris, *The Gospel According to John*, rev. ed., NICNT (Grand Rapids: Eerdmans, 1995), 167–69.

Interpreting and Applying Luke 3:23

Some interpreters have tried to find a significant meaning in Jesus' being thirty-three years old. I've been in several Bible studies where someone will contribute the following piece of background information: Jewish children were bound to the authority of their parents until the age of thirty; now that Jesus is thirty, he can begin functioning outside his mother's authority. The problem with this interpretation is twofold. First, I have yet to see any reliable source indicating this background information was valid for first-century Israel. Second, Jesus wasn't thirty, he was probably thirty-three or thirty-four. Several commentators mention the link to other biblical figures being thirty years old: priests began serving at thirty (Num 4:3), Joseph began serving Pharaoh at thirty (Gen 41:46), and Ezekiel was possibly thirty when he began his prophetic ministry (Ezek 1:1). Possibly more significant is that King David's reign began when he was thirty (2 Sam 5:4). Regardless, Luke never says Jesus was exactly thirty, so the most that can be safely understood is that Luke might have been connecting Jesus to prominent Old Testament figures. Most likely, the number should simply be understood at face value (for example, see John 2:6 ["six"] and 5:2 ["five"]).

One of the fascinating aspects of Scripture is that the authors don't write like they are making up stories. The details they provide would be curious if they were simply writing fairy tales. Why provide genealogies or an approximate age of Jesus in Luke 3:23 if this is simply made up? The authors of Scripture consistently ground the narratives in a historical context, referencing historical figures that can be studied in sources outside of Scripture itself, like Herod the Great, Caesar Augustus, and Pontius Pilate. We can have confidence that the accounts about Jesus' life in the New Testament are historically reliable and accurate, despite the numerous attacks of critics.

Annotated Bibliography

Commentaries

Bock, Darrell L. *Luke 1:1–9:50*. BECNT. Grand Rapids: Baker, 1994.

Bock's discussions are at times technical but very helpful. His discussions on chronology are insightful. See especially pages 281–82, 351–52, 903–13.

Books

Hoehner, Harold W. *Chronological Aspects of the Life of Christ*. Grand Rapids: Zondervan, 1978.

This book directly addresses the issue of this legend. It is one of the best books on chronology and the New Testament. See especially pages 11–28, 95–114.

Maier, Paul L. "The Date of the Nativity and the Chronology of Jesus' Life." Pages 113–30 in *Chronos, Kairos, Christos: Nativity and Chronological Studies Presented to Jack Finegan*. Edited by Jerry Vardaman and Edwin M. Yamauchi. Winona Lake, IN: Eisenbrauns, 1989.
Maier's chapter covers a wealth of information. Highly recommended. Available online at www.inchristus.files.wordpress.com/2010/12/maier-date-of-the-nativity.pdf.

Articles

Hoehner, Harold W. "Chronology." Pages 118–22 in *Dictionary of Jesus and the Gospels*. Edited by Joel B. Green and Scot McKnight. Downers Grove: InterVarsity, 1992.
This article summarizes Hoehner's study mentioned above.

Websites

Köstenberger, Andreas J. "When Was Jesus Born, and When Did He Die?" *Biblical Foundations*. December 23, 2010. Accessed July 16, 2014. www.biblicalfoundations.org/when-was-jesus-born-and-when-did-he-die.
Köstenberger's summary of this issue is clear and succinct.

CHAPTER 6

All Giving Must Be Done in Secret

Matthew 6:3

The Legendary Teaching on Matthew 6:3

Jesus clearly prescribed how we are to give of our finances. He said you should not "let your left hand know what your right hand is doing" (Matt 6:3). In contrast to that command, Christians today give to have their names put on fellowship halls and buildings. These "philanthropists" appear to be motivated by seeing their names honored rather than Christ's name honored. One of the ways this manifests itself is through "giving envelopes." People justify giving through the modern envelope system because it helps them get a tax break. But think of all the people that will be aware of how much you give when you use this system: the church treasurer, the person doing your taxes, and the government! And that's just the minimum.

Jesus calls us to secret giving. You should never let anyone know how much you give or any of the details of your giving. If you tell people about your giving, you've just received all the reward you'll ever get: praise from people. Any eternal rewards will be forfeited. Give to the Lord, and give generously, but give secretly, as Jesus prescribed.

Introduction: Unraveling the Legend

Can you really do something with one hand while the other hand doesn't know? What does it even mean for a hand *not to know*? I've actually accomplished this: I did something with my right hand and my left hand didn't know. My wife and I were in my car, and after parking it, I took the keys out of the ignition. Apparently I put them on the seat, which is not very wise. I got out of the car, and not having power locks, I locked the car door with my right hand and closed the door with my left hand. As my left hand slammed the door shut, my right hand "saw" the keys and reached for them. The locked door slammed closed on my right hand. Praise the Lord that my car was cheaply made, for as the door closed and locked on my right hand, none of my bones were broken. I could wiggle my fingers, but it was totally stuck. My wife quickly reached across the car to open the door; thank goodness she hadn't closed her door yet, or I would have had to wait for AAA to come! That's as close of an example I know to the left hand not knowing what the right hand is doing. What does Jesus mean when he says, "Don't let your left hand know what your right hand is doing"?

Jesus is using a common rhetorical device called hyperbole: intentional exaggeration to make a point. An effective hyperbole is actually an impossible statement. If I said, "I want you to go to that door, turn the door knob with your right hand, but don't tell your left hand what you're doing," you'd say, "I can't do it!" You will never be able to keep it a secret. One commentator said it's only possible for someone who has had a lobotomy![1]

The Context of Giving in Matthew 6

Matthew 6:1–18 contains Jesus' teaching on three topics: giving, prayer, and fasting. The introductory statement for the section is Matthew 6:1: "Be careful not to practice your righteousness in front of people, to be seen by them. Otherwise, you will have no reward from your Father in heaven." This verse is important as Jesus supplies the underlying principle to the three teachings that follow. He says that if your intention in giving/praying/fasting is for others to see your righteous acts, then your reward has been received. The key here is the intention: if your purpose in giving/praying/fasting is to be seen by people, you have a heart problem.

He illustrates this underlying principle with these three examples. For prayer (especially vv. 5–8), Jesus commands his disciples to pray in secret. If taken (over)literally, this means all forms of public prayer would be disobedience. For fasting (vv. 16–18), some people have interpreted Jesus' words to mean you *can't* tell anyone when you're fasting or you've *invalidated* the fast. I've heard this from several people throughout my life. But again, Jesus is speaking in hyperbole.

Jesus provides the underlying principle of something to avoid: don't do righteous acts to be seen by people. He illustrates this with three exaggerated examples on giving, praying, and fasting. Jesus uses hyperbole in several

---

[1]   See Craig Blomberg, *Matthew*, NAC (Nashville: B&H, 1992), 117.

other places in Matthew's Gospel as well: Matthew 5:29–30; 7:3–5; 18:8–9; 19:23–24.[2]

Interpreting Matthew 6:2–4

Jesus' main point is that his followers should give to the poor without being motivated by receiving praise from other people. If what motivates your giving is the hope of others seeing you give and taking notice of your giving, then you have a heart problem connected to your giving. I am not saying it is problematic if you give and someone sees you. You don't have to sneak your giving into the "offering plate" or collection box in your church. That misunderstands the point to this passage: what is the motivation of your heart?

I know people that won't put anything on their tax returns about how much they gave because then the government will know. If your motivation for giving is a tax break, or so the president of the United States knows how much you gave, or that you can show your tax forms to someone and say, "I am a generous giver," then it *is* a problem. But you need to ask yourself about the purpose and the motivation for your giving. That's what Jesus is trying to teach when he says, "Don't let your left hand know what your right hand is doing." Blomberg concludes that Jesus commands "that we should give in such a way that there is no temptation for others to glorify the giver rather than God."[3]

Application

Christians should be responsible in their financial stewardship. This passage cannot be appropriately used to justify haphazard giving. In fact, nothing in this passage would prohibit a financial accountability partner: someone who holds you accountable in what you spend your money on.

Jesus is warning against hypocritical giving, that is, giving not to glorify God or to help the one receiving the gift but to receive praise from people. Be careful about giving so your name will be on a list of generous givers.

What does proper giving look like? Three concepts should be the driving forces for our giving: grace driven, relationship driven, and love driven. Giving should be a response to the grace God has shown believers through sending his Son to die for our sins on the cross (2 Cor 8–9). The more we meditate on the cross, the greater our desire to give should grow. Giving should also be relationship driven, that is, based on one's relationship with the Lord. God is not seeking for you to simply balance a budget or crunch numbers in a calculator;

---

[2] See ibid., 109, 128, 275, and 299 for comments on all those verses being examples of hyperbole.

[3] Ibid., 117.

he is seeking a relationship with you (2 Cor 8:5). Go to him in prayer and earnestly seek his heart for the amount and receiver of your gifts. Finally, giving should be driven by a believer demonstrating love for God (2 Cor 8:8–9).

This passage is primarily countering hypocritical motivations for giving. However, Scripture offers at least four proper motivations for giving: (1) We should give to express our thankfulness to God (2 Cor 9:12). If you find yourself giving begrudgingly and bitterly, your motivation is dubious. (2) Giving causes one to grow in holiness (2 Cor 9:6, 8). As we learn to give more generously, it will help us to "excel in every good work" (2 Cor 9:8). (3) Christians should recognize that God praises sacrificial giving, and receiving praise from God is a valid motivation for giving (Mark 12:42–44; 2 Cor 8:2–3). (4) After Jesus teaches about giving, praying, and fasting, he explains that giving will store up eternal rewards (Matt 6:19–21).

Much more could be said on this subject,[4] but these are the foundational principles for biblical giving that place Christians on the right track toward bringing glory and honor to God through generous, sacrificial giving.

Annotated Bibliography

Commentaries

Blomberg, Craig. *Matthew*. NAC. Nashville: B&H, 1991.
Blomberg provides a sound interpretation of this passage. See especially page 117.

Books

Croteau, David A. *You Mean I Don't Have to Tithe? A Deconstruction of Tithing and a Reconstruction of Post-Tithe Giving*. Eugene, OR: Pickwick, 2010.
A work on the wider question of the applicability of tithing to the Christian, technical at times. See pages 238, 243 where the legend above is addressed.

Websites

Krell, Keith. "Secret Service (Matthew 6:1–18)." *Bible.org*. March 23, 2010. Accessed July 16, 2014. www.tinyurl.com/SSKrell.
Krell interprets this passage in a helpful way, elucidating the underlying principles exceptionally well.

---

[4] For more information on giving, see David A. Croteau, "Giving after the Cross," in *Tithing after the Cross* (Gonzalez, FL: Energion, 2013), 55–70.

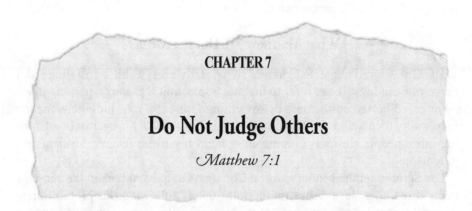

CHAPTER 7

Do Not Judge Others

Matthew 7:1

The Legendary Teaching on Matthew 7:1

I've talked to many people who refuse to go to church because of the hypocrisy of Christians. And if there's any one area that is most cited for the hypocrisy it's judging others. Jesus prohibited judging in Matthew 7:1: "Do not judge, so that you won't be judged." All forms of judging are commanded to cease. Don't judge other people, believers or unbelievers, based on what you see them doing, on their lifestyle, on how they dress, or on what music they listen to. Jesus is calling us to a higher standard, to put aside our differences and live in unity with one another. Judging others disrupts unity; it divides the church. The world is looking at us wondering if we'll ever be united, if we'll ever demonstrate love for one another. The more we judge one another, the weaker our witness will be.

Introduction: Unraveling the Legend

The importance of the legendary interpretation of this verse is underscored by Carson, who says that Matthew 7:1 has displaced John 3:16 "as the only verse in the Bible the man in the street is likely to know."[1] Every time someone quotes it to me (along with many of these legends), I think of the words of the great philosopher Inigo Montoya: "I do not think it means what you think it means." The context of this verse rules out certain interpretations. Its context includes the following: (1) the context of Jesus' Sermon on the Mount (Matthew 5–7); (2) the context of Matthew's Gospel; and (3) the context of the New

---

[1] D. A. Carson, *The Gospel According to John*, PNTC (Grand Rapids: Eerdmans, 1991), 317.

Testament. Each of these three contexts will show that the above superficial reading of this text is problematic.

What Matthew 7:1 Doesn't Mean

The Greek word translated "judge" by virtually every Bible translation has a range of meanings. It can refer to making a selection ("prefer"), passing judgment based on the correctness of something ("discern"), or judging someone to be guilty ("condemn").[2] The prohibition in Matthew 7:1 is against condemning other people. Jesus is commanding them not to be severely critical and judgmental.

The Sermon on the Mount calls on Christians to judge others in the sense of being discerning. Jesus' illustration immediately following this prohibition is primarily intended to communicate the hypocritical penchant humans have for criticizing others while tolerating the same (or worse) behavior in themselves (Matt 7:3–5). Jesus concludes that illustration by saying that after the log is removed from your own eye, then you will be able to see clearly enough to help your friend by removing the speck from his eye. This means that you will have to *see* the speck, the "minor shortcoming,"[3] in order to remove it. This involves judging (in the sense of discernment) on some level. In Matthew 7:6, Jesus prohibits his followers from giving "what is holy to dogs" or from tossing "your pearls before pigs." Obedience to Jesus' words requires discerning the identity of the "dogs" and of the "pigs." Finally, how are Jesus' followers expected to watch out for "false prophets" (Matt 7:15) if they are prohibited from discerning who is false?

From the larger context of Matthew's Gospel, one passage in particular sticks out as relevant: Matthew 18:15–20. Jesus commands his followers to rebuke fellow followers when they sin.[4] The process outlined in these verses involves much judging, again, in the sense of discernment. John Stott aptly concludes that "the command to *judge not* is not a requirement to be blind."[5]

In the context of the entire New Testament, a prohibition against discernment appears to fail as well. Jesus' own teaching in John 7:24 appears to contradict Matthew 7:1 on the surface: "Stop judging according to outward appearances;

---

[2] See Louw and Nida, 30.75, 56.30; and BDAG, 567–68.

[3] David L. Turner, "The Gospel According to Matthew," in *Cornerstone Biblical Commentary*, ed. Philip W. Comfort (Carol Stream, IL: Tyndale, 2005), 110.

[4] See chapter 12 for a brief summary of this passage. It is possible that the text says, "If your brother sins against you" (HCSB, ESV, KJV) rather than "If your brother sins" (NIV, NASB, NET). Regardless of which reading is deemed as original, the point made above remains relevant.

[5] John R. W. Stott, *The Message of the Sermon on the Mount* (Downers Grove: InterVarsity, 1985), 177.

rather judge according to righteous judgment." Here is an explicit command from Jesus to "judge," using the same word as in Matthew 7:1. In the context Jesus is discussing how the Jews (or possibly the Jewish leaders) were passing judgment on Jesus (referring to discernment) regarding his actions on the Sabbath (see John 7:23). So he commands them to cease discerning based on "mere appearances" (NIV), a phrase that refers to a "superficial"[6] discernment. Instead of discerning superficially, they are commanded to discern based on a "righteous judgment." Jesus is explaining that a right or correct judgment of himself will lead them to conclude that he is actually fulfilling the laws of circumcision and Sabbath (cf. John 7:22–23).

Paul discusses the process for disciplining a Christian who is involved in public sin in 1 Corinthians 5:1–13 (similar to Matthew 18:15–20). Several places in this chapter call for Christians to be discerning. Paul commands the sinning person to be removed from the congregation (5:2) and turned over to Satan (5:5). He reminds them "not to associate with anyone who claims to be a believer who is sexually immoral or greedy, an idolater or verbally abusive, a drunkard or a swindler" (5:11). The only way to follow Paul's exhortation is to be discerning of those with whom you associate. Other verses that exhort Christians to be discerning include Galatians 1:8–9 (discernment about a false gospel); Philippians 3:2 (discernment over the "dogs," evil workers, and mutilators of the flesh); 1 John 4:1 (discernment about "the spirits" and false prophets); and 2 John 10 (discernment about false teachers).

A strong case can be made that the overall teaching in the New Testament is for Christians to be discerning in areas including others' sin and false teaching. Christians should diligently discern in at least both of these areas. If Matthew 7:1 does not prohibit discernment, what is Jesus prohibiting?

What Matthew 7:1 Does Mean

In contrast to interpreting Matthew 7:1 as a prohibition against discernment, it is a prohibition against an overly judgmental attitude. Jesus' disciples are to be committed to a righteous life, but he does not authorize them to have a judgmental attitude. The reason Jesus prohibits this is spelled out in the second half of 7:1: "so that you won't be judged."

While this phrase could mean that by being censorious you invite others to be overly critical of yourself, it most likely means that when you are overly critical of others, God will judge you with those same standards. Being quick to condemn others is inviting the condemnation of God on your life. People are incapable of knowing with any certainty another person's heart, nor can we

---

[6] See Carson, *John*, 316.

know their motives.[7] Stott concludes: "To be censorious is to presume arrogantly to anticipate the day of judgment, to usurp the prerogative of the divine Judge, in fact to try to play God."[8]

Rather than requiring blindness, Matthew 7:1 is "a plea to be generous."[9] Augustine summarizes Jesus' teaching this way: "We are taught nothing else, but that in the case of those actions respecting which it is doubtful with what intention they are done, we are to put the better construction on them."[10] This is what some call giving "the charitable assumption."

Application

While many of us are quick to criticize and condemn other Christians, we should be more generous in our assumptions about others' actions. You might see another Christian doing something that appears sinful, but we shouldn't conclude too quickly that our judgment is correct. While sometimes it could be obvious, other times reality is much more complicated than what we think. Try to give the charitable assumption when possible.

Paul appears to be applying the principle of Matthew 7:1 in Romans 14:3–4: "One who eats must not look down on one who does not eat, and one who does not eat must not *criticize* one who does, because God has accepted him. Who are you to *criticize* another's household slave?" (emphasis added). Both words translated "criticize" above are the same Greek word as in Matthew 7:1. Paul is prohibiting the overly critical attitude of condemning others' actions on "doubtful issues" (Rom 14:1). The context of this prohibition probably relates to Jewish dietary laws and the difficulty of obtaining kosher meat.[11] Therefore, be all the more open to adopting the charitable assumption in areas that are "doubtful," that is, grey areas in Christian living.

Annotated Bibliography

Commentaries

Carson, D. A. "Matthew." In *The Expositor's Bible Commentary: Matthew and Mark*. Edited by Tremper Longman III and David E. Garland. Grand Rapids: Zondervan, 2010.

---

[7] Cf. Stott, *Sermon on the Mount*, 177.

[8] Ibid. Cf. D. A. Carson, "Matthew," in *The Expositor's Bible Commentary: Matthew and Mark*, ed. Tremper Longman III and David E. Garland (Grand Rapids: Zondervan, 2010), 219.

[9] Stott, *Sermon on the Mount*, 177.

[10] Cited in Leon Morris, *The Gospel According to Matthew*, PNTC (Grand Rapids: Eerdmans, 1992), 164, n. 2.

[11] See Douglas J. Moo, *The Epistle to the Romans*, NICNT (Grand Rapids: Eerdmans, 1996), 837.

Carson's excellent commentary has some brief but insightful comments on this issue. See especially page 219.

Stott, John R. W. *The Message of the Sermon on the Mount*. Downers Grove: InterVarsity, 1985.

Stott's book has some penetrating and pastoral thoughts. See especially page 177.

Websites

Chaffey, Tim. "Commonly Misused Bible Verses: Matthew 7:1." *Midwest Apologetics*. July 22, 2011. Accessed July 17, 2014. www.midwestapologetics.org/blog/?p=618.

Chaffey provides a few good reasons to avoid the legend above.

Warren, Michael H., Jr. "Judge Others. Jesus Said To." *Christian Civilization*. Accessed July 17, 2014. www.christianciv.com/Judge_Others.htm.

This article discusses the legend above but also discusses the theme of judging throughout the New Testament.

CHAPTER 8

Jesus' Most Famous Quote Is John 3:16

John 3:16

The Legendary Teaching on John 3:16

I am excited this week because I get to preach in the paint, teach from the words of Jesus himself. Now I love all of Scripture, but nothing equals teaching from the words of Jesus Christ. Jesus said in John 3:16, "For God loved the world in this way: He gave His One and Only Son, so that everyone who believes in Him will not perish but have eternal life." These words speak of God's love and Jesus' coming so those who believe can have eternal life. Nothing is more important in Scripture than the words in red, so pay close attention to them.

Introduction: Is John 3:16 the Most Famous Bible Verse?

Some interesting studies have been done on what verses in the Bible are the most popular. Bible Gateway does an article every year about the most searched for Bible verse on their website. In 2011 the top verses were: (1) Jeremiah 29:11; (2) John 3:16; and (3) Philippians 4:13. In 2012, the King James Version Online had these as their top three popular verses: (1) Psalm 23:4; (2) Philippians 4:13; (3) John 3:16. Another study concluded that John 3:16 was the most highlighted verse in the Kindle ESV, being highlighted twice as many times as the verse that came in second place: Philippians 4:13. Every study I looked at had John 3:16 near the top of the list for popular verses in the Bible.[1] Therefore, it appears justifiable to say that John 3:16 is probably the

---

[1] For the above studies, see "The Top Five Bible Verses of 2011," *Bible Gateway* (January 30, 2012), accessed June 3, 2014, www.biblegateway.com/blog/2012/01/the-top-five-bible-verses-of-2011; Audrey Barrick, "Most Popular Bible Verses of 2012; 'I Will Fear No Evil' Tops List," *The Christian Post* (January 3, 2013), accessed June 3, 2014, www.christianpost.

most popular verse in the Gospels. So how could I say that it is not true that Jesus' most famous quote is John 3:16?

John 3:16 appears in red letters in most Bibles, and red letters are used to indicate that Jesus is speaking. The practice of publishing the Bible with Jesus' words in red ink began in 1899 with Lewis Klopsch, an American editor for a magazine called *The Christian Herald*.[2] Today it can be hard to find a Bible where Jesus' words are *not* in red.

The Accuracy of the Red Letters

Since the inspiration and inerrancy of Scripture do not extend to the format of publication (for example, the color of the words on a page), can we be absolutely confident all the words in red were actually spoken by Jesus? Many issues are involved in this discussion,[3] but for the current purposes we are going to focus on whether Jesus actually spoke the words in John 3:16.

Since the original Greek manuscripts did not contain quotation marks, there is some debate as to what the indicators might be in the Greek text that would clue the reader in to the fact that a quote is about to be given. This is an interpretation about whether the words are a quote by someone speaking or a comment by the author of the book.

Is This a Valid Question? Of Course Jesus Spoke John 3:16!

Even though John 3:16 might be in red letters and quotation marks in your Bible, since that was an interpretive decision made by a Bible translation committee, we need to ask whether their interpretation was correct. One way to investigate this is to look at different translations to see if there is any wrestling among them, any disagreements or footnotes to clue the reader in that there is an issue or controversy. The following five translations put the verse in quotation marks: NASB, ESV, NKJV, NLT, and HCSB. But the HCSB, after verse 21, has a footnote that says, "It is possible that Jesus' words end at verse 15." This means they are saying that it's possible John 3:16–21 is not a quote of Jesus but the apostle John reflecting upon the previous verses: Jesus' encounter

---

com/news/most-popular-bible-verses-of-2012-i-will-fear-no-evil-tops-list-87676; Paul Ellis, "The 7 Most Popular Verses in the Bible," *Escape to Reality* (May 16, 2012), accessed June 3, 2014, www.escapetoreality.org/2012/05/16/7-most-popular-bible-verses. Also note that the results for Bible Gateway in 2009 were: (1) John 3:16; (2) Jeremiah 29:11.

² Steve Eng, "The Story Behind: Red Letter Bible Editions," *Bible Collectors' World* (January/March, 1986), accessed June 3, 2014, www.biblecollectors.org/articles/red_letter_bible. htm. Klopsch claimed Luke 22:20 for his inspiration: "This cup is the new covenant established by My blood. It is shed for you."

³ For example, the *Ipsissima Verba* and *Ipsissima Vox* debate and the issue of the language(s) Jesus spoke (see chap. 20) and the translation of his words.

with Nicodemus. The ESV has a footnote after verse 15 that says, "Some interpreters hold that the quotation ends at verse 15." This is similar to the HCSB, which has the footnote earlier in the chapter.

Both the NIV[4] and the NET *do not* have the verse in quotation marks, and both have footnotes after verse 15 saying that the quote might continue to verse 21. By looking at seven translations, we see significant evidence that the committees who translated the Bible were divided over whether John 3:16–21 was spoken by Jesus.

The Evidence from John 3

There are three main reasons John 3:16 was probably not spoken by Jesus. First, it would create redundancy between John 3:15 and 3:16: "So that everyone who believes in Him will have eternal life. For God so loved the world in this way: He gave His One and Only Son, so that everyone who believes in Him will not perish but have eternal life." If the quotation ends after verse 15, then the author is beginning a summarizing section in verses 16–21. However, if Jesus is continuing to speak in verse 16, then John 3:16 becomes somewhat redundant with 3:15. Essentially everything that is stated in 3:15 is repeated in 3:16. It seems more likely that a change is taking place: Jesus is no longer speaking, and we are now reading John's thoughts.

Second, the writing style and vocabulary used in John 3:16 seem to indicate that the apostle John was speaking here and not Jesus. Here are four pieces of evidence: (1) Some of the translations say Jesus is the "only begotten," and some say he is the "One and Only."[5] Both of these phrases are translating one Greek word, and the only other places it occurs outside of John 3:16–21 in the Gospel of John are in John 1:14 and 1:18. In both of those verses, the apostle John is speaking, not Jesus.[6] This is a word more comfortable on the lips of the Beloved Disciple, John, than our Savior. (2) The phrase "believed in the name" occurs in John 3:18. Similar phrases occurred previously in John 1:12 and 2:23; Jesus was not speaking in either of those contexts.[7] (3) John 3:21 refers to practicing the truth, a phrase that, in the New Testament, only elsewhere occurs in 1 John 1:6. (4) The weakest argument is regarding the phrase "the light." It occurs six times in the Gospel of John before John 3:19–21. All six are in chapter 1 and are statements by the apostle John.[8]

---

4   This is a reference to the 2011 NIV. The 1984 NIV puts John 3:16 in quotes.
5   The issue of the meaning of this word is beyond the purview of the current study.
6   It is also used by John in 1 John 4:9.
7   The phrase also occurs in 1 John 5:13.
8   After this passage it is found spoken by Jesus and in John's voice.

The final reason relates to the content of the verse. John 3:16 says that God's love was demonstrated by the giving of his Son; those who believe in his Son, based on God's act of giving, will be saved. What does it mean that God *gave* his Son? There are two main options in this context for the meaning of "gave." The first is based on the verse that follows John 3:16: "For God did not send His Son into the world." This could lead you to think that the *giving* in John 3:16 refers to the incarnation: Jesus leaving heaven and taking the form of a man. But think about this question: if Jesus left heaven, took the form of a man, preached the good news of the kingdom of God, but never died as a sacrifice for sin, would believing in him result in eternal life? In other words, did Jesus have to die for believers to receive eternal life? If you say yes, then you need to look at option two: the *giving* refers to Jesus' death.

John 3:14–15, the verses leading right up to John 3:16, say, "Just as Moses lifted up the snake in the wilderness, so the Son of Man must be lifted up, so that everyone who believes in Him will have eternal life." The words seem to be referencing Jesus' forthcoming death. Jesus is referring to his own death somewhat cryptically so that those who were there (and the readers of the Gospel of John) may not have understood what Jesus was talking about.[9] This is why John decides he needs to clarify Jesus' words about being lifted up. John wanted his readers to grasp that Jesus was talking about his death and about providing eternal life for all who believe. Therefore, when John says God *gave*, Jesus' death must be included in that giving. But Jesus hadn't died by the time we read John 3. This can't be Jesus talking about his death in the past, so it must be the apostle John, after Jesus had died, thinking about Jesus' death and writing about it.

Does It Really Matter?

The reason this matters is because the meaning of the word "gave" is at stake. Once you declare that Jesus said the words in John 3:16, then logically you must believe He did not need to die on the cross. Now I know people don't usually mean this when they say that Jesus said John 3:16, but what other meaning are you going to give to the word "gave"? Jesus' purpose in coming into the world was to seek and save the lost. But his death on the cross becomes just an interesting addition to his story, not really the climax, if the giving that causes those of us who believe in him to have eternal life was his incarnation.

For the Gospel writers and the authors of the rest of the New Testament, Jesus' death, burial, and resurrection seem to be the key cornerstone of all of Christian theology, not an additional note at the end. This is the reason He

---

[9] Jesus was actually referencing a story in Numbers 21:4–9.

came: to live a life of obedience and die on the cross as a sacrifice for us, paying a penalty we could never pay. It wasn't the incarnation; it was his death.

Application

Jesus' death on the cross is an essential part of all gospel presentations. Without the cross there would be no forgiveness of sins, no reconciliation of God with man, and God's wrath would not be appeased. We must never downplay the importance of the cross, for in John 3:16 the cross is the ultimate demonstration of God's love for us.

Annotated Bibliography

Commentaries

Carson, D. A. *The Gospel According to John*. PNTC. Grand Rapids: Eerdmans, 1991.
Köstenberger, Andreas J. *Encountering John: The Gospel in Historical, Literary, and Theological Perspective*. Encountering Biblical Studies. Grand Rapids: Baker, 1999.
    A very accessible and brief commentary on John's Gospel.

Journals

Steele, Mary. "Where Does the Speech Quotation End in John 3:1–21?" *Notes on Translation* 2.2 (1988): 51–58.
Trudinger, P. "Jesus' 'Comfortable Words' in John 3:16: A Note of Disappointment to Some?" *St Mark's Review* 147 (1991): 30–31.

Websites

Mounce, Bill. "John 3:16 (quotation marks)." *Teknia*. February 5, 2008. Accessed June 23, 2014. www.teknia.com/blog/john-3-16-quotation-marks.
    Mounce's blog doesn't exactly come to a conclusion on this but raises the issue in a helpful way.

CHAPTER 9

Hell Referred to a First-Century Garbage Dump near Jerusalem

Mark 9:47

The Legendary Teaching on Mark 9:47

A few different words used in the Greek New Testament are translated "hell." The word used in Mark 9:47 is the Greek word *gehenna*: "And if your eye causes your downfall, gouge it out. It is better for you to enter the kingdom of God with one eye than to have two eyes and be thrown into hell."

> Gehenna, in Jesus's day, was the city dump. People tossed their garbage and waste into this valley. There was a fire there, burning constantly to consume the trash. Wild animals fought over scraps of food along the edges of the heap. When they fought, their teeth would make a gnashing sound. Gehenna was the place with the gnashing of teeth, where the fire never went out. Gehenna was an actual place that Jesus's listeners would have been familiar with. So the next time someone asks you if you believe in an actual hell, you can always say, "Yes, I do believe that my garbage goes somewhere."[1]

Introduction: Unraveling the Legend

Some interpreters have used this (supposed) background information to explain the excruciating eternal torment of hell and others to communicate doubts about an eternal hell. *Gehenna* is derived from a Greek word based on the Hebrew phrase "Valley of Hinnom." Where is the evidence that this place was used as a trash dump during the first century?

---

[1] Rob Bell, *Love Wins: A Book about Heaven, Hell, and the Fate of Every Person Who Ever Lived* (New York: HarperOne, 2011), 68.

49

The legendary background information is taken from Rabbi David Kimhi's (died around 1235) commentary on Psalm 27: "Gehenna is a repugnant place, into which filth and cadavers are thrown, and in which fires perpetually burn in order to consume the filth and bones; on which account, by analogy, the judgement of the wicked is called 'Gehenna.'"[2] Bailey concludes that Kimhi's conclusion "finds no support in literary sources or archaeological data from the intertestamental or rabbinic periods. There is no evidence that the valley was, in fact, a garbage dump, and thus his explanation is insufficient."[3] If the "trash dump" theory is not the background for *Gehenna*, then what is?

What Is the Background for *Gehenna* in the Old Testament?

Joshua 15:8 places the Valley of Hinnom near Jerusalem. It was probably southwest of Jerusalem. Second Kings 23:8–10 explains that King Josiah defiled the Valley of Hinnom (also called Topheth) to prevent Israelites from worshipping false gods and sacrificing their children to Molech by burning them. This practice may have been introduced to the Israelites by King Ahaz (eighth century BC), who had his own son pass through the fire (2 Kgs 16:3; 2 Chron 28:3; cf. with Manasseh [seventh century BC] in 2 Chron 33:6).

Jeremiah (seventh-sixth century BC) describes this practice in his time as well. In Jeremiah 7:30–34, he prophesied that the name of Topheth/Valley of Hinnom would be changed to "Valley of Slaughter," becoming "a cemetery, because there will be no other burial place" (7:32).

The last chapter of Isaiah (eighth-seventh century BC) provides the background from which Jesus speaks in Mark 9:47. Isaiah 66 prophesied judgment for those rebelling against God. Those who worship God will observe the dead corpses of those who rebelled and were judged. They are in a condition of eternal death and eternal destruction. Isaiah 66:24 says, "As they leave, they will see the dead bodies of the men who have rebelled against Me; for their worm will never die, their fire will never go out, and they will be a horror to all mankind." Isaiah emphasizes the permanence of God's judgment against those who rebelled.

How Was Gehenna Understood in the Time of Jesus?

Jewish thought around the time of Jesus related the concepts of the Valley of Hinnom with judgment from these Old Testament texts. Hence, Gehenna became a word for eternal torment. Jesus is adopting contemporary terminology

---

[2] Cited from Lloyd R. Bailey, "Gehenna: The Topography of Hell," *Biblical Archaeologist* 49, no. 3 (1986): 188.

[3] Ibid., 189.

when he refers to hell with the Greek word for *Gehenna*. According to Peter Head, Jesus' use of this word "suggests a durative aspect to the unquenchable fire and continuing destructive activity of the worm."[4]

Several writings by Jews between the Old and New Testament help explain the understanding of *Gehenna* in Jesus' time. The apocryphal book of Judith (probably written by a Jew in the Second Temple period) interprets Isaiah 66:24 as a reference to eternal torment: "Woe to the nations rising up against my people; the Lord Almighty will take vengeance on them in the day of judgment, putting fire and worms into their flesh and they will weep in pain forever." In 1 Enoch 27:2–3 (maybe second century BC), Uriel says:

> This accursed valley is for those accursed forever; here will gather together all (those) accursed ones, those who speak with their mouth unbecoming words against the Lord and utter hard words concerning his glory. Here shall they be gathered together, and here shall be their judgment, in the last days. There will be upon them the spectacle of the righteous judgment, in the presence of the righteous forever.[5]

There are several other places where the Valley of Hinnom is apparently referred to as a place of judgment in 1 Enoch (54:1–6; 56:1–4; 90:24–27). Fourth Ezra 7:26–38, probably written by a Jew around AD 100, uses Gehenna to refer to hell. Sibylline Oracles 4.179–91 (though extremely difficult to date, probably written by a Jew in the late first century AD) references Gehenna and Tartarus together in discussing hell.

Tying It Together

What caused a valley that was associated with worship of the god Molech to become a word for hell? Bailey provides two possibilities. It could be that the geographical location of the Valley of Hinnom evolved, via the prophecies of Jeremiah and Isaiah, to "a place for the disposition of the living wicked. It becomes a vital solution to the problem of a wicked, rebellious world."[6] While this solution is altogether possible, Bailey finds the second option slightly more likely. The sacrifice of humans was offered in Hinnom to the god Molech; those who practiced this worship may have believed an entrance

---

4   Peter M. Head, "The Duration of Divine Judgment in the New Testament," in *Eschatology in Bible and Theology: Evangelical Essays at the Dawn of a New Millennium*, ed. Kent E. Brower and Mark W. Elliott (Downers Grove: InterVarsity, 1997), 223.

5   E. Isaac, "1 (Ethiopic Apocalypse of) Enoch: A New Translation and Introduction," in *The Old Testament Pseudipigrapha*, ed. James H. Charlesworth, 2 vols. (New York: Doubleday, 1983), 1:27.

6   Bailey, "Gehenna," 189.

to the underworld of Molech was in this valley. The name of the valley transferred to the name of the underworld location of Molech.[7]

The Legend Continues

Besides the excellent article by Bailey, New Testament scholar Beasley-Murray concluded similarly that besides Kimhi, this concept "is not attested in any ancient source."[8] Similarly, Peter Head concluded that "there is no convincing evidence in the primary sources for the existence of a fiery rubbish dump in this location."[9] Postdating the 1986 works of Beasley-Murray and Bailey, books are still being written advocating this viewpoint. Besides Rob Bell's book cited above, N. T. Wright says, "Gehenna was Jerusalem's smouldering rubbish-heap, and thence became a metaphor for the place of fiery judgment after death."[10] He says this immediately preceding a reference to Bailey's article! Only a few years ago, Wright used this background material to argue that once Christians realized that Gehenna was only a trash dump Jesus was referring to, then we could rid ourselves of the thought that unless we repent in this life we will burn in the next one.[11] I've been told that the legendary information is regularly given by tour guides in Israel. Recognize that many interpreters who hold to a traditional Christian view of hell also advocate the Gehenna-trash dump theory.[12]

---

[7] Ibid., 190–91.

[8] G. R. Beasley-Murray, *Jesus and the Kingdom of God* (Grand Rapids: Eerdmans, 1986), 376–77n92.

[9] Head, "Duration of Divine Judgment," 223. See also Francis Chan and Preston Sprinkle, *Erasing Hell: What God Said about Eternity, and the Things We've Made Up* (Colorado Springs: David C. Cook, 2011), 59–60.

[10] N. T. Wright, *Jesus and the Victory of God* (Minneapolis: Fortress, 1996), 183n142.

[11] See N. T. Wright, *Surprised by Hope: Rethinking Heaven, the Resurrection, and the Mission of the Church* (New York: HarperOne, 2008), 175–76. Note that two recent books by Andrew Perriman, *The Coming of the Son of Man: New Testament Eschatology for an Emerging Church* (London: Paternoster, 2005), 92n18, and *Hell and Heaven in Narrative Perspective* (n.p.: CreateSpace Independent Publishing, 2012), 39–40, recognize the evidence stacked against him, but he still believes this theory is "plausible."

[12] For example, Douglas Moo, "James," in *Zondervan Illustrated Bible Backgrounds Commentary: Hebrews to Revelation* (Grand Rapids: Zondervan, 2002), 104–5. Many evangelical interpreters reference the Valley of Hinnom being used as a trash dump after the time period of the Old Testament, but in an ambiguous way to the time of Christ. For example, see Michael J. Wilkins, "Matthew," in *Zondervan Illustrated Bible Backgrounds Commentary: Matthew, Mark, Luke* (Grand Rapids: Zondervan, 2002), 39; Craig Blomberg, *Matthew*, NAC (Nashville: B&H, 1992), 107. For an interesting example of rising doubt regarding this belief, compare R. T. France, *The Gospel According to Matthew: An Introduction and Commentary* (Grand Rapids: Eerdmans, 1985), 120, to R. T. France, *The Gospel of Matthew*, NICNT (Grand Rapids: Eerdmans, 2007), 202, where France seems less sure of his earlier understanding.

Interpreting Mark 9:47–48

Jesus' reference to Gehenna in Mark 9:47 is based on contemporary Jewish usage. It referred to the place of torment for those who did not worship God. He is saying this is a place to avoid at all costs, hence the hyperbolic statement about gouging out an eye. The allusion to Isaiah 66:24 is used to demonstrate the permanence and unending nature of the final judgment. Jesus paints an appalling picture of Gehenna to try to get his hearers to do all they can to avoid it.

Application

Hell is real and gruesome. It is a place of eternal torment, separated from fellowship with God, but with His wrath being poured out on the unrepentant forever. Jesus' words in Mark 1:15 encapsulate an application for this reality: "Repent and believe in the good news!" One final application is to spread the gospel near and far, to the ends of the earth, that at all costs people are given the opportunity to respond in repentance and faith to God's Son who died for them.

Annotated Bibliography

Books

Beasley-Murray, G. R. *Jesus and the Kingdom of God*. Grand Rapids: Eerdmans, 1986.
   A short discussion but very helpful regarding the legend above. See pages 376–77n92.
Chan, Francis, and Preston Sprinkle. *Erasing Hell: What God Said About Eternity, and the Things We've Made Up*. Colorado Springs: David C. Cook, 2011.
   In a very nontechnical way, they explain the legend and refute it. See pages 59–60.

Journals

Bailey, Lloyd R. "Gehenna: The Topography of Hell." *Biblical Archaeologist* 49, no. 3 (1986): 187–91.
   Probably the best resource on this topic.

Websites

Bolen, Todd. "The Fires of Gehenna: Views of Scholars." *BiblePlaces.com Blog*. April 29, 2011. Accessed July 17, 2014. blog.bibleplaces.com/2011/04/fires-of-gehenna-views-of-scholars.html.

CHAPTER 10

The Gospel of John Never Refers to Repentance

John 12:40

The Legendary Teaching on Repentance in the Gospel of John

John's Gospel has only one condition for receiving eternal life: believing in Jesus. John seems to avoid the word *repentance* intentionally. If I summarized John the Baptist's preaching in one word, I'd say, "Repent!" But John the Baptist's message in the Gospel of John ignores that word and instead focuses on the idea of being a "witness."
Two common words are used in connection to "believe" in John's Gospel, and neither of those has any connotations to the concept of repentance: *know* and *receive*. John 3:16 provides the consistent message in John's Gospel for how eternal life is attained: "For God loved the world in this way: He gave His One and Only Son, so that everyone who believes in Him will not perish but have eternal life." Nothing is required except believing in Jesus.

The word and concept of repentance are missing from John's Gospel. Because of this, Lewis Sperry Chafer said: "No thoughtful person would attempt to defend such a notion against such odds. And those who have thus undertaken doubtless have done so without weighing the evidence or considering the untenable position which they assume."[1] Chafer is responding to the idea that repentance should be part of a gospel presentation. How could you even think about attempting to demonstrate that when repentance doesn't even occur in John's Gospel! Therefore, the concept of repentance can be ignored in gospel presentations because the Gospel of John doesn't discuss it. Unless you think John has misrepresented the gospel himself.

---

[1] Lewis Sperry Chafer, *Systematic Theology*, 8 vols. (Dallas: Dallas Seminary Press, 1947–48), 3:376–77.

Introduction: Unraveling the Legend

"It is only through that man who died on a tree 2,000 years ago that you can be put into a right relationship with God." If, after reading that sentence, someone said to you, "Dave doesn't believe Jesus is the only way to God because he didn't actually mention Jesus," would that be accurate? What if he said, "Dave doesn't believe the cross is essential for salvation because he doesn't mention the cross"? What if he said, "Dave denies the reconciling power of Jesus' death on the cross because he doesn't mention that"? How would you respond? Hopefully you would say something like this: "He referred to all those concepts even though he didn't use the words." By using the phrase "that man," I am hoping the context makes clear that I am talking about Jesus. By mentioning a tree, I was referring to the cross. I might have avoided the technical jargon of *saved* or *reconciled*, but when I say a "right relationship with God," the conceptual similarity should be obvious.

Sometimes people look for a particular word when doing a Bible study, and when they can't find the exact word, they assume the concept is absent as well. That is a tragic mistake. Though a specific word might not be used, the concept might be prominent. The noun for "repentance" occurs twenty-two times in the New Testament while the verb for "repent" occurs thirty-four times; together they occur fifty-six times.

Occurrences of the Word "Repent/Repentance" in the New Testament

	Matthew	Mark	Luke-Acts	Paul	Hebrews	2 Peter	Revelation	TOTAL
Noun for *repentance*	2	1	11	4	3	1		22
Verb for *repent*	5	2	14	1			12	34

People could draw several possible conclusions from the chart above. For example, since Paul only used the verb and noun a total of five times, maybe he didn't think repentance was an important aspect of salvation or the Christian life. In fact, its absence in much of the New Testament could lead to this conclusion, as well. But how could someone possibly explain the absolute silence in John's Gospel? Though John also didn't use it in his letters, the book of Revelation uses it twelve times. But in the Gospel of John, he completely avoided the word. He is familiar with it since he uses it in Revelation, so why would he totally ignore it in the Gospel of John?

Answering an Objection

The absence of a word doesn't equal the denial of a concept. For example, just because John doesn't mention the virgin birth doesn't mean he was ignorant of it or denied it. Also, two common words are used for hell in the New Testament (three words overall), and neither of them occurs in John's Gospel. Paul doesn't use them either. Does that mean they denied that there was a hell? Jesus is never given the title Savior in Matthew's or Mark's Gospel, nor in Romans, Colossians, Hebrews, or Revelation. Does that mean the authors didn't view Jesus as Savior because they didn't use that particular word? That is an untenable position based merely on silence. Therefore, the absence of the word doesn't necessitate the absence of a concept. When the word is not there, the concept *might* also not be there. One scholar said regarding repentance and the gospel, "Let the debate over the gospel begin with John's Gospel, unless you would accuse him of preaching half a gospel or easy believism."[2] I agree. Let that debate begin with the Gospel of John.

Searching for the Concept

The definition of repentance needs to be clear in order to properly search for the concept. *Repentance* is defined as "turning away from sin."[3] There are two main categories related to repentance: Christian living and salvation. Repentance in Christian living is often included in what theologians call progressive sanctification: growing more Christlike throughout one's Christian life. However, repentance regarding salvation is the concept being searched for in John's Gospel. The proper response to the gospel is at stake in this study.

While six compelling passages in John's Gospel discuss the concept of repentance, only the top two will be discussed now: John 3:19–21 and 5:14.[4] On the tails of the most recognized verse in the New Testament, we find a solid argument for the concept of repentance. John 3:16 is a wonderful verse, which is part of the problem. It's actually a mesmerizing verse. Many people read John 3:16 and love it so much they stop reading. They don't see the verses around it because they are so focused on John 3:16. The verses following John 3:16 are unpacking the meaning of that verse, verses 19–21 in particular. Here is where we will find the concept of repentance: "This, then, is the judgment: The light has come into the world, and people loved darkness rather than the

---

[2] Charles C. Bing, "The Condition for Salvation in John's Gospel," *Journal of the Grace Evangelical Society* 9, no. 16 (1996): 33.
[3] See chapter 17 on Acts 2:38 for evidence for this definition.
[4] For discussion of all relevant passages, see David A. Croteau, "Repentance Found? The Concept of Repentance in the Fourth Gospel," *Master's Seminary Journal* 24, no. 1 (Spring 2013): 97–123.

light because their deeds were evil. For everyone who practices wicked things hates the light and avoids it, so that his deeds may not be exposed. But anyone who lives by the truth comes to the light, so that his works may be shown to be accomplished by God." There is a contrast between two groups in these verses: those who are believing and those who are unbelieving. The believing are described as those who come to the light. The unbelieving are described as those who hate or avoid the light. Why would one person come to the light and another person hate or avoid the light? Those who believe come to the light because they have works that were accomplished by God. They don't have a reason to be embarrassed by the exposure light will give. So they come to the light because they have works. Why do the unbelieving avoid the light? Because they don't want their evil deeds exposed. The reason they are called unbelieving is because they have not *turned from their sin* and are still doing evil deeds. There is a lack of turning from sin and, instead, an embracing of sin. This is the concept of repentance. The unbelieving are defined as non-repentant. John is wrapping up the concept of repentance in his definition of what he means by "believe." That is why the concept is present even though he doesn't use the word.

Probably the best passage that refers to the concept of repentance is John 5:14. This verse takes place in the context of Jesus' healing a man who was unable to walk for thirty-eight years. Jesus tells the man to pick up his mat and walk. Many Jews believed it was sinful to carry a mat on the Sabbath. He blamed his Healer when he was questioned about why he was carrying his mat on the Sabbath, though he didn't know the identity of his Healer. Then Jesus went up to the man and said, "See, you are well. Do not sin anymore, so that something worse doesn't happen to you" (John 5:14). Jesus states plainly what this man is supposed to do: don't sin anymore. Saying "do not sin" is conceptually equivalent to saying, "Turn from sin." The idea of turning from sin is the idea of not doing it any longer. This is essentially a command to repent. Jesus is telling him, "Change your ways. Turn your life around. Turn to God." This is in the context of a man who shows no evidence of saving faith. Therefore, it is in the context of calling someone to salvation. I have yet to read any scholar reference this verse when searching for the concept of repentance in the Gospel of John.

Repentance Found?

Virtually everyone seems to have conceded the point that the word for repentance does not occur in John's Gospel. But what if the word was in the text and people kept missing it for some reason? I believe John explicitly refers to repentance but by using a less common word for it. The key text is John 12:39–40: "This is why they were unable to believe, because Isaiah also said:

He has blinded their eyes and hardened their hearts, so that they would not see with their eyes or understand with their hearts, and be converted, and I would heal them." John 12:40 is a paraphrase of Isaiah 6:9–10. John seems to expect that his audience would have been familiar with Isaiah. Two verses earlier, in John 12:38, he quotes Isaiah as well. The Greek word translated "converted" in John 12:40 is not one of the two most common words related to repentance: *metanoia* (a noun) or *metanoeō* (a verb). Instead, John uses *strephō*, a verb meaning "to turn." The concept of repentance, turning away from sin, and this verb, meaning "to turn," are fairly close in meaning. But there is more evidence.

The Hebrew word in Isaiah 6:10 is *shuv*. This verb can mean "repent" or "turn back from evil." For example, Jeremiah 15:7b says, "They did not *repent* of their ways" (NASB, emphasis added). Isaiah 59:20b is another example: "In Jacob who repent of their sins" (NIV). There are others, but these two should be sufficient. Here is how some translations translate *shuv* in Isaiah 6:10:

> NASB: "return"
> ESV, NIV: "turn"
> HCSB: "turn back"
> NET: "repent"

Isaiah 6:9–10 is discussing the concept of repentance. When John cites the passage, he may not use *metanoia* or *metanoeō*, but he uses a word that can refer to the same idea. To the man who said, "Let the debate over the gospel begin with John's Gospel unless we would accuse him of preaching a half gospel or easy believism," I agree. Let it start with John's Gospel because John references the concept of repentance, the idea of turning from sin, when he describes the unbelieving as refusing to turn from their sins (John 3:19–21); when he tells the healed man in John 5:14, "Do not sin"; and by referencing Isaiah 6:9–10, which contains a word that can be used to refer to the concept of repentance. Let's preach the gospel here and abroad, and remember that the proper response to the gospel is both faith and repentance.

Annotated Bibliography

Journals

Croteau, David A. "Repentance Found? The Concept of Repentance in the Fourth Gospel." *Master's Seminary Journal* 24, no. 1 (Spring 2013): 97–123.

This is a much longer study on repentance, which includes a section on defining the word *repentance* and discusses several more texts that have repentance conceptually present. It is available at www.tms.edu/tmsj/msj24e.pdf.

Websites

MacArthur, John. "Repentance in the Gospel of John." *Grace to You.* November 24, 2009. Accessed on July 14, 2014. www.gty.org/resources/articles/a238/repentance-in-the-gospel-of-john.

CHAPTER 11

The "Eye of a Needle" Was a Gate in Jerusalem

Mark 10:25

The Legendary Teaching on Mark 10:25

Some of Jesus' words in the Gospels are difficult to understand. Many times the reason for the difficulty is that we don't understand the culture and historical setting for his words. For example, Jesus said, "It is easier for a camel to go through the eye of a needle than for a rich person to enter the kingdom of God" (Mark 10:25). It could seem like Jesus is saying all rich people will go to hell; a camel is never going to fit through the eye of a needle. However, since it's obvious that not all rich people are going to hell, we need to look deeper and not settle for a superficial understanding.

In the ancient Near East cities had large gates that had small and low openings called "needle's eyes." These tiny gates were too narrow and too short for a camel to get through in the regular way, especially if they were loaded. If a camel was going to go through a needle gate, it had to kneel down, have its burden removed, and shuffle on its knees through the gate. It would also need to bow its head to squeeze through. In like manner, for a rich person to enter heaven, he must be willing to get rid of his wealth and material possessions, kneel in prayer, and humbly lower his head before the sovereign God of the universe.

Introduction: Unraveling the Legend

This is one of the most popular urban legends in this book. It has been preached and repeated countless times. Some scholars say that this interpretation arose in the fifteenth century; others say the ninth century. Some scholars specifically name Theophylact (a Greek archbishop who died in 1107) as the originator of this interpretation; I've yet to be convinced he ever advocated this.

Popular commentator Matthew Henry proposed two possible interpretations for Mark 10:25. He first mentioned the idea of a small gate in Jerusalem as discussed above. He introduced that interpretation by saying, "Some imagine there might be," probably indicating some doubt about the existence of the gate. The second possible interpretation relates to the connection between the Greek word for *camel* and the Greek word for *rope*; only one letter distinguishes them. These words were mixed up at some point, and Jesus was really discussing the difficulty of a rope going through the eye of a needle, not a camel. Both Theophylact and the Geneva Bible suggested this interpretation as well.[1]

The evidence for the Greek word originally being *rope* is weak. The evidence for the existence of a "needle gate" in first-century Jerusalem is confusing. A NET Bible footnote says the gate didn't exist *until* the Middle Ages. However, several commentators claim there is no evidence whatsoever that a gate with this name *ever* existed in Jerusalem.[2] While it's hard to prove the absence of evidence, there is a hint in the text of the Gospels that there wasn't a gate with that name in Jerusalem during Jesus' earthly ministry. If Matthew, Mark, and Luke were referring to the title of a gate, the name of the gate should be (at least somewhat) consistent between them. While it might look consistent in English translations, it isn't in the Greek. First, the Greek words signifying a *hole* or *eye* are different in Matthew, Mark, and Luke, with three different words being used for the idea of the "eye" or "hole" of the needle. Second, Luke uses a different word for *needle* than Matthew or Mark. Therefore, Luke's reference to the "eye of a needle" is a completely different name/ expression. If they were referring conceptually to a needle and to the hole of the needle, they referred to it in a way that anyone could have understood. But if it was the title of a gate, it could be confusing. Garland concludes, "If a gate

---

[1] Matthew Henry, *Matthew Henry's Commentary on the Whole Bible*, 6 vols. (Peabody, MA: Hendrickson, 1991), 5:421. For the reference on the Geneva Bible and Theophylact, see the footnote in the Geneva Bible on Matthew 19:24.

[2] David Garland, "Mark," in *Zondervan Illustrated Bible Backgrounds Commentary: Matthew, Mark, Luke* (Grand Rapids: Zondervan, 2002), 265; Craig Blomberg, *Matthew*, NAC (Nashville: B&H, 1992), 299–300; David L. Turner, "The Gospel According to Matthew," in *Cornerstone Biblical Commentary*, ed. Philip W. Comfort (Carol Stream, IL: Tyndale, 2005), 252; Leon Morris, *The Gospel According to Matthew*, PNTC (Grand Rapids: Eerdmans, 1992), 493; Arthur Carr, *The Gospel According to St Matthew*, Cambridge Greek Testament for Schools and Colleges (Cambridge: Cambridge University Press, 1896), 231; G. F. Maclear, *The Gospel According to St Mark*, Cambridge Greek Testament for Schools and Colleges (Cambridge: Cambridge University Press, 1892), 137; James A. Brooks, *Mark*, NAC (Nashville: B&H, 1991), 164. Leo Percer pointed out to me that in two visits to Jerusalem he asked his tour guides about the "needle gate," and both guides said they had no knowledge of it.

had been known as the Needle's Eye it seems likely that only one Greek term would have been used to describe it."[3] Third, there is no mention of a gate in any of the passages. Matthew 19:24; Mark 10:25; and Luke 18:25 neglect to reference a gate. None of them says Jesus was pointing to a gate in Jerusalem. In fact, Mark 10:32 says they started on the road toward Jerusalem. Jesus was not even in Jerusalem when referring to this supposed "Needle Gate." The whole concept of a gate is entirely imported into the text.

Interpreting Mark 10:25

The context for this verse is Mark 10:23–27. The passage occurs after Jesus encounters a rich man. Jesus eventually tells this man to sell everything he has and give it to the poor; then he can follow Jesus. Mark 10:22 says, "[The man] went away grieving, because he had many possessions." Jesus then says that entering the kingdom of God is hard for the wealthy. The encounter with the rich man was surely on his mind. His disciples were shocked so Jesus said it is easier for a camel to go through the eye of a needle than for a wealthy person to enter the kingdom of heaven. His disciples were all the more astonished. The passage concludes with Jesus saying, "With men it is impossible, but not with God, because all things are possible with God" (v. 27).

The rich man in the previous passage asked Jesus about inheriting eternal life. Jesus' reaction to that encounter is a discussion about entering the kingdom of God. The phrases "eternal life" and "the kingdom of God" appear to be closely related. When Jesus talks about the difficulty for a rich man to enter the kingdom of God, the disciples respond by asking, "Who can be saved?" Therefore, Jesus' words about entering the kingdom of God were understood as a reference to salvation. There is probably a relationship between the kingdom of God and salvation. Finally, having eternal life, entering the kingdom of God, and being saved are all similar concepts, overlapping in meaning.

The reason the disciples were shaken to their core when Jesus said this is that, in Jewish thinking, having great wealth was a sign God was blessing you. Deuteronomy 28:1–14 says the man who is obedient to God in the Mosaic covenant will be blessed. Therefore, when people living in Israel were blessed and had a surplus of possessions, Jews concluded that *God* must be blessing them; they must be part of God's people. That is why the disciples were shocked. If the people who show evidence of salvation by being (financially/materially) blessed can't be saved, then who can? Since Jesus' disciples were so utterly astonished, Jesus illustrates how hard it really is for a wealthy person to get saved. This provides the context for Mark 10:25—salvation.

---

[3] Garland, "Mark," 265.

Mark 10:25 is an example of Jesus' speaking in hyperbole: intentional exaggeration to make a point. This is a common rhetorical device. The disciples immediately realized a camel will *never* be able to go through the eye of a needle. A camel was considered the largest land animal in Palestine, and the needle was considered the smallest opening. The Babylonian Talmud, written in Babylon by Jews about 450 years after the time of the New Testament, has a saying about an elephant going through the eye of a needle. In Babylon the largest land animal was an elephant. This is essentially a message about a large animal going through a small opening. Jesus was speaking in hyperbole to illustrate the difficulty of a wealthy person's coming to salvation. Leon Morris says, "This does not mean that he will not enter at all, but it certainly means that wealth so far from being an unmixed blessing poses a problem for all but the flippant."[4]

There was probably never a gate in Jerusalem called "Needle Gate." Using this pseudo-background material to interpret Jesus' saying is inappropriate.

Application

Wealth is fraught with danger so the New Testament provides warnings about it. It's not sinful to be wealthy, but it is dangerous. One of the struggles of the Christians in Laodicea was their overdependence on their own wealth instead of relying on God (Revelation 3). Paul warns about the love of money (1 Tim 6:10) and the dangers associated with that. We need to be careful about trusting in riches. The antidote for trusting in riches is to be ready and willing to part with our material possessions at any time for the sake of seeking first God's kingdom. Think about specific possessions in your life that you treasure. Can you part with them for the sake of God's kingdom?

Salvation is only possible because of God. Jesus affirmed two things following Mark 10:25. First, there is nothing a human being can do in order to guarantee the salvation of a wealthy person (or anyone). Second, while people are limited in this way, God is not. Salvation is a work of God in the hearts of those who are His enemies. God is the initiator and sustainer of salvation. Never think you can do anything to *cause* others to get saved apart from God doing a work in their hearts. We have a role to play: proclaim the gospel. That role is going to be entirely fruitless without God working in their hearts. No methodology can bypass what is necessary for salvation: God working in someone's heart. Salvation is impossible apart from the working of God, whether you are rich, middle class, or poor.

---

[4]   Morris, *Matthew*, 492.

Annotated Bibliography

Commentaries

Blomberg, Craig. *Matthew*. NAC. Nashville: B&H, 1992.
Blomberg summarizes the *legend* and counters it directly. See especially pages 299–300.

Books

Kaiser, Walter C., Jr., Peter H. Davids, F. F. Bruce, and Manfred T. Brauch. *Hard Sayings of the Bible*. Downers Grove: InterVarsity, 1996.
This classic addresses many difficult passages directly and helpfully, including the legend of the Needle Gate. See especially pages 437–39.

Websites

Houdmann, S. Michael. "What Did Jesus Mean When He Said It Is Easier for a Camel to Go Through the Eye of a Needle than for a Rich Man to Get into Heaven?" *Got Questions*. Accessed July 16, 2014. www.gotquestions.org/camel-eye-needle.html.
This is a brief and nontechnical article directly addressing the legendary interpretation.

CHAPTER 12

When Two Are Gathered in Prayer, God Will Be There

Matthew 18:20

The Legendary Teaching on Matthew 18:20

Some verses in the Bible are especially comforting. They make you feel warm because you realize who God is and how much he loves you. Matthew 18:20 is one of the most comforting verses in the Bible: "For where two or three are gathered together in My name, I am there among them." God loves us and cares deeply for us. Some of us would say, if we are honest, that we are lonely. Some of us are struggling, and we need some encouragement. God makes a promise in this verse. If we will put aside our individualism and isolationism and come together and pray, then God will be in our midst. There is power in the gathering of the saints. Let's unite and, as we do, know that God will be in our midst.

Introduction: "In My Name"

While the origin of this legend remains a mystery to me, it appears that the phrase "in My name" was probably connected to the idea of prayer. This seems all the more likely when verse 19 is considered because it explicitly references prayer. The phrase "in My name" is used several times in the New Testament in the context of prayer, as in John 14:13: "Whatever you ask *in My name*, I will do it" (emphasis added; see also John 14:14; 15:16; 16:23–24, 26).

However, that phrase is never used in reference to prayer in Matthew's Gospel. There are only two other occurrences. Matthew 18:5 says, "And whoever welcomes one child like this *in My name* welcomes Me" (emphasis added). Jesus is not saying, "Whoever welcomes a child by praying for them." It doesn't make any sense in that context for that phrase to be related to prayer.

The second passage is Matthew 24:5: "For many will come *in My name*, say-ing, 'I am the Messiah,' and they will deceive many" (emphasis added). They are not coming in prayer. The one time Paul used the phrase was not a refer-ence to prayer (1 Cor 1:15). Only the Gospel of John connects the phrase "in My name" to prayer.

Instead of being a reference to prayer, the phrase means "under/in the author-ity of." When John's Gospel uses it in the context of prayer, he is saying you should recognize that you are praying under the authority of someone else. In Matthew 18:5, it refers to welcoming a child under the authority of Jesus. In Matthew 24:5, these people are coming and pretending to be functioning under the authority of Jesus, claiming they themselves are the Messiah. A similar phrase is used in Matthew 28:19, saying disciples should be baptized "in the name of the Father and of the Son and of the Holy Spirit." Again this refers to authority, not prayer.

The Context for Matthew 18:20

To appropriately grasp the main point of Matthew 18:20, we need to under-stand verses 15–17. Matthew 18:15–17 is a description of what to do when a fellow believer sins. First, go and privately rebuke the person in love. When done appropriately, many times that is all that needs to be done. If after the confrontation the person confesses the sin and repents, the confrontation ends. But if there is no repentance, then go again with one or two more people. Try lovingly to rebuke the person for his or her sin, with the goal being repentance. If the sinner still refuses to repent, then the situation is taken to the entire con-gregation. If repentance is still not evidenced, the person is to be considered an unbeliever.

Matthew 18:20 functions to provide the theological underpinnings for this process. After Jesus instructs them on what to do when someone sins, verses 18–20 provide the reason, the authority, and the theological underpinnings to that process.

A Closer Look at Matthew 18:18–20

Jesus said to his disciples, "I assure you: Whatever you bind on earth is already bound in heaven, and whatever you loose on earth is already loosed in heaven. Again, I assure you: If two of you on earth agree about any matter that you pray for, it will be done for you by My Father in heaven. For where two or three are gathered together in My name, I am there among them." The idea of binding and loosing, or as the NLT translates it, "forbid" and "per-mit," is reminiscent of Matthew 16:19 where these words are also used. These words relate to the authority given to the church. The idea is to communicate the seriousness of church discipline because church discipline relates to the concepts of forgiveness of sins and one's eternal destiny. Commentator David Turner expresses the seriousness this way: "Successively rejecting the overtures of a brother, two or three witnesses, and the church is tantamount to rejecting Jesus and the Father."[1] All the actions taking place in the local church in accordance with the process Jesus outlined, including its outcome, are within God's sovereign will.

The "two" mentioned in verse 19 probably refers back to the representatives of the church that have confronted the sinning person (cf. Matt 18:16). Jesus is explaining that the decision made by the church will be confirmed by God in heaven. Verse 19 also mentions "any matter that you pray for" (HCSB). Nearly every other translation says "anything," but the HCSB brilliantly states "any matter." The typical Greek word used to say "anything" is not used in this verse (*tis*). For example, Matthew 21:3 contains the common word: "If anyone says *anything* to you" (emphasis added). But in Matthew 18:19, the words are a little different. The Greek word translated "matter" (HCSB) or "-thing" (most English versions) is a fairly uncommon word in the New Testament, occurring only eleven times (*tis* occurs a few hundred times). The word in Matthew 18:19 can carry a legal connotation. The setting in Matthew is sin and confrontation. Jesus mentions bringing two or three *witnesses*, which brings to mind a legal or courtroom setting, especially for Jews in the first century. Deuteronomy says that a legal dispute requires multiple witnesses (see Deut 17:6; 19:15). This is the evidence for Matthew 18:20 being in a legal or courtroom context.

For example, the word for "matter" occurs in 1 Corinthians 6:1 and is translated "a legal dispute." That's the passage about a Christian's having a lawsuit against another Christian. In Matthew 18 it refers to the issue of disciplining the brother in sin, specifically pointing back to the issue of church discipline.

Confidence in Discipline

How can the church be sure their decisions are correct or they are taking the right approach? That question plagues leaders when they are going through the process of confronting an unrepentant person. As they approach the final stage of a public rebuke and removing the person from church membership, even considering the person as separated from God, they ask themselves: "Is this really the right thing to do? Is this person really evidencing that he or she doesn't know Christ?" That is what verse 20 is about. Jesus says, "I am there among them." Disciplining people is a difficult process, turning them over to Satan for the destruction of their flesh (cf. 1 Cor 5:5), hoping they will be

---

[1] David L. Turner, "The Gospel According to Matthew," in *Cornerstone Biblical Commentary*, ed. Philip W. Comfort (Carol Stream, IL: Tyndale, 2005), 241.

restored to the faith and that their souls will be saved on the day of judgment. Jesus provides comfort: his presence.

God's Presence as a Theme in Matthew's Gospel

This idea that Jesus will be "with them" or "among them" is a minor motif in Matthew's Gospel. Matthew begins his Gospel in 1:23, saying, "See, the virgin will become pregnant and give birth to a son, and they will name Him Immanuel, which is translated '*God is with us*'" (emphasis added). In Matthew 28:20, Jesus says, "And remember, *I am with you always*, to the end of the age" (emphasis added). Matthew bookends the entire Gospel with the concept of God's presence.

In this process of church discipline, Jesus says to the people who are involved in it, "I am here; I am with you; I will be guiding this process." Verse 19 has a reference to prayer because Jesus is saying people can have a right heart in this process or a wrong heart. Those involved need to have a prayerful, submissive, broken heart. Some people can be belligerent, unloving, and uncaring, having the wrong mind-set for church discipline. Jesus is saying that if it's done in the way he has commanded, by following the proper procedures with the proper attitude, he will be with them.

Conclusion

If this passage is saying Jesus is present when two or three pray together, what happens if you pray alone? Is Jesus not there? I received an e-mail from a friend while I was working on this passage. He asked about my upcoming move. I sent him back a response and asked for prayer. About ten minutes later I received another e-mail saying, "I just prayed for you." Since I was working on this passage, I *almost* responded to him (in a sarcastic way), "I hope you weren't alone because Jesus wasn't there!" That would be unbiblical because God is present everywhere. This passage is not about prayer.

Jesus does mention praying over a matter of church discipline, but the main idea is that the church has the authority to enact discipline, and Jesus will be present as the guidelines he sets forth are followed. David Turner concludes:

> The flippant way in which Matthew 18:19 is often cited to assure small meetings of Christians that God is with them is disturbing because it twists a solemn passage into a *cliché*. No doubt God is present with any legitimate meeting of his people, whatever its size, and there is no need to mishandle Scripture to prove it. Taking this solemn passage out of context cheapens it and profanes the sacred

duty of the church to maintain the harmony of its interpersonal relationships.[2]

Application

Christians (and churches) need to obey Matthew 18:15–17. The purity of Christ's bride is of utmost importance. Therefore, the purity of every member of the church is important. We attempt to preserve that purity as we confront and expose sin.

The seriousness of church discipline should be remembered. If it is done harshly or vindictively, the consequences can be horrific. But when it is done lovingly, gently, and patiently, it can be beautiful, even when repentance doesn't occur. It's a serious issue, and steps should be taken slowly and cautiously. I have heard stories where a church has gone through all the stages of discipline, removed the person from church membership, and the person walked away from God. However, a few years later the sinner repented, was truly saved, came back to the church, and lived a transformed life. I have heard *several* of those stories, and they are absolutely glorious.

The authority to discipline church members rests in the local church. This can be hard to grasp in an individualistic society. While this might offend some people, Jesus himself delegated this authority to the church.

The church should take comfort that the sovereign Lord of the universe is involved in the process because the consequences of the outcome are paramount. While discipline can be a scary process to begin, those involved in the process, as they prayerfully proceed, should be comforted in knowing that Jesus is sovereign and is involved in the process. He has not left us alone; he has not left his church unattended.

Annotated Bibliography

Commentaries

Turner, David. "The Gospel According to Matthew." In *Cornerstone Biblical Commentary, Vol 11: Matthew and Mark*. Carol Stream, IL: Tyndale, 2005.
  This nontechnical commentary confronts the legend head-on. See pages 240–41.

Websites

Patton, C. Michael. "'Where Two or Three Are Gathered' . . . and Other Bad Interpretations." *Parchment & Pen Blog*. August 10, 2012. Accessed July 14, 2014. www.tinyurl.com/2or3gathered.

---

[2] Ibid.

Patton does a great job placing this verse in context.

Jackson, Wayne. "Does Matthew 18:20 Sanction 'Personal' Assemblies?" *Christian Courier*. Accessed July 14, 2014. www.tinyurl.com/1820assembly.

Jackson correctly interprets the thrust of this passage in addressing another legend unrelated to the one above.

CHAPTER 13

Jesus Sweat Drops of Blood

Luke 22:44

The Legendary Teaching on Luke 22:44

Jesus was coming upon the hour of his arrest, trial, flogging, crucifixion, and death. The reality of what he was about to face began to set in. He went to the garden of Gethsemane to pray. It was an intense time of prayer, so much so that Luke the doctor says he sweat blood: "Being in anguish, He prayed more fervently, and His sweat became like drops of blood falling to the ground" (Luke 22:44). Some people have tried to use this verse to demonstrate the foolishness of the Bible, to say it's not historical and can't be trusted. However, this moment of prayer in the garden of Gethsemane was so intense for Jesus that he suffered from *hematohidrosis*. This is a medical condition where a person appears to sweat blood. It typically occurs when someone is under extreme stress, and it has been associated with a few historical figures. When someone experiences extreme stress, the capillaries that go to the sweat glands can rupture causing the blood from the capillaries to pour into the sweat glands. When the person starts to sweat, the blood comes out through the sweat glands. This is what happened to Jesus. An article in the *Journal of the American Medical Association* diagnosed Jesus with this condition. It wasn't a miracle that he sweat blood. It was simply an uncommon medical condition that the good doctor Luke was reporting.

The verse itself says Jesus was in anguish. The Greek word is *agōnia*. It's where we get the English word *agony*. Jesus was in such intense agony that the capillaries in his forehead burst and caused blood to come out of his sweat glands. Jesus was about to go to the cross and have the Father's wrath poured out on him. This is what caused such intense, extreme stress. It is what caused his absolute agony, and it is why he suffered from *hematohidrosis*. This is what it cost the Son of God when our eternal destinies hung in the balance. Jesus decided to go to the cross for us.

Introduction

Hematohidrosis is a real, but rare, medical condition.[1] I have no problem with the idea of Jesus sweating blood and of Gethsemane being an extremely stressful time. There are no biblical or theological problems with those ideas. Regardless, the conclusion that Jesus sweat blood brings up two important questions: (1) Should Luke 22:44 be in the Bible? (2) What does the verse say about Jesus sweating blood?

Was Luke 22:44 in the Original Gospel of Luke?

When scholars say Scripture is inerrant, they are referring to the original manuscripts. The original manuscript of the Gospel of Luke was without error; but it has been lost in time, and scholars are left with copies. These copies contain mistakes. The problem with trying to figure out what the original copy of the Gospel of Luke said is not that there is not enough information but that there is so much! There are so many copies of the New Testament from so many different time periods throughout church history that synthesizing all the data can be an overwhelming task.

The Greek New Testament used by most scholars puts Luke 22:43–44 in brackets to indicate that the editors of the Greek New Testament were not confident the verses were original. The ESV, NIV, and NASB all contain footnotes mentioning that some ancient manuscripts don't have these verses. The HCSB puts these verses in brackets and provides a similar footnote after verse 44. The translations are not ignoring or trying to cover up this issue.

The initial question of Jesus' sweating blood relates to the originality of this verse. The best and earliest manuscripts either do not have the verses; or, if they have it, they put an asterisk or some other symbol next to it to indicate the person making the copy didn't think those verses were original. However, there is more evidence from four church fathers: Justin (d. 165), Irenaeus (d. 202), Hippolytus (d. 235), and Eusebius (d. 339). All of these men date to the time of those earliest manuscripts or earlier; all of them are familiar with these verses. Therefore, either an independent historical account was circulating containing these verses, or early copies of Luke had them. So where does that leave us?

---

[1] See William D. Edwards, Wesley J. Gabel, and Floyd E. Hosmer, "On the Physical Death of Jesus Christ," *Journal of the American Medical Association* 255, no. 11 (1986): 1455–63.

Robert Stein, concluding that these verses should not be regarded as part of the original Gospel of Luke, comments:

> For some believers who have been raised on the *King James Version* of the Bible, to speak of "omitting" certain verses from the Bible seems heretical, and the warning of Rev 22:19 comes to mind. What is at issue here, however, is not "omitting" something from the sacred text but rather not allowing something that was never in the sacred text to be added to it. It is just as wrong to add something to the Scriptures as it is to take away something from them. When we therefore speak of "omitting" Luke 22:43–44 from the text, we mean that we should not include what some later scribe added to the original Gospel penned by the Evangelist Luke.[2]

While I tend to agree with Stein, who summarizes the issue brilliantly, I am not as confident that these verses probably weren't original.

What Does Luke Say About Jesus Sweating Blood?

What do these verses actually say about Jesus' sweating blood, regardless of whether they are original? Luke 22:44 says, "Being in anguish, He prayed more fervently, and His sweat became *like* drops of blood falling to the ground" (emphasis added). Notice the word *like* in this verse. Virtually all major modern translations include this word as a translation of the Greek word *hōsei*. This Greek word is a relatively weak marker of a relationship between two things.[3] Luke uses a different word in his Gospel when he wants to communicate a more emphatic marker of similarity between two things: *hōsper*. For example, Luke 18:11 says, "The Pharisee took his stand and was praying like this; 'God, I thank You that I'm not *like* other people—greedy, unrighteous, adulterers, or even like this tax collector'" (emphasis added). The Pharisee was being emphatic; he is absolutely not like the sinner he is about to discuss. The Greek language provides ways to mark the degree of similarity between things, and the word Luke chose in Luke 22 does *not* communicate a strong relationship but a weak relationship.

It would be odd for someone to say he saw something *kind of like* blood if he knew it was *actually* blood. In fact, there would probably be no word of comparison. Luke would have simply stated, "Jesus sweat blood." The mistake of skipping over the word *like* occurs in other places in the New Testament as well. For example, Matthew 3:16 says, "The heavens suddenly opened for Him, and He saw the Spirit of God descending *like* a dove and coming down on Him" (emphasis added). Every time I have seen this verse depicted in a

---

2 Robert H. Stein, *Luke*, NAC (Nashville: B&H, 1992), 559n55.
3 See Louw and Nida, 64.12.

movie or a picture, it is always a literal dove. But Matthew 3 does not say the Holy Spirit possessed a dove. Matthew is saying the way that the Holy Spirit came down from the sky reminded him of the way that a dove descends from the sky.[4]

In what way was Jesus' sweat like the drops of blood? There are three main options: (1) It could refer to color, that the sweat was like blood because it was red. However, if it was red, it probably would not be *like* blood; it would *be* blood itself. Therefore, the comparison is probably not about color. (2) It could be about consistency. In talking with medical personnel, they affirm that blood is thicker than sweat. So it could refer to the thickness of the sweat. (3) It could refer to size, the most likely option. I am not sure how easy it would be to see the consistency of sweat from a distance unless that consistency manifested itself in large drops of sweat. Notice what the following translations say:

- "His sweat became like *great* drops of blood" (ESV, emphasis added).
- "His sweat was as it were *great* drops of blood" (KJV, emphasis added).
- "His sweat became like *great* drops of blood" (NKJV, emphasis added).
- "His sweat fell to the ground like *great* drops of blood" (NLT, emphasis added).

These translations are interpreting the comparison ("like") as being about size. They all believe the sweat drops were large. Luke is saying that, in the intensity of the moment, Jesus sweat large drops of sweat. My main point is that Luke 22:44 does not say Jesus sweat drops of blood. We have no indication of whether Jesus sweat blood because no verse actually says he did.

Application

First, the text of Scripture is reliable even though in some places deciding on the original reading is difficult. No major doctrine is impacted by the different readings available. We can trust the Bible we have. Second, read the footnotes in your Bibles. Many modern translations have footnotes in them. Pay attention to them. Read the introduction to your Bible so you know what the abbreviations in the footnotes mean. Some of the footnotes in your translations on these verses contain this abbreviation: MSS. If you don't read the introduction to your Bible, you won't know that *MSS* means manuscripts. Third, pay attention to the small words like *as* and *like*. Every word of Scripture is inspired, and every word is important for a correct interpretation. Missing one little word can change the entire meaning of a passage. Fourth, understanding the extreme sacrifice of Jesus should lead to a thankful, obedient life. Jesus

---

[4] Acts 2:3 contains another great example.

truly did have an intense time of prayer in the garden of Gethsemane. That is clear with or without Luke 22:43–44. Knowing that God's wrath was going to be poured out on him for the sake of those who place their trust in him, Jesus endured the cross. And this fact should drive us to being thankful that the Son of God willingly suffered by laying down his own life for us. This thankfulness should pour out into our lives by living in a way that brings glory to God for all he has done for us, truly seeking to be obedient to the One who saved us.

Annotated Bibliography

Commentaries

Carroll, John T. *Luke: A Commentary*. Louisville, KY: Westminster John Knox Press, 2012.
   Carroll does not believe Luke 22:43–44 is original to the Gospel.
Bock, Darrell L. *Luke 9:51–24:53*. BECNT. Grand Rapids: Baker Books, 1996.
   One of the best and most thorough commentaries on Luke.

Journals

Green, Joel B. "Jesus on the Mount of Olives (Luke 22:39–46): Tradition and Theology."
   Journal for the Study of the New Testament 26 (1986): 29–48.
   Green's analysis touches on issues related to textual criticism, Greek syntax and grammar, and discourse analysis. This is a highly technical article. He touches on the issue at hand and refers to it as a simile.
Edwards, William D., Wesley J. Gabel, and Floyd E. Hosmer. "On the Physical Death
   of Jesus Christ." *Journal of the American Medical Association* 255, no. 11 (1986): 1,455–63.
   While disagreeing with the conclusion of this chapter, the authors provide the medical background for *hematohidrosis*.

Websites

Ray, Jerry C. "His Sweat Became as It Were Great Drops of Blood." *Truth Magazine* VIII,
   no. 4 (1964). Accessed July 12, 2014. www.truthmagazine.com/archives/volume8/TM008074.htm.
   Short, helpful article summarizing the issue.

CHAPTER 14

Jesus Was Flogged Once

John 19:1

The Legendary Teaching on John 19:1

Jesus began the painful punishment for our sins with a flogging: "Then Pilate took Jesus and had him flogged severely" (John 19:1 NET). Matthew 27:26 says, "Then he released Barabbas for them. But after he had Jesus flogged, he handed him over to be crucified" (NET). Roman soldiers administered three types of flogging: (1) *fustigatio*: the least severe beating given for light offences, typically accompanied by a severe warning not to commit the light offence again; (2) *flagellatio*: a severe flogging given to criminals who committed more serious crimes; not a precursor to capital punishment but a more severe flogging than the first kind; and (3) *verberatio*: the most severe form of flogging, always associated with another punishment, usually capital punishment, including crucifixion. This third kind is what Jesus received. The flogging was so horrible that some men would die from the flogging alone. The scourge would typically be constructed of a wooden handle and have several leather straps with metal, glass, or bone tied into the straps. The criminal typically had his hands tied to a post so that his back would be stretched out, making the skin tight so that when the whip came across the back with the metal, glass, or bones in it, it would easily tear the flesh.

Introduction: Unraveling the Legend

Much of the legendary teaching is true. There were three main categories for Roman floggings, and they were described fairly accurately. There weren't always clear-cut divisions between them, but those were the three categories. However, do John 19:1 and Matthew 27:26 refer to the same flogging?

A Closer Look at Matthew 27:26

To answer this question, we need to go through the Gospel accounts and their descriptions of floggings to compare them with each other. In Matthew 27, Jesus was on trial before Pontius Pilate. After Pilate finished interrogating Jesus, Matthew mentioned that the custom of the Roman governor was to release one prisoner during the Passover festival and release him. Pilate asked if they wanted Barabbas released, a notorious prisoner, or if they wanted Jesus. The Jewish rulers persuaded the crowds, and they asked for Barabbas. Pilate asked them what he should do with Jesus. The crowds demanded that he be crucified. At this point Pilate seemed reluctant to crucify Jesus. He washed his hands, symbolically saying he was not really responsible, and then said, "See to it yourselves!" (Matt 27:24). When Pilate said this, he had made his decision to have Jesus crucified and Barabbas released. Then Matthew 27:26 says, "Then he released Barabbas to them. But after having Jesus flogged, he handed Him over to be crucified." Matthew is clear that the crowds asked for Barabbas (v. 21). The decision to crucify Jesus was made in verse 25; in 26a Barabbas was released; and in 26b Jesus was flogged. That is the order of events in Matthew.

The verb used in Matthew 27 to describe Jesus' flogging is *phrageloō*, meaning "to flog or to scourge." One Greek lexicon defines it this way: "a punishment inflicted on slaves and provincials after a sentence of death had been pronounced on them."[1] This word is used when a flogging would take place after the sentence of death, possibly crucifixion, had been given. Regarding the account in Mark 15:15, it reads the same as Matthew. Mark uses the same words, terminology, and order though he doesn't include as many details as Matthew.

A Closer Look at Luke 23:16, 22

Luke describes the flogging in 23:16 and 22. Luke follows a similar pattern as Matthew, but he has some differences. After Pilate interrogates Jesus and he is provided with no reason to find Jesus guilty (Luke 23:4), he sends Jesus to Herod Antipas to get a second opinion. Herod Antipas was the ruler in Galilee (where Jesus was from), so Pilate was allowed to send Jesus for a second opinion (Luke 23:7). Herod talks to Jesus and sends him back to Pilate. Pilate explains to the crowds that neither he himself nor Herod found Jesus guilty of anything (Luke 23:14–15). In verse 16, Pilate says, "Therefore, I will have Him whipped and then release Him." Pilate was going to have Jesus flogged and released, not crucified. The Greek word for "whipped" in Luke

---

[1] BDAG, 1,064.

23:16 refers generically to the concept of punishment, possibly by a whip. The verse does not actually state that Jesus was flogged; it just states that Pilate's plan was to flog Jesus and then have him released.

After Luke 23:16, the crowd started asking for Barabbas to be released, and Luke states in 23:20: "Pilate, wanting to release Jesus, addressed them again." Pilate's desire was to punish Jesus and then have him released. But Pilate was being pressured by the Jewish crowds to release Barabbas instead. After insisting that Jesus had done nothing wrong, Pilate declared again in 23:22, "Therefore, I will have Him whipped and then release him." This is identical to what was stated in 23:16. Jesus had not yet been flogged, but Pilate was planning on having Jesus punished by flogging and then release him. This most likely refers to the first kind of flogging discussed in the beginning: *fustigatio*.[2]

The account continues in 23:23–25: "But they kept up the pressure, demanding with loud voices that He be crucified. And their voices won out. So Pilate decided to grant their demand and released the one they were asking for, who had been thrown into prison for rebellion and murder. But he handed Jesus over to their will." If the only Gospel account of Jesus' trial was from Luke, we wouldn't know if Jesus was ever flogged. Luke doesn't say. It was Pilate's intention to have him flogged, but the time period between verses 23 and 24 is unknown. Since we can't answer this from Luke's Gospel, let's take a look at what John has to say.

A Closer Look at John 19:1

Pilate interrogated Jesus and concluded in John 18:38 that Jesus had done nothing wrong. Pilate offered to release Jesus according to the custom of the festival. The crowds shouted back that instead they wanted Barabbas. In response to their request for Barabbas, Pilate had Jesus flogged. The verb used to describe Jesus' flogging is *mastigoō*. Matthew and Mark use *phrageloō* (a flogging that occurred after a sentence of death had been given); Luke uses the verb *paideuō* (a general term for punishment, but it could include punishment by [light] whipping); and John uses *mastigoō* (a punishment typically decreed by a synagogue). In fact, one Greek lexicon recognizes the confusion over what is specifically being referred to in John 19:1, saying that it might be equivalent to the flogging of Luke 23:16, 22.[3] John 19:1 appears to be referring to *fustigatio*, the light flogging discussed in Luke 23. While Luke never said it took place, John says it did occur.

---

[2] Cf. Mark Strauss, "Luke," in *Zondervan Illustrated Bible Backgrounds Commentary: Matthew, Mark, Luke* (Grand Rapids: Zondervan, 2002), 490. See also Stein, *Luke*, 580.

[3] BDAG, 620.

If John 19:1 was referring to the *verberatio* (the most severe form of flogging followed by a further punishment), then the following verses are difficult to explain: "Pilate went outside again and said to them, 'Look, I'm bringing Him outside to you to let you know I find no grounds for charging Him'" (John 19:4). Pilate declared *after* the flogging in 19:4 that he found no reason for Jesus to be crucified. Would Pilate say this after having him flogged in such a way that he could have died? Would he command the *verberatio* and then bring him out and say he did nothing wrong?

John 19:6 says, "When the chief priests and the temple police saw Him, they shouted, 'Crucify! Crucify!' Pilate responded, 'Take Him and crucify Him yourselves, for I find no grounds for charging Him.'" Pilate is still trying to get Jesus released without further punishment. Then John says, "From that moment Pilate made every effort to release Him" (John 19:12). John does not describe a sentence of crucifixion followed by a flogging, as in Matthew and Mark. Instead, Pilate had Jesus lightly flogged, and then he attempted to release him. John 19:16 says, "So then, because of them, [Pilate] handed Him over to be crucified. Therefore they took Jesus away." Pilate decided in John 19:16 to have Jesus crucified.

Putting It All Together

Let's compare the order of events in Matthew and John. Matthew: (1) the crowds asked for Barabbas; (2) a decision to crucify was made; (3) Barabbas was released; and (4) Jesus was flogged. John: (1) crowds asked for Barabbas; (2) Jesus was flogged; (3) a decision to crucify was made. The main difference is that in Matthew there is a decision to crucify followed by a *flogging*, and in John there was a flogging followed by *a decision to crucify*. By going through the order of events in all four Gospels in the following way, they fit together well.

There are eight steps to the flogging reconstruction:

1. Pilate threatens to flog Jesus lightly and then release Him (Luke 23:16).
2. The crowd asks for Barabbas instead (Matt 27:21; Luke 23:18; John 18:40).
3. Pilate threatens (again) to flog Jesus lightly and then release Him (Luke 23:22).
4. The crowd pressures Pilate (Matt 27:22–24a; Luke 23:23).
5. Pilate has Jesus lightly flogged (*fustigatio*) (John 19:1).
6. Pilate tries to release Jesus after the flogging (John 19:2–15).
7. Pilate gives in to the pressure and sentences Jesus to crucifixion (Matt 27:25; Luke 23:24; John 19:16).
8. Pilate has Jesus flogged again (*verberatio*) (Matt 27:26).

Jesus received two floggings: the least severe and the most severe. Some scholars have postulated, based on Deuteronomy 25:1–3, that Jesus was whipped thirty-nine times. While that could be true, why would a Roman soldier constrain himself in the amount of lashes given to a criminal based on the Mosaic law? Roman law didn't necessitate the instrument used or the number of lashes. The soldiers themselves decided on the severity of the lashing. Jesus might have been lashed thirty-nine times, but it could have been much higher, maybe fifty or sixty lashes. This reconstruction does help explain why Jesus struggled to carry the cross beam to the site of the crucifixion: he had been flogged twice.

Application

The Bible is trustworthy in its description of historical events. Christians need not fear *apparent* contradictions in Scripture, even though much work is sometimes involved in order to uncover how the apparent contradiction can be resolved. When a new "contradiction" is introduced, do not panic. Through study and with time, an answer can be found. In all likelihood someone has answered the question before, and there is a reasonable explanation.

Jesus suffered greatly for my sins. When I think about the suffering Christ endured for my sins—the flogging, the precrucifixion humiliation, and the cross itself—it drives me to worship and reminds me of how much my sin cost Him and how little I deserve his forgiveness. That quickly leads me to reflect on areas where I have struggled in forgiving others. Forgiving others becomes easier as I meditate on the suffering of Christ in the flogging, precrucifixion events, and the crucifixion itself.

Annotated Bibliography

Commentaries

Borchert, Gerald L. *John 12–21*. NAC. Nashville: B&H, 2002. See pages 245–47.

Borchert is not technical and agrees with the conclusions here. He is probably overly optimistic on there being a sharp distinction between *flagellatio* and *verberatio*.

Carson, D. A. *The Gospel According to John*. PNTC. Grand Rapids: Eerdmans, 1991. See page 597.

This section of Carson's commentary is accessible; he agrees with the conclusion presented here.

Köstenberger, Andreas. *John*. BECNT. Grand Rapids: Baker Academic, 2004.

Books

Sherwin-White, A. N. *Roman Law and Roman Society in the New Testament: The Sarum Lectures 1960–1961*. Grand Rapids: Baker, 1963.

Articles

Douglas, J. D., and F. F. Bruce. "Scourging, Scourge." Pages 1,067–68 in *New Bible Dictionary*. Edited by I. Howard Marshall, A. R. Millard, J. I. Packer, and D. J. Wiseman. 3rd ed. Downers Grove, IL: InterVarsity, 1996.

Short, accessible summary of the evidence.

Bruce, F. F. "The Trial of Jesus in the Fourth Gospel." Pages 7–20 in *Gospel Perspectives: Studies of History and Tradition in the Four Gospels*. Volume 1. Edited by R. T. France and D. Wenham. Sheffield: JSOT, 1980.

The best summary of the two-flogging theory. See especially page 15.

CHAPTER 15

Agapē Is a Superior Love to *Phileō*

John 21:15–19

The Legendary Teaching on John 21:15–19

When they had eaten breakfast, Jesus asked Simon Peter, "Simon, son of John, do you love Me more than these?"

"Yes, Lord," he said to Him, "You know that I love You."

"Feed My lambs," He told him.

A second time He asked him, "Simon, son of John, do you love Me?"

"Yes, Lord," he said to Him, "You know that I love You."

"Shepherd My sheep," He told him.

He asked him the third time, "Simon, son of John, do you love Me?"

Peter was grieved that He asked him the third time, "Do you love Me?" He said, "Lord, You know everything! You know that I love You."

"Feed My sheep," Jesus said. "I assure you: When you were young, you would tie your belt and walk wherever you wanted. But when you grow old, you will stretch out your hands and someone else will tie you and carry you where you don't want to go." He said this to signify by what kind of death he would glorify God. After saying this, He told him, "Follow Me!" (John 21:15–19)

These verses have two Greek words for *love*. You might have heard of *"agapē* love" and *"phileō* love." While *"agapē* love" is the common phrase used, in this passage it is actually the verb form of the Greek word, so it is actually *agapaō* love. *Agapaō* love is the highest, greatest, most noble, divine kind of love. It is an unconditional, self-sacrificing, God-type love. It is the more exalted term for love in the Greek language. *Phileō* is a lesser form of love, dealing more with a human friendship-type of love. The back-and-forth between the use of *agapaō* and *phileō* is the key to understanding this passage. It unlocks everything that is going on in the dialogue between Peter and Jesus.

Look at the passage again, but this time notice the switch between *agapaō* and *phileō*. Jesus says to Simon, "Do you *agapaō* me?" Do you unconditionally love me with a Godlike love? Peter responds, "You know that I *like* you a lot." Peter does not respond with the unconditional love but the lesser love, the *phileō* love. Jesus comes back a second time and says, "Peter, do you *agapaō* me?" Do you love me unconditionally? Do you have a self-sacrificial love for me? Peter responds, "We're buds. I like you, but I don't have that kind of love." Then Jesus says, "OK, I understand. Peter, do you have a friendship-type love for me" (*phileō* love). Peter says, "We're good friends." Then John says that Peter was grieved that Jesus asked him a third time. Why was he grieved?

Peter was sad because he knew his weakness. He had just experienced the high point of his own weakness when he denied Christ. Peter did not have the audacity to claim a God-type love for Jesus. Peter knew himself. He did not think more of himself than he should have. We also need to recognize our weaknesses. We need to recognize where we are weak and frail and admit those things to God and be comforted. Jesus did not say to Peter, "Well, tough. I am looking for *agapaō* love. Is all you have to offer me *phileō* love? I am through with you." No, Jesus says, "If what you have to offer me is *phileō* love, I'll take *phileō* love." And He makes Peter a leader in the early church. Be comforted in knowing that Jesus will meet us where we are.

Introduction: Unraveling the Legend

The main problems with this interpretation of John 21 are a misuse of Greek and a lack of attention to the narrative context of John's Gospel. This is not a critique of the theology or application above but of the interpretation. The first question we must answer is this: Are these the correct definitions of the Greek words?

The Disciple Jesus Loved

These two Greek words are used interchangeably throughout the Gospel of John. The apostle John wrote the Gospel of John, but he doesn't say, "I, John, write these things." Instead, he typically refers to himself with the phrase "the disciple Jesus loved." Studying that phrase throughout the Gospel of John yields interesting results. For example, John 19:26 says, "When Jesus saw

His mother and the *disciple He loved* standing there, He said to His mother, 'Woman, here is your son'" (emphasis added). Which Greek word would you expect to be here: *agapaō* or *phileō*? Does Jesus have an unconditional, God-like love or a brotherly love for John? Not surprisingly, Jesus, being fully God, has an *agapaō* love for John—this supposed unconditional, Godlike love. A few verses later in John 20:2, John says: "So she ran to Simon Peter and to the other disciple, *the one Jesus loved*" (emphasis added). You might expect *agapaō* here, but it is *phileō*. My question is this: Why, between John 19:26 and 20:2 did Jesus' love for John decrease? Does this mean Jesus ceased having unconditional love for him? Did John do something to cause Jesus to love him less? If so, does that mean we could do things to cause Jesus to love us less? Is that what is going on here? The fact that in 19:26 John used *agapaō* and a few verses later he used *phileō* strongly suggests that John uses these words to refer to the same kind of love.

The Father Loves the Son

This is not the only time these words are used synonymously in John's Gospel. John 3:35 describes God's love for Jesus: "The Father loves the Son and has given all things into His hands." The word used there is *agapaō*. Using the vocabulary of the legendary interpretation, the Father has unconditional love for his Son in John 3:35. Jesus says in John 5:20: "For the Father loves the Son and shows Him everything." The Greek word used for love there is *phileō*. If the legendary interpretation of John 21 is true, then I ask: Did Jesus make a mistake between John 3:35 and John 5:20 so the Father loved him less? I am uncomfortable with this line of reasoning, and I hope you are too.

Amnon's Love for Tamar

There is another problem with interpreting these words this way. Is *agapaō* love correctly defined as a self-sacrificial, Godlike love? The translation of the Old Testament into Greek, the Septuagint, was influential on many of the authors in the New Testament. It was completed before Jesus was born. Understanding words in the Septuagint can help us understand the way words were used in the New Testament. The story in 2 Samuel 13 about Amnon having *love* for Tamar is helpful to study. Amnon is said to have loved Tamar in verses 1 and 4 utilizing the Greek word *agapaō*. Verses 14–15 say: "But he refused to listen to her, and because he was stronger than she was, he raped her. After this, Amnon hated Tamar with such intensity that the hatred he hated her with was greater than the love he had loved her with. 'Get out of here,' he said." So Amnon is described as loving Tamar four times in these verses, and every single time it is using either *agapaō* (the verb) or *agapē* (the noun). And what does he do with that love? He rapes her. So if *agapaō* is an unconditional, self-sacrificial, Godlike love, how could it lead to rape? The fact is that *agapaō* doesn't always refer to a Godlike, sacrificial love.

Husbands, Love Your Wives

While *agapaō* can refer to a sacrificial love, that definition is decided based on the context the word is in. For example, Ephesians 5:25 says, "Husbands, love your wives," and the Greek word there is *agapaō*. How do we know what kind of love that is? Because Paul tells us that husbands are to love their wives "just as Christ loved the church and gave Himself for her." Paul himself defined *love* in this context as sacrificial love. *Agapaō* doesn't necessarily mean that every time, but it does in Ephesians 5:25.

Interpreting John 21:15–19

If this passage is not about the interplay between two Greek words, then what does it mean? It is about the restoration of Peter. Peter denied Christ *three times*. Jesus asked Peter to declare his love *three times*. Then John 21:17 says Peter was grieved. What was the source of Peter's grief? It is not because Jesus asked, "Do you love me?" It says he asked *the third time* if Peter loved him. When Jesus said it the third time, that reminded Peter that he denied Jesus three times. Peter is remembering his denials, and that is what is grieving Peter.

Another piece of evidence for this interpretation is the word *charcoal*. The Greek word for *charcoal* occurs only twice in the entire New Testament and never in the Septuagint. The two occurrences are fascinatingly linked. The first time it occurs (John 18:18), John describes Peter standing by a charcoal fire right after a slave girl questioned him and he denied Jesus. In John 21:9, the disciples came ashore, stepped onto the land, and saw a charcoal fire with fish cooking. These are the only times this Greek word is used. Besides the literary link, it is possible that when Peter smelled that charcoal fire, it reminded him of his denials. There is a very strong link between smell and memories.[1]

To what is Jesus restoring Peter? Jesus connects the concepts of abiding in him (John 15:4) and abiding in his love (John 15:9). Then he connects love to keeping his commandments (John 15:10). Jesus brings the concept of obedience into the picture. Remaining in Jesus, remaining in his love, is demonstrated by obedience to his commands. The question of loving Jesus

---

[1] See, for example, Tom Stafford, "Why Can Smells Unlock Forgotten Memories?," *Future* (March 13, 2012), accessed May 21, 2014, www.bbc.com/future/story/20120312-why-can-smells-unlock-memories.

is a question of obedience. Therefore, Peter is being restored to obey Christ's commands.

Second, Peter is restored to discipleship. *Follow* is an important word in John's Gospel occurring nearly twenty times. Some of Jesus' initial words to his disciples were to follow him (John 1:43). The word is used several times in this way throughout the Gospel, all the way to John 13:36, where Jesus says: "Where I am going you cannot follow Me now, but you will follow later." For three and a half years the disciples have been following Jesus, and then Jesus says, "You cannot follow Me." I imagine some major internal panic broke out among the disciples. And what does Peter say? "Oh, OK. I guess we can't follow him." No! Peter says, "Why can't I follow You now? I will lay down my life for You!" He objects to Jesus' words, and then Jesus prophesies that Peter is going to deny him three times. That is the context to the denial. Then, in John 21, after Peter is restored, in verse 19 Jesus clinches the restoration by saying to Peter, "Follow Me!" Jesus is inviting Peter to enter back into a discipleship relationship he had with Jesus before the denials. Peter is restored to obedience and discipleship.

Application

We should be comforted by this account in Peter's life because we make mistakes too. We have sin in our lives, and we can know that, like Peter, we can be restored to discipleship and obedience. God will take us back when we turn from our sin. And notice it says that Peter was grieved. Repentance and grief are not the same thing, but repentance will include grief. When you turn from your sin, you will experience grief over the fact that you did sin. If you don't have grief over your sin, then you do not have true repentance. Repentance includes feelings of grief and sorrow over the fact that you sinned.

A few weeks later we find Peter in Jerusalem preaching the sermon at Pentecost and 3,000 people are saved. Was he restored to service? Was he restored to obedience? Was he restored to following Christ? Absolutely. And we can be too. Are there aspects of your life that you don't want to hand over to Jesus? Turn and Christ will restore you.

Annotated Bibliography

Commentaries

Carson, D. A. *The Gospel According to John*. PNTC. Grand Rapids: Eerdmans, 1991.
    This is a largely accessible volume from a reputable scholar. Easily accessible to the interested layperson and informative for the scholar.
Köstenberger, Andreas J. *John*. BECNT. Grand Rapids: Baker Academic, 2004.

This volume is typical of the Baker Exegetical Commentary series as it is accessible to a large audience.

Morris, Leon. *Expository Reflections on the Gospel of John*. Grand Rapids: Baker, 1988.

Very accessible for a lay audience. The Greek text is transliterated throughout, and Morris keeps the discussion understandable for a broader audience.

Journals

Freed, Edwin D. "Variations in the Language and Thought of John." *Zeitschrift für die neu-testamentliche Wissenchaft und die Kunde der älteren Kirche* 55, no. 4 (1964): 167–97.

Somewhat technical, Freed reviews the issues of John's use of synonyms and variations throughout the Gospel. A working knowledge of Greek is required for reading this article.

Oladipo, Caleb O. "John 21:15–17: Between Text and Sermon." *Interpretation: Essays on Bible and Theology* 51 (1997): 65–66.

This article is written with interpretation in mind but toward a theologically and exposi-tionally robust end. The article is short and accessible.

Websites

Scott, Shane. "Do You Love Me? Feed My Sheep (Part 1)." *Focus Online*. August 20, 2013. Accessed June 23, 2014. www.focusmagazine.org/do-you-love-me-feed-my-sheep-part-1.php.

CHAPTER 16

"Go" Is Not a Command in the Great Commission

Matthew 28:19

The Legendary Teaching on Matthew 28:19

Jesus said in Matthew 28:19: "Go, therefore, and make disciples of all nations, baptizing them in the name of the Father and of the Son and of the Holy Spirit." Many sermons have been preached on this well-known verse. The problem is that most translations, and therefore sermons, understand this verse incorrectly. The word translated as  "go" is not translated correctly. Greek, as does English, has -*ing* words known as participles. Both languages also contain imperatives, verbs that are commanding something. If I said to you, "Buy some milk as you are running to the store," the word *buy* is a command and the word *running* is a description but not a command. I found two Bible translations that accurately translated this verse: the ISV and YLT. The ISV says, "Therefore, *as you go*, disciple people in all nations" (emphasis added), and the YLT says, "*Having gone*, then, disciple all the nations" (emphasis added). Jesus is saying that *as you are going* about your daily life you should be making disciples. It is not as much a call for intentionally, specifically reaching out to lost people that are distant from you as a call to be involved in the lives of those around you, to have a mindset of making disciples. So let's be disciple makers in everything we do and in every arena of our lives.

Introduction: Using Greek as a "Trump Card"

One of the problems with teaching future pastors *a little* Greek is that sometimes they get enough in their training to be dangerous but not enough to use it effectively. At times you will hear someone from a pulpit appeal to the Greek; that is fine. However, never allow the use of Greek to trump the context. If you see someone using the Greek in a way that doesn't fit the context, then be suspicious. Context is probably going to triumph over the use of the Greek. Sometimes the preacher is using the Greek incorrectly. Sometimes those who have a little knowledge of Greek accidentally ignore the context and rely on their little knowledge.

We are going to approach this legend in two ways: (1) we will analyze the Greek construction to see if the argument above is valid; and (2) we will examine the context. This verse actually contains another legend, besides the one introduced above, which understands the command to make disciples as "make converts." This is practiced way too often in the church. Therefore, we need to discuss the meaning of "make disciples" as well. When someone becomes a Christian, have we taken part in the Great Commission because they have converted, or is this passage saying there is more to do?

Analyzing the Greek Construction

Technically "go" is one of those *-ing* verbs like "running." The only explicit command in this verse is "make disciples," and "make disciples" is one word in the Greek. That is all true. The reason I encourage people going into ministry to learn Greek is *not* because they can learn to do word studies but so they can understand the relationships *between* the words. When you look at the way these words ("go" and "make disciples") are put together, the relationship is much more complicated than saying one is a command and one is a participle. Looking at parallel constructions, examples from the Gospel of Matthew with the same verb for "go" being used, will be helpful in deciding what Jesus meant when he said "go." Matthew has five helpful examples, but we will look at three. All of these have the verb for "go" preceding a command, just like Matthew 28:19.

1. Matthew 11:4: "Jesus replied to them, 'Go and report to John what you hear and see.'" John the Baptist had sent his disciples to Jesus to make sure Jesus was truly the Messiah. Jesus responded by telling them to go (the supposed *-ing* verb) and report (the explicit command) to John. Are we expected to believe that Jesus was saying, "As you go about your life, if you happen to see John, the guy in prison, make sure you report to him what you hear and see"? It's doubtful that we are supposed to understand that from "go and report." Could he have meant, "Be ready to report to John as you are going about your life"? Again, this is doubtful. The only way the disciples can obey the command to "report" is to "go" to John. Going is not really optional; it must be done in order to obey the command to report.

2. Matthew 17:27: "But, so we won't offend them, go to the sea, cast in a fishhook, and take the first fish that you catch. When you open its mouth you'll find a coin. Take it and give it to them for Me and you." If the legendary teaching above is correct, Jesus must be saying something like, "As you are going about your life, if you happen to pass a sea, cast in a fishhook." Or maybe he is saying, "Make it your mind-set to be casting in fishhooks when you pass a sea." Those are fairly ridiculous ideas for what Jesus is actually saying. The command is to cast a fishhook. But the only way they could obey that command is to go to the sea.

3. Matthew 28:7: "Then go quickly and tell His disciples, 'He has been raised from the dead. In fact, He is going ahead of you to Galilee; you will see Him there.' Listen, I have told you." An angel is speaking to the women at the tomb. The angel commands the women to tell Jesus' disciples that he was raised from the dead. According to the legendary understanding of Greek, we are to believe the angel commands them to tell Jesus' disciples as they are going about their lives. These women have found out that the resurrection has taken place, and now they are supposed to go about their normal lives, and if they happen to run into a disciple, they are to mention the resurrection! One key to this interpretation's being extremely unlikely is the presence of the word "quickly." That word makes it clear that "go" is functioning like a command. You wouldn't say, "As you are going about your life quickly." The idea of going, even though it is a participle (like *running*), still carries more force to it than some of these interpreters believe. So the phrase "as you are going" is used to try to communicate that it is not a command but simply a lifestyle. How do you do a lifestyle "quickly"? The point is that they are to tell Jesus' disciples, and the only way they can do that is to go. Going is required to obey the explicit command of telling.[1]

The same pattern is present in Matthew 28:19. Jesus is commanding the disciples to make disciples, but the only way they can do that is to go. While the explicit command is to make disciples, "go" is an *implied command*. It takes on the same force as an imperative because it is connected to "make disciples," just like "go and report" or "go quickly and tell." Because of the connection of "go" to an explicit command, it carries the same force as the command does.

Examining the Context

The same conclusion could have been reached without knowledge of Greek. While the Greek helps us analyze the construction, the context is fairly clear. The command is not only to "make disciples" but to make disciples "*of all*

---

[1] The other two examples are Matt 2:8 and 9:13. They demonstrate the same pattern.

nations" (emphasis added). How do you get to all those nations? You go! This is not going to happen unless you are intentional and go. So the going is not referencing a lifestyle; it's not about having a discipleship mind-set. It's about intentionally seeking to disciple the world, and the context explicitly says this. New Testament scholar Craig Blomberg strikes a brilliant balance between the "going" and the "making disciples" regarding this verse: "To 'make disciples *of all nations*' does require many people to leave their homelands, but Jesus' main focus remains on the task of all believers to duplicate themselves wherever they may be."[2] Both concepts are present in the verse. Why didn't Jesus give a command to go and a separate command to make disciples? Probably because He was emphasizing the command to make disciples but not to the exclusion of a command to go and reach a lost world.

Application

The focus of this verse is the explicit command to make disciples. Therefore, we need to ask: What does discipleship entail? Is it just conversion to Christ? The Greek word for "making disciples" is somewhat vague. Therefore, Jesus provides two vital aspects of discipleship that distinguish making disciples from merely converting the lost: baptism and teaching.

Baptism is a key to discipleship as it is the symbol externally of what has taken place internally. The cleansing of sins has occurred internally, and baptism pictures this externally. It is a picture of salvation. It is done in the likeness of Jesus' burial and resurrection; thus a new disciple is proclaiming upon baptism their allegiance to Jesus, and the baptizer is affirming that the one being baptized has a valid profession of faith. When it is done well, it can be an invigorating event in the life of a church, which should cause a passion for evangelism to grow and a passion for further discipleship to burn even stronger.

Teaching is the essence of disciple making. In this context it clearly refers to teaching them the commands of Christ. But more generally it refers to instructing the new disciple in the Christian life. It should never be limited to a classroom but would include teaching them by example. Teaching can be done in many environments and contexts. The classroom is a great environment for passing along data for information, but as life rubs against life, a deeper discipleship can occur. So let's not settle for discipleship as distributing information in a classroom. If transformation is not taking place, discipleship is not occurring. Let's be disciple makers and not convert makers.

---

[2] Craig Blomberg, *Matthew*, NAC (Nashville: B&H, 1992), 431.

Annotated Bibliography

Commentaries

Hagner, Donald A. *Matthew 14–28*. WBC. Dallas: Word Books, 1995.

As with the rest of the Word Biblical Commentary series, this volume is technical and thorough. Hagner's discussion on Matthew 28:19 is not too involved.

Luz, Ulrich. *Matthew 21–28*. Hermeneia. Translated by James E. Crouch. Edited by Helmut Koester. Minneapolis: Fortress Press, 2005.

This is a thick and technical commentary; however, the discussion on Matthew 28:19 is brief and not too involved. Requires knowledge of Greek.

Journals

Blue, J. Ronald. "Go, Missions." *Bibliotheca Sacra* 141 (1984): 341–53.

Blue's article is intended for a broad audience and is highly accessible to a lay audience. No prior knowledge of Greek is required.

Kvalbein, Hans. "Go Therefore and Make Disciples . . . The Concept of Discipleship in the New Testament." *Themelios* 13.2 (1988): 48–53.

Kvalbein's treatment of the issues is rather accessible to almost any interested layperson. No prior knowledge of Greek is required.

Rogers, Cleon. "The Great Commission." *Bibliotheca Sacra* 130, no. 519 (1973): 258–67.

Knowledge of Greek would be helpful for reading this article. He discusses the relationship of the verbs for "go" and "make disciples." He also has a helpful section on the meaning of "make disciples."

Websites

Wallace, Daniel B. "The Great Commission or the Great Suggestion?" February 17, 2014. Accessed May 30, 2014. www.tinyurl.com/dbwallace1.

Wallace, Daniel B. "The Great Commission, Part 2: Historical Setting." February 22, 2014. Accessed May 30, 2014. www.tinyurl.com/dbwallace2.

Wallace, Daniel B. "The Great Commission, Part 3: Application." February 26, 2014. Accessed May 30, 2104. www.tinyurl.com/dbwallace3.

Wallace does a brilliant job of analyzing this issue. He also demonstrates how translations have correctly translated this type of construction in other places in Matthew's Gospel.

PART II

Urban Legends in
The Acts of the Apostles,
the Epistles, and Revelation

CHAPTER 17

Repent Means "to Change Your Mind"

Acts 2:38

The Legendary Teaching on Acts 2:38

Repent!' Peter said to them, 'and be baptized, each of you, in the name of Jesus Christ for the forgiveness of your sins, and you will receive the gift of the Holy Spirit'" (Acts 2:38). Repentance is merely a change of mind whereby a person recognizes his sinfulness and need of salvation. Therefore, an alcoholic should not be told he needs to change his lifestyle in order to obtain salvation. The only form of repentance required for eternal salvation is a change of mind about Christ. The idea that *repentance* means "to turn from sins for salvation" amounts to salvation by works. If people need to turn from their sins in order to obtain salvation, then no one could ever attain eternal life. Not only is this view a distortion of the gospel, but it also completely undermines any confidence Christians could have that they have been saved.

The Greek word for *repentance* is *metanoia*, a compound word made of two different Greek words: *meta* means "after," and *noia* (*nous*) means "mind" or "thought." It contains the concepts of "an afterthought" or "a second thought." When you have an afterthought, you might change the way you think about something. Therefore, the Greek word means "a change of thought" or "to change your mind about something."

If I say the word *earthquake*, you know I am referring to the earth shaking since that is what *earthquake* means. If I reference the "moonlight," you know I am talking about light that comes from the moon. That's how words work.

When Peter tells the crowd in Jerusalem to repent, he is commanding them to change their minds about Jesus Christ. We need to protect the gospel from being distorted by those who would try to add to the gospel, specifically adding works like "turning from sins."

Introduction: The Importance of the Meaning of Repentance

I took an anecdotal survey at a church I previously attended on the definition of *repent*. I received several different responses: "to feel sad about something," "to feel remorse," and "to change your mind." One person said, "To do a 360." What they meant was "to do a 180," referring to the idea of turning from sin. This survey demonstrated to me that there is much confusion over the English word *repent*, not to mention the meaning of the Greek word. However, the first command Jesus gave according to the Gospel of Mark was, "Repent and believe in the good news!" (1:15). If Jesus commanded repentance, then what exactly did he command? Three issues need to be addressed: (1) the meaning of the Greek word; (2) repentance as work of man or work of God; and (3) the relationship of repentance to the gospel.

The Way Words Work

Two Greek words are usually discussed[1] when referring to the idea of repentance: (1) a noun, *metanoia*, usually translated "repentance"; and (2) a verb, *metanoeō*, usually translated "repent." It is true that *meta* can mean "after" and that *noia* probably comes from the Greek word *nous* meaning "mind" or "thought." It is possible that when this word was originally formed it meant "an afterthought" or "a change of mind." But there are two problems with equating the Greek words for repentance with "a change of mind."

First, words change in meaning through time. For example, take the word *bimbo*. It comes from an Italian word that means "little child" or "baby." In contemporary usage it usually means "an attractive but stupid woman." When it was first used by Italian Americans, it referred to "a tough, contemptible man." I'm not sure how or why that word changed in meaning through time, but I do know it changed. Another example is the word *peruse*. It comes from fifteenth-century Middle English and meant "to use up" or "to wear out." Today it most commonly means "to browse" or "read through without detail." A few decades ago it meant "to examine carefully," almost the exact opposite of what it means today. Words change in meaning through time. Even though *metanoia* might have originally meant "a change of mind," the real question is what it meant at the time of the writing of the New Testament.

Second, compound words are more complicated than doing simple addition. Sometimes it works, like with the words *earthquake* or *moonlight*. However, sometimes it does not work, like the words *butterfly* or *honeymoon*. Splitting a

---

[1] Other Greek words would need to be discussed for a more comprehensive analysis, like *metamelomai*, *strephō*, and *epistrephō*.

word into two parts to discover its meaning is an unreliable method for word studies.[2]

The correct meaning of a word is discovered through examining that word in many contexts. The more contexts available for analysis, the clearer the meaning will be. Some words occur hundreds or thousands of times in the New Testament. It can take a long time to figure out what they mean. The noun (22 times) and the verb (34 times) for *repentance* occur a total of fifty-six times. The three occurrences of this word discussed below will help determine its meaning.

Analyzing the Greek Word

Matthew 3:7–9 is discussing John the Baptist: "When he saw many of the Pharisees and Sadducees coming to the place of his baptism, he said to them, 'Brood of vipers! Who warned you to flee from the coming wrath? Therefore produce fruit consistent with repentance. And don't presume to say to yourselves, "We have Abraham as our father." For I tell you that God is able to raise up children for Abraham from these stones!'" John the Baptist scolds the scribes and Pharisees for their poor character using the phrase "brood of vipers." Then he calls for fruit consistent with repentance before they would be allowed to be baptized. He is looking for concrete evidence of repentance. What does concrete evidence of repentance look like? When someone has repented, it will be demonstrated by their lifestyle. It will flow from a changed heart. One scholar said that repentance in this passage refers to "an ethically transforming event" resulting in "changed behavior."[3] Therefore, a connection exists between repentance and the evidence of it: good fruit.

Jesus' description of the Ninevites in Matthew 12:41 indicates that they repented at the preaching of Jonah: "The men of Nineveh will stand up at the judgment with this generation and condemn it, because they repented at Jonah's proclamation; and look—something greater than Jonah is here!" Jesus uses the Greek verb for *repentance* discussed above. The book of Jonah describes the reaction of the Ninevites in Jonah 3:5: "The men of Nineveh believed in God. They proclaimed a fast and dressed in sackcloth—from the greatest of them to the least." Their belief is then demonstrated by a call for a fast and putting on sackcloth and ashes, followed by a declaration by the king for the people to turn from their wicked ways. Therefore what Jesus calls "repenting," Jonah describes as "believing" and "turning." This provides more evidence

---

[2] See D. A. Carson, *Exegetical Fallacies*, 2nd ed. (Grand Rapids: Baker, 1996), 29–30.

[3] Robert C. Tannehill, *The Shape of Luke's Story: Essays on Luke-Acts* (Eugene, OR: Cascade Books, 2005), 88.

that the Greek word for *repentance* includes more than just a change of mind; it includes the concept of "turning" and in some way relates to believing.

Finally, in Acts 26:20, Paul summarizes his preaching ministry: "Instead, I preached to those in Damascus first, and to those in Jerusalem and in all the region of Judea, and to the Gentiles, that they should repent and turn to God, and do works worthy of repentance." The word *repent* is used to indicate the initial act of coming to faith. It contains the idea of turning and will produce good deeds, which demonstrate that the repentance was genuine. Repentance stresses the concept of a change in *direction*. Notice the explicit connection between repentance and works: true repentance will bring about works. Clinton Arnold says, "Repentance in this passage includes a sorrow for sin but also a re-orientation of the whole of one's life around the Kingdom of God and the work of the Messiah. True repentance can be seen in a changed lifestyle."[4] Repentance is "turning away from sin."

Is Repentance a Work of Man or of God?

Two verses in Acts and one in 2 Timothy describe the source of repentance. Peter and the apostles declared in Acts 5:31, "God exalted this man to His right hand as ruler and Savior, to grant repentance to Israel, and forgiveness of sins." Peter, in Acts 11:18, says something similar: "When they heard this they became silent. Then they glorified God, saying, 'So God has granted repentance resulting in life even to the Gentiles!'" This chapter began in Acts 2:38, a sermon by Peter; Acts 5 and 11 were spoken by Peter. He does not describe repentance as something we muster up but as something granted by God. The Greek word for *grant* means "to give" or "to bestow."[5] Peter is explicitly declaring that repentance is a gift from God, not a work of man.

The final verse was written by Paul in 2 Timothy 2:25: "Perhaps God will grant them repentance leading them to the knowledge of the truth." Paul uses the same Greek word to communicate that repentance is a gift. The idea that repentance leading to salvation is something man does is not supported by Scripture.[6]

---

4 Clinton E. Arnold, "Acts," in *Zondervan Illustrated Bible Backgrounds Commentary: John, Acts* (Grand Rapids: Zondervan, 2002), 466.

5 BDAG, 242 (see definition 2).

6 For a few more references that are a little less clear, see Romans 2:4 and Acts 3:19 with 3:26.

How Does Repentance Relate to the Gospel?

Repentance and faith are not part of the gospel[7] but proper responses to the gospel. When I explain the gospel and say that the proper response is repentance and faith, I don't mean "fix up your life and then you can get saved." First, salvation is a work of God in the hearts of people. Those who don't believe in Christ are dead, so they are unable to muster up faith or repentance. God has to do a work in their hearts to make them able to believe and repent. Second, this work of God in the hearts of those hearing the gospel will make them willing to repent and believe. Third, when I explain the concept of repenting from sins, I tell people they have to *turn away* from something. In my experience in witnessing to people, I don't have to focus on turning away from sins because after I have presented the gospel and explained that they are lost and that sin has separated them from God, I then lift up the glory of Jesus Christ and talk about what Jesus has done for them (dying on the cross to pay for their sins, paying a debt they could never pay). Then they understand the call to turn away from sin. I don't even have to say it because they understand that sin separated people from God in the first place.

New Testament scholar D. A. Carson says this: "Repentance is not a merely intellectual change of mind or mere grief, still less doing penance, but a radical transformation of the entire person, a fundamental turnaround involving mind and action, and including overtones of grief which result in spiritual fruit."[8] It's a radical transformation of the entire person. It includes a change of mind, a sorrow over sin, but it is more than that. It is a transformation of all you are because everything about you is radically changed when you are made alive with Christ, what theologians call regeneration.

Application

When presenting the gospel, remember to explain the impact of sin on humanity. Once someone properly understands sin, then referencing the concept of turning from sin makes sense. This provides a context for them to understand repentance. Don't shy away from talking about sin when you share the gospel. People need to know why they need a Savior.

Also, we want to avoid confusing words when doing evangelism. The word *repentance* is a confusing word in English. I try to avoid using that specific word when I am witnessing to someone. Instead, I describe the concept. If we

---

[7] Cf. D. A. Carson, "Editorial," *Themelios* 34, no. 1 (2009): 1–2.

[8] D. A. Carson, "Matthew," in *The Expositor's Bible Commentary: Matthew and Mark*, ed. Tremper Longman III and David E. Garland (Grand Rapids: Zondervan, 2010), 128.

are looking at Scripture passages and the word *repentance* occurs, I define it for them.

Annotated Bibliography

Commentaries

Blomberg, Craig L. *Matthew*. NAC. Nashville: Broadman, 1992.
    See comments on Matthew 3:2.
Nolland, John. *Luke*. WBC. Dallas: Word Books, 1989.

Journals

Croteau, David A. "Repentance Found? The Concept of Repentance in the Fourth Gospel."
    Master's Seminary Journal 24, no. 1 (2013): 97–113.
    See especially pages 98–107. This article can also be found online at www.tms.edu/tmsj/
msj24e.pdf.
Nowell, Irene. "Bible Terms Today: Metanoia." *Bible Today* 30 (1992): 68–72.
    This is an accessible article. No prior knowledge of Greek or Hebrew is required.
Hägerland, Tobias. "Jesus and the Rites of Repentance." *New Testament Studies* 52, no. 2
    (2006): 166–87.
    This is a technical and nuanced discussion on both Semitic backgrounds and the Greek
and Hebrew languages. Not all conclusions are advocated, but the discussion on defining
repentance is helpful.

Websites

Pink, Arthur W. *Repentance*. Accessed July 12, 2014. www.the-highway.com/repenttoc_
    Pink.html.
    This booklet by Pink has been published online.
"What Is Repentance and How Do I Do It?" *New Life Community Church*.
    Accessed July 12, 2014. www.new-life.net/growth/other-articles/
    what-is-repentance-and-how-do-i-do-it.
    A helpful online article summarizing the issue at hand.
"True Repentance." *Ligonier Ministries*. Accessed July 12, 2014. www.ligonier.org/learn/
    devotionals/true-repentance.
    I wouldn't follow the route to this conclusion, necessarily, but it ends at the right
destination.

CHAPTER 18

The Philippian Jailer
"Just Believed" and Was Saved

Acts 16:31

The Legendary Teaching on Acts 16:31

The gospel is a call to faith in Jesus Christ. Nowhere is this more clearly stated than in Acts 16:31. When the Philippian jailer asked Paul and Silas, "What must I do to be saved?" (Acts 16:30), they responded with all that needs to be said: "Believe on the Lord Jesus, and you will be saved—you and your household" (Acts 16:31).

Do not add works to the free message of the gospel. Do not add repentance or turning from sins. In order for repentance to be a necessary response to the gospel, it would have to be mentioned alongside faith every time in the New Testament. Do not lay a burden on those who wish to follow God. As one theologian said, repentance

> is not there, and no amount of theological casuistry can put it there. . . . [T]he effort to find the concept of repentance and surrender in the word "believe" is totally without linguistic foundation. The word "believe" means "believe"—both in English and in Greek. . . . Eternity alone will reveal how many thousands of souls have rested their eternal happiness and well-being on this uncomplicated declaration. Their ranks will certainly include many who appropriated this promise as very young children, as well as countless others who did so at every age of life.[1]

---

[1] Zane Hodges, *Absolutely Free! A Biblical Reply to Lordship Salvation* (Grand Rapids: Zondervan, 1989), 144–45, 169.

Introduction: Unraveling the Legend

As is the case with many of the legends, the literary context of Acts 16:31 provides the key to understanding the meaning of this verse. Acts 16:12–40 is the entire story of Paul and Silas's missionary trip to Philippi, a city of Macedonia. They arrive in Philippi (16:12), and shortly afterward Lydia is converted (16:14). Then they encounter a slave girl who was demon possessed.

Acts 16:16–22 explains Paul and Silas's encounter with the demon-possessed slave girl. Luke said that she "cried out" for "many days" while Paul and Silas proclaimed "the way of salvation." The word for "cried out" refers to her speaking in a loud voice. After Paul became greatly aggravated, he cast the demon out of her. Since her owners realized they could no longer make a profit from her with the demon gone, they grabbed Paul and Silas and brought them before the authorities. They were charged with "seriously disturbing" the city before the magistrates, and a mob attacked them.

The next major section describes Paul and Silas in prison (16:23–29). They responded to being beaten with rods by praying and singing hymns to God. The prisoners were listening to Paul and Silas.[2] An earthquake shook the prison, the doors were opened, and the prisoners' chains unfastened. The jailer woke up and, seeing that the doors were open, prepared to kill himself, supposing the prisoners had escaped. Paul stopped him from committing suicide, explaining that all the prisoners were still inside the prison. The jailer entered the prison and was terrified, falling before Paul and Silas.

Verse 29 raises a few questions. Why did the jailer fall before Paul and Silas if he knew nothing about them or their message? When Paul called to him, how did he know it was Paul? The jailer couldn't even see inside the prison at that point so he had to call for lights. This response by the jailer implies that he must have known something about Paul and the message he preached.

The next section describes Paul and Silas being released from jail (16:30–34). The jailer asks, "What must I do to be saved?" While some interpreters believe his question referred to the expected punishment he would receive for allowing prisoners to escape, this interpretation fails for two primary reasons. First, he was already made aware that none of the prisoners had escaped. Second, why would the jailer ask prisoners this question? If he had asked his

---

[2] While some people have pointed out that the jailer could have heard the content of the prayers and songs to help inform him of the question he is about to ask in verse 31, that conclusion becomes difficult when realizing that verse 27 says the jailer was sleeping. Whether he was sleeping the entire time or part of the time is impossible to know. Clinton E. Arnold, "Acts," in *Zondervan Illustrated Bible Backgrounds Commentary: John, Acts* (Grand Rapids: Zondervan, 2002), 377, speculates that the jailer may have heard some of the songs Paul and Silas had sung. Similarly, John B. Polhill, *Acts*, NAC (Nashville: B&H, 1995), 355, says, "Perhaps he had fallen asleep to the sound of Paul and Silas's hymns to God."

superiors, it would make more sense, but to ask the prisoners this question does not. Since the word *saved* does not refer to being rescued from punishment in this context, it most likely refers to his response to having heard the gospel proclaimed: "saved" in the sense of being rescued from the eternal punishment of God. The jailer seems to know more about the gospel than some give him credit. New Testament scholar Darrell Bock concludes: "In the logic of the narrative, the jailer surely knows why the men are there. Their religious claims must have registered with him when the quake came and they preserved his life by staying. . . . This is more than a request to save his life."[3]

The answer to his question is, "Believe on the Lord Jesus" (16:31). Understanding this as the all-incorporating response necessary to the gospel has at least two problems. First, the jailer must have had more understanding than is explicitly stated in the passage in order to ask the question. Second, Luke does not provide everything stated in the dialogues contained in Acts. He is summarizing what took place. The correct way to interpret narrative literature is to recognize that the author is crafting the stories he includes in a way that they build upon each other. Readers of Acts have 1:1–16:30 already in their minds by the time they get to Acts 16:31. A competent reader will take all of that into consideration.

The idea that stories are summarized in the New Testament shouldn't be shocking. To see a great example of this, read through the accounts of Peter and Cornelius. In the first explanation of their encounter, Luke uses forty-eight verses to tell the story (Acts 10:1–48). The apostles and believers in Judea heard about Peter's encounter with the Gentiles (Acts 11:1), and they were surprised (Acts 11:3). So Peter explained what had happened in "an orderly sequence" (Acts 11:4). Acts 11:5–16 (twelve verses) provides Peter's summary of what happened. Of course, with any summary certain details were left out. Whether Peter left out these details or Luke did is not of much concern, for the reader of Acts had just completed reading the story and wouldn't need all the details again. Peter again recounted his encounter with Cornelius in Acts 15:7–9, just three verses. Luke went from forty-eight verses, to twelve verses, to three verses. It was not improper for ancient writers of history to summarize accounts.

Going back to the response of Paul and Silas in Acts 16:31, Luke explicitly tells his readers that "believe" was not the entirety of their answer. Verse 32 says they "spoke the message of the Lord to him along with everyone in his house." Luke only quotes the words in 16:31, but he states that Paul and Silas explained more to him and to his household than simply "believe." Verse 32 declares that Paul and Silas had more content to explain than what was said in

---

[3]   Darrell L. Bock, *Acts*, BECNT (Grand Rapids: Baker, 2007), 541.

verse 31. As Bock states, "Clearly, Luke is summarizing here. The jailer would have the meaning of such a confession explained to him (v. 32 says as much)."[4]

Before the jailer was baptized (16:33) and the declaration that he believed was given (16:34), notice the act of repentance: "He took them the same hour of the night and washed their wounds" (16:33). Only after this was he baptized, and *then* Luke says, "He had believed God" (16:34). The jailer had taken a journey from suicide to salvation.

Application

The content of the gospel is necessary in order for someone to have a true response to the gospel. To ask people if they are saved but give them no (theological) context for that question is unhelpful.[5] People need to understand what they are being saved from; they need to understand that they are sinners; and they need to understand sin. But sin itself does not make much sense to people who don't believe God created them and that they are therefore accountable to God. Of course, you can't share an entire systematic theology while witnessing to someone, but some excellent resources are available to help you understand the content necessary in gospel presentations, like Greg Gilbert's book *What Is the Gospel?* and Trevin Wax's book *Counterfeit Gospels.*[6]

Current American Christianity appears to have a focus on quick evangelistic encounters. Discipleship materials and courses are being taught to help Christians share the gospel as quickly as possible so a call to decision can be made. I. Howard Marshall wisely instructs us "that it is not enough simply to face people with gospel proof-texts; there is normally need for careful instruction adapted to their particular situation and for personal, pastoral care if the task of evangelism is to be successful and lasting in its effects."[7] Let's make sure as we share the gospel with unbelievers that we take the time to patiently explain to them all that is needed for eternal life, as Paul and Silas did in Acts 16:31–32.

Annotated Bibliography

Commentaries

Bock, Darrell L. *Acts*. BECNT. Grand Rapids: Baker, 2007.
    Bock's comments on this narrative are helpful. See especially pages 540–41.

---

[4] Ibid., 542. Similarly, I. Howard Marshall, *Acts* (Downers Grove: InterVarsity, 2008), 273, concludes, "But all this needed fuller explanation than could be given in a brief formula."

[5] See R. C. Sproul, *Saved from What?* (Wheaton: Crossway, 2002), especially 13–14.

[6] Greg Gilbert, *What Is the Gospel?* (Wheaton: Crossway, 2010); Trevin Wax, *Counterfeit Gospels: Rediscovering the Good News in a World of False Hope* (Chicago: Moody, 2011).

[7] Marshall, *Acts*, 273.

Marshall, I. Howard. *Acts*. Downers Grove: InterVarsity, 2008.

Marshall's easy-to-read commentary does a good job reading this verse in context. See especially page 273.

Websites

Erickson, Millard. "Is Belief in Christ's Lordship Essential?" *Southwestern Journal of Theology* 33, no. 2 (1991): 107–25.

Erickson summarizes the overarching debate, making particularly insightful analyses along the way. See especially pages 120–21. Also available online at www.cslewisinstitute.org/webfm_send/360.

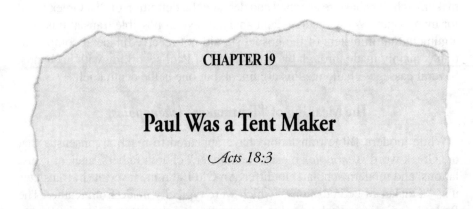

CHAPTER 19

Paul Was a Tent Maker

Acts 18:3

The Legendary Teaching on Acts 18:3

In a few places in the New Testament, Paul mentions the idea that he worked to support himself. In 1 Corinthians 4:12, Paul says, "We labor, working with our own hands," and in 1 Thessalonians 2:9, he says, "For you remember our labor and hardship, brothers. Working night and day so that we would not burden any of you." Luke also says this regarding Paul, quoting him in Acts 20:34: "You yourselves know that these hands have provided for my needs and for those who were with me." What did Paul do, exactly, in order to provide for himself (and those with him)?

Acts 18:3 appears to provide a clear answer, referring to Aquila and Priscilla as "being of the same occupation . . . tentmakers by trade." Every major modern translation says Paul was a tentmaker. While this most likely refers to the obvious, that Paul made tents, there is another possible meaning for this word.

A lesser-known Bible translation, The Power New Testament, says that Paul was a prayer shawl maker. The glossary to this translation says that the prayer shawl was referred to by Jewish men as a tent or prayer closet, being placed over the head during prayer. Therefore, it is possible that Paul spent his days earning his living by making prayer shawls or prayer tents. Regardless, the main idea is that Paul supported himself and didn't depend on others' support. This has given rise to the modern concept of missionaries being "tentmakers."

Introduction: Unraveling the Legend

The idea of Paul working with his hands needs to be addressed from two avenues: (1) the definition of the Greek word underlying the common translation "tentmaker;" and (2) the idea that ministers of the gospel should not be financially supported. While every major Bible translation calls Paul a "tent-maker," scholars have researched and debated the definition of that Greek word for many years. We will survey and analyze several possible translations. The argument that ministers of the gospel should not receive financial compensation is mainly made through the implication of Paul's working with his hands. Several passages challenge this argument, but one is the death knell.

The Meaning of "Tentmaker" (*skēnopoios*)

While modern Bible translations have appeared to reach a consensus that the Greek word *skēnopoios* means "tentmaker," church fathers, ancient translations, and modern scholarship differ. An Old Latin manuscript (h) translates it as "a maker of bed cushions," which were typically made from leather. The Peshitta (a Syriac translation that became the standard translation for Syrian churches by the fifth century) rendered it "maker of leather thongs," referring to items like bridles.[1]

The church fathers provide three main options for Paul's trade.[2] Origen (third century), Rufinus (third century), and Theodoret (fifth century) refer to Paul as a shoemaker, connecting his trade to working with leather. Gregory of Nyssa said that Paul stitched together tents. Chrysostom believed Paul worked in both of those areas. Some have proposed that Paul was a "maker of stage properties," working in the theater. Due to the religious objections Jews had toward the theater, it's unlikely that Paul (along with Priscilla and Aquila) would have been involved in that.[3]

A popular theory in the 1800s suggested that Paul was a weaver of cloth for tents made from goats' hair. The region Paul was from (Cilicia) was known for its *cilicium* (goats' hair). This theory has fallen out of favor since Theodor Zahn (a German New Testament scholar from the late nineteenth and early twentieth centuries) attacked it on several grounds. He stated that goats' hair was seldom used for tents. He also noted that if Paul moved to Jerusalem as a boy (cf. Acts 22:3), his connection to Cilicia becomes less relevant. Finally, Zahn concluded that weaving was a despised trade among Pharisees, making it unlikely as a trade for Paul.[4]

---

[1] See Ronald F. Hock, *The Social Context of Paul's Ministry: Tentmaking an Apostleship* (Minneapolis: Fortress, 190), 20.

[2] See ibid., 20–21, for the following information on the church fathers.

[3] See BDAG, 928 (see definition 1).

[4] See Theodor Zahn, *Die Apostelgeschichte des Lukas. Kap. 13–24* (Leipzig: Diechert, 1921), 633–34. For an appropriate critique of Zahn's analysis, see H. Szesnat, "What Did the ΣΚΗΝΟΠΟΙΟΣ Paul Produce?" *Neotestimentica* 27, no. 2 (1993): 396.

The dominant view today is that Paul was a leatherworker.[5] The designation of "tentmaker" is not technically incorrect but simply too narrow. While Paul probably was involved with tent making, *he was more than a tent maker*. The main objection to the idea that Paul was a leatherworker is the association it would have with the despised profession of tanning leather. Not only were many Jews repulsed by this profession because of the terrible stench of working with dead animals, but they were also concerned with the ritual purity of tanners since they were in consistent contact with dead animal carcasses.[6] However, there is no reason to believe Paul was involved in the tanning process himself.

Therefore, the best word to describe Paul's trade was a leatherworker.[7] What exactly he made as a leatherworker is not known, but, as Hock concluded, "Tents were usually made of leather, and leather goods were associated with Cilicia."[8] Similarly, German historian Martin Hengel concluded that we "should not understand the designation 'tentmaker' in too narrow a sense. The goods produced in this trade may have included a variety of leather articles or comparable products, just as a 'saddler' does not produce only saddles."[9] It's even likely that Paul would have used other material besides leather to make his products, such as goats' hair and linen.[10]

The theory that Paul was a maker of prayer shawls has zero support in any scholarly research. Conceptually connecting the way Jews referred to the prayer shawl with the word used in Acts 18:3 is pure speculation.

---

[5] For evidence that this is the dominant view, see Todd D. Still, "Did Paul Loathe Manual Labor? Revisiting the Word of Ronald F. Hock on the Apostle's Tentmaking and Social Class," *Journal of Biblical Literature* 125, no. 4 (2006): 781, and Hock, *Paul's Ministry*, 73n14.

[6] See Clinton E. Arnold, "Acts," in *Zondervan Illustrated Bible Backgrounds Commentary: John, Acts* (Grand Rapids: Zondervan, 2002), 300–301. The HCSB has a footnote at Acts 9:43 saying, "Tanners were considered ritually unclean because of their occupation." In the Mishnah *Ketuboth* 7:10 says, "In Sidon there was a tanner who died, and he had a brother who was a tanner. Sages ruled, 'She can claim, "Your brother I could take, but I can't take you [as my levir].""" This tradition could postdate the New Testament.

[7] Note that two scholars have concluded that Paul worked both with leather *and* canvas. Jerome Murphy-O'Connor, *Paul: A Critical Life* (Oxford: Oxford University Press, 1996), 86–89, and Morna Hooker, *Paul: A Short Introduction* (Oxford: Oneworld, 2003), 19n18.

[8] Hock, *Paul's Ministry*, 21.

[9] Martin Hengel, *The Pre-Christian Paul*, trans. John Bowden (London: SCM, 1991), 17. Similarly, see Hock, *Paul's Ministry*, 21. See also the conclusion by P. W. Barnett, "Tentmaking," in *Dictionary of Paul and His Letters*, ed. G. F. Hawthorne and R. P. Martin (Downers Grove: InterVarsity, 1993), 926.

[10] See Szesnat, "Paul Produce," 395–400.

Paul Worked a Trade, So Ministers Must Today

The main way I have heard the second legend argued is by saying that since Paul supported himself and did not depend on churches to support him financially, ministers of the gospel today are required to do the same. One way of avoiding this application is to take the line of interpretation of Hock: wealthy Greco-Romans despised hard labor; Paul was raised in a wealthy family; therefore Paul despised hard labor.[11] However, as Still has demonstrated, it's far from certain that Paul was raised in a wealthy family, and the text of Paul's letters doesn't support this claim.[12]

One of the problems with the second legend is the underlying hermeneutic. A central maxim to proper interpretation is that *description does not equal prescription*. In this case, the fact that Paul is *described* as trying to support himself as much as possible does not necessitate that all ministers of the gospel are *prescribed* to do that as well. But beyond that, one specific passage explicitly undermines this legend.

First Corinthians 9 is an illustration of the teaching in chapter 8. In 1 Corinthians 8, Paul explains the principle of sacrificing freedoms that Christians have for the sake of other Christians. The specific example he was addressing was food sacrificed to idols. The illustration in chapter 9 is regarding the support of ministers of the gospel. He (rhetorically) asks in 1 Corinthians 9:6 if only he and Barnabas "have no right to refrain from working?" In other words, other ministers are not working, but Paul and Barnabas are working. He provides several illustrations between verses 7–10. Then in verse 11 he says, "If we have sown spiritual things for you, is it too much if we reap material benefits from you?" In verse 12, he specifically refers to receiving compensation for serving as a minister of the gospel as a "right," but a right that they "have not made use of" for the sake of the gospel. He concludes in 9:14, saying that "the Lord has commanded that those who preach the gospel should earn their living by the gospel."

Ministers of the gospel have a right to earn their living by preaching the gospel. However, they also have the freedom to forgo that right if they desire. Paul's practice of working with his hands as a leatherworker does not, in any way, preclude ministers of the gospel today from receiving compensation.

---

[11] See Hock, *Paul's Ministry*, 66–67.
[12] See Still, "Did Paul Loathe Manual Labor?," 781–95.

Annotated Bibliography

Books

Hock, Ronald F. *The Social Context of Paul's Ministry: Tentmaking an Apostleship*. Minneapolis: Fortress, 1980.

While not all of the theses of Hock's book are trustworthy, his discussion on Paul's trade is easy to read and well done. See especially pages 20–21.

Rapske, Brian. *The Book of Acts and Paul in Roman Custody*. BAFCS 3. Grand Rapids: Eerdmans, 1994.

Rapske's summary of the issue is masterful. His footnotes provide ample opportunity for further study on the issue. See pages 106–8.

Dictionary Articles

Michaelis, W. "σκηνοποιός." Pages 393–94 in *Theological Dictionary of the New Testament*. Vol. VII. Edited by Gerhard Kittel and Gerhard Friedrich. Translated by Geoffrey W. Bromiley. Grand Rapids: Eerdmans, 1971.

P. W. Barnett, "Tentmaking." Pages 925–27 in *Dictionary of Paul and His Letters*. Edited by G. F. Hawthorne and R. P. Martin. Downers Grove: InterVarsity, 1993.

Barnett's easy-to-read article summarizes the issue well.

Journals

H. Szesnat, "What Did the ΣΚΗΝΟΠΟΙΟΣ Paul Produce?" *Neotestimentica* 27, no. 2 (1993): 391–402.

Szesnat is critical of the historicity of Acts (and the New Testament), but his discussion on Paul's trade and the material he worked with is balanced. Available online at www.academia.edu/625092/What_Did_the_ΣΚΗΝΟΠΟΙΟΣ_Paul_Produce.

Websites

McKee, J. K. "Paul, Tentmaker." *Theology News Network Online*. September 26, 2006. Accessed July 12, 2014. www.tnnonline.net/faq/P/Paul_Tentmaker.pdf.

A fine online article addressing the issue of Paul's trade and the legend in the introduction.

CHAPTER 20

Jews (and Jesus) Primarily Spoke Hebrew in Jesus' Day

Acts 26:14

The Legendary Teaching on Acts 26:14

Jesus primarily spoke Hebrew. In the first place, denying this contradicts the Bible (see John 5:2; 19:13, 17, 20; 20:16; Acts 21:40; 22:2; 26:14; Rev 9:11; 16:16). Acts 26:14 says, "And when we had all fallen to the ground, I heard a voice saying to me in the Hebrew language, 'Saul, Saul, why are you persecuting me? It is hard for you to kick against the goads'" (ESV). The footnote in the ESV says "or *the Hebrew dialect*." In fact, the HCSB, NASB, and KJV all say that Jesus spoke in Hebrew. Realize that this means the movie *The Passion of the Christ* was incorrect in having Jesus speak Aramaic and Latin. This is one reason it is important to have a New Testament translated into Hebrew.

Introduction: The Four Languages of Israel[1] Defined

This legend deals with an underlying assumption by many people: Jesus primarily spoke Hebrew. The first item to clarify is that the ESV footnote cited above actually says "or *the Hebrew dialect* (that is, Aramaic)." Also, the NIV, NET, and NLT all translate the underlying Greek word "Aramaic" and not "Hebrew."

Hebrew and Aramaic are both Semitic languages. Evidence of their existence dates back a few thousand years in the Mesopotamia area. Most Semitic languages omit vowels since the consonants carry most of the meaning. Hebrew and Aramaic are related languages, like Spanish and French. The rise of the Neo-Assyrian (eighth century BC) and Persian Empires (sixth–fourth century

---

[1] The words *Israel* and *Palestine* will be used interchangeably with no difference intended.

BC) resulted in Aramaic becoming the primary language in the region. The debate over the use of Aramaic and Hebrew in the first century becomes muddled when the possibility of a mixing of the languages is considered.[2]

Koine Greek is the language used in the New Testament. The word *koine* comes from a Greek word meaning "common," thus referring to the common language of the people. It's the precursor to medieval and modern Greek. Ancient writers such as Plutarch and Polybius wrote in Greek, and the Old Testament translation called the Septuagint is in Greek. Many church fathers wrote in Greek.

Latin found its origin in ancient Rome and surrounding areas. It's related to many Indo-European languages and is still used by scientists (biological taxonomy), some scholars, and clergy.

A Brief History of the Four Languages in First-Century Israel[3]

Aramaic

Hebrew started fading out as the primary language in Israel after the Persian Empire conquered the land and they went into exile. Aramaic eventually surpassed Hebrew in much of Israel. At least four pieces of evidence are found in the Old Testament itself. Nehemiah 8:8 says, "They read out of the book of the law of God, *translating* and giving the meaning so that the people could understand what was read" (emphasis added). The people apparently needed the Scriptures translated in order to understand them. Ezra 4:18 says, "The letter you sent us has been *translated* and read in my presence" (emphasis added).[4] Nehemiah 13:23–24 says, "In those days I also saw Jews who had married women from Ashdod, Ammon, and Moab. Half of their children spoke the language of Ashdod or the language of one of the other peoples *but could not speak Hebrew*" (emphasis added). Hebrew was fading out after the Jews went into exile. Finally, even portions of Daniel were written in Aramaic (Dan 2:4–7:28).

Aramaic was becoming the primary language in Judea by the first century AD. Prior to the writing of the New Testament, the Old Testament was being

---

[2] See the immensely helpful article by Seth Sanders, "Jesus' Language More Complicated than Experts Claim," *Religion Dispatches* (June 9, 2014), accessed July 15, 2014, www.religiondispatches.org/jesus-language-more-complicated-than-experts-claim. He compares it to "Splanglish" in some pockets of America.

[3] Much of the information below has been taken from the informative article by Joseph A. Fitzmyer, "The Languages of Palestine in the First Century A.D.," *Catholic Biblical Quarterly* 32 (1970): 501–31.

[4] It is possible that the word "translating" in Nehemiah and "translated" in Ezra should be understood as "clearly" or "plainly," per various translations (cf. ESV, NIV, and KJV).

translated into Aramaic. At first these translations were done in the synagogue when the Hebrew text was read out loud so the congregation could understand the Scripture. The synagogue leader would translate the Hebrew text into Aramaic, and eventually these translations were written down. The translations were known as the Targumim. Even grave inscriptions around Judea were written in Aramaic. In northern Israel, around Galilee, where Jesus was raised, Aramaic was the most commonly spoken language since it became the official language of the area in the sixth century BC. Though, as we'll see, the Greek culture and language also heavily influenced this region.

Josephus claims he originally wrote *The Wars of the Jews* in his "native tongue" and that it was intended for Parthians, Babylonians, remotest Arabians, and the Adiabeni.[5] This "almost certainly implies that it was originally written in the *lingua franca*, Aramaic."[6]

The fact that Aramaic manuscripts have been found at Qumran *at all* can be considered instructive. For a Jewish separatist group, it could be expected that the only language used would be Hebrew. But the presence of Aramaic manuscripts, though they are the minority, demonstrates the presence of Aramaic in first-century Israel. Ossuary (bone boxes used in burials around the time of the writing of the New Testament) inscriptions and even an IOU were written in Aramaic around AD 55–56.

Greek

Though Greek culture had been influencing Jews in Israel prior to Alexander's conquest in 332 BC, his conquest caused Greek language to be more prominent in Israelite society. The conquerors even built Greek cities and transformed existing cities into Greek cities; as many as thirty cities were like this.[7] In the New Testament era, Greek was the *lingua franca* of the Near East. Intertestamental works such as 2 Maccabees and 1 Esdras were written in Greek. The book of Esther was translated into Greek in Jerusalem 100 years before Jesus was born. Many ossuaries have Greek inscriptions. In some places the Greek inscriptions outnumber the Aramaic or Hebrew. This could be a strong indicator of the *lingua franca* of a people. Large portions of the Minor Prophets were translated into Greek near the Dead Sea (e.g., the Greek Minor Prophets Scroll from Nahal Hever).

Some evidence indicates that some first-century Jews may have spoken *only* in Greek. While the identification of the groups in Acts 6:1 is controversial, a

---

[5] Josephus, *Jewish War* 1.6.

[6] Fitzmyer, "Languages of Palestine," 511.

[7] See ibid., 508. Josephus's testimony about his learning and understanding of Greek, as well as serving as a translator for Titus, seems to indicate that Greek was not widespread in first-century Israel. However, his testimony overall is unclear. See analysis by ibid., 510–12.

likely interpretation is that the Hellenistic Jews were Jewish Christians who spoke primarily or habitually only Greek and were therefore more heavily influenced by Hellenism. The Hebraic Jews would be those who characteristically spoke in Aramaic.[8]

Greek was the language of business and trade. Jews that were well educated or part of the upper class would have been able to converse in Greek. Other Jews would probably have had a basic knowledge of it, enough for use in trade and travel. Matthew even refers to the region of Galilee as "Galilee of the Gentiles" (Matt 4:15).

Finally, Jesus' disciples have a distinct Greek influence on them. Matthew/ Levi was a tax collector, requiring a knowledge of Greek in order to conduct business with the officials of Herod Antipas. Four of His disciples were fishermen (Simon Peter, Andrew, James, and John) who did business at the Sea of Galilee. They would have needed to conduct much of their business in Greek to be successful. For Jesus to have been a competent businessman as a builder (see ch. 4), He would have needed to use Greek.

Hebrew

While Greek and Aramaic continued to grow in popular usage, Hebrew never entirely disappeared from the Israelite language scene. The Wisdom of Sirach is evidence of this, written in Hebrew probably between 200 and 180 BC. Hebrew was not only a written and a scholarly language since some Jews in society continued using it as a spoken language. The vast majority of the documents at Qumran were written in Hebrew but possibly in a literary form of Hebrew that was not spoken.[9] Mostly Jews in Judea and Jewish separatists (like those at Qumran) used Hebrew. But even among these people, Aramaic was common. We have no good evidence for the everyday use of Hebrew in Galilee or Nazareth. Scribes and rabbis may have used Hebrew. The lack of Hebrew inscriptions from the first century (outside of Qumran) is rather surprising.

---

[8] For example, see C. F. D. Moule, "Once More, Who Were the Hellenists?" *Expository Times* 70 (1958–59): 100–102; Stanley E. Porter, "Did Jesus Ever Teach in Greek?" *Tyndale Bulletin* 44, no. 2 (1993): 211n34; Fitzmyer, "Languages of Palestine," 515.

[9] Mark D. Roberts, "What Language Did Jesus Speak? Why Does It Matter?" *Patheos* (2010), accessed July 11, 2014, www.patheos.com/blogs/markdroberts/series/what-language-did-jesus-speak-why-does-it-matter, comments perceptively, "Assuming that the Dead Sea Scrolls tell us something about the average Jew in the time of Jesus would be a little like arguing that since Amish people speak Pennsylvania Dutch (German) that language is used throughout the United States." Hebrew scholars differentiate between Classical and Mishnaic Hebrew.

Latin

As Alexander's conquest caused the Greek language to spread in Israel, Pompey's conquest in 63 BC introduced Latin. The earliest evidence available is from the first century AD, but Latin would have been present when the events of the New Testament were taking place. It was mainly used by the Romans and can be found on the tombstones for Roman military leaders who died in Israel and on inscriptions on the buildings built by Romans. One of the most famous inscriptions found was on a building called the Tiberieum that Pontius Pilate built to honor Tiberias. It mentions Pilate by name. When describing the temple, Jewish historian Josephus explains that a sign stating that "no foreigner should go within that sanctuary" was written "some in Greek, and some in Roman letters"[10] (referring to Latin). Josephus also referenced a letter written to the Jews by Julius Caesar as "both in Greek and in Latin."[11] This coheres well with John 19:20, which states that one of the three languages used to write the sign that was placed on the cross was Latin.

Four prominent languages were present in Israel in the first century AD. Aramaic would have been the most common language, followed closely by Greek. Hebrew had a limited use, and Latin was mostly used by Romans.

The Language Jesus Taught In: The New Testament Evidence

Most scholars (for good reasons) believe Jesus primarily spoke Aramaic. All the references in the legendary introduction, particularly Acts 26:14, are most likely references to Aramaic, not Hebrew. One Greek lexicon says of the word used in all three of the Acts passages: "These pass[ages] refer to the Aramaic spoken at that time in Palestine."[12]

A few texts in the New Testament appear to indicate that Aramaic was the common language and Jesus spoke primarily in Aramaic. John 19:13 says, "When Pilate heard this, he brought Jesus out and sat down on the judge's seat at a place known as the Stone Pavement (which in Aramaic is Gabbatha)" (NIV). *Gabbatha* is an Aramaic word that refers to an "elevated place." Also, John 19:17 says, "Carrying his own cross, he went out to the place of the Skull (which in Aramaic is called Golgotha)" (NIV). The word *golgotha* is Aramaic for *skull*. Acts 1:19 is an example outside the Gospels: "This became known to all the residents of Jerusalem, so that in their own language that field is called *Hakeldama* (that is, Field of Blood)." Again, *Hakeldama* is an Aramaic

---

[10] Josephus, *Jewish War* 5.194.
[11] Josephus, *Antiquities* 14.191.
[12] BDAG, 270.

expression.[13] If locations in Jerusalem had Aramaic names, then the common language was likely Aramaic. Also, Jesus is recorded in a few passages using Aramaic: Mark 5:41; 7:34; 15:34 (paralleled in Matt 27:46).

Jesus probably also taught in Greek.[14] In Matthew 8:5–13, Jesus seems to communicate directly with a Roman centurion. It's unlikely the centurion spoke Aramaic (or Hebrew), so they probably communicated in Greek. There could have been a translator, but none is mentioned. Jesus spoke with Pontius Pilate before being crucified (see Matt 27:11–14; John 18:33–38). While a translator could have been present, none is mentioned. More likely Pilate and Jesus spoke in Greek. In this account Porter ventures to say (against Fitzmyer's advice[15]) that we have actual words of Jesus spoken in Matthew 27:11: "You have said it." Mark 7:25–30 discusses Jesus speaking to a Syro-Phoenician woman (a Gentile). This conversation most likely took place using Greek. Another possibility advocated by Porter is the wordplay on Peter's name in Matthew 16:13–20.[16]

While the primary language spoken in Nazareth was probably Aramaic, Sepphoris was only a one-day walk. It was a major Greek city, and if Jesus did any of his general contracting business there, he most likely would have spoken in Greek. This data cannot be pressed too hard, however. We have no proof that Jesus spoke Greek, only the implications that (1) a normal Jew from Galilee would know Greek, (2) Jesus spoke with those who may have required the knowledge of Greek to speak to them, and (3) certain phrases may imply that Jesus had conversations in Greek. Porter concludes:

> The arguments for this position rest firmly on the role of Greek as the lingua franca of the Roman Empire, the linguistic and cultural character of lower Galilee during the first century, the linguistic fact that the New Testament has been transmitted in Greek from its earliest documents, a diversity of epigraphic evidence, significant literary evidence, and several significant contexts in the Gospels that give plausibility to this hypothesis.[17]

Some scholars have proposed that Jesus would have only taught in Hebrew; but since he regularly spoke to common people, Aramaic and Greek are more likely choices for the languages of his teaching. Two passages may indicate

---

[13] So John B. Polhill, *Acts*, NAC (Nashville: B&H, 1995), 92; Clinton E. Arnold, "Acts," in *Zondervan Illustrated Bible Backgrounds Commentary: John, Acts* (Grand Rapids: Zondervan, 2002), 229.

[14] This is the main thrust of Porter's article ("Teach in Greek"). The following arguments are based on his research.

[15] Fitzmyer, "Languages of Palestine," 516.

[16] Porter, "Teach in Greek," 230–32. The use of *anōthen* in John 3 is another possible example.

[17] Ibid., 205.

that Jesus knew Hebrew. First, when he read from the Isaiah scroll in Luke 4:17–20, that most naturally appears to have him reading from a Hebrew scroll. Second, it's possible that his conversation with the Samaritan woman took place in Hebrew (John 4:4–26).

In summary, it's not a matter of which singular language Jesus spoke. I view the options like this:

> 1a. Aramaic
> 1b. Greek
> 3. Hebrew
> 4. Latin (unlikely)

Jesus probably used Aramaic and Greek commonly with Hebrew used sparingly. I have seen no good evidence that he ever used Latin.

Application

Jesus did not speak English. This should remind all Christians that work is needed to interpret the original words of the New Testament. While not everyone needs to learn Greek and Hebrew, remembering that Scripture was written in a different language (with a different culture) is important.

However, the English translations available today are excellent. At this point I'm hoping you recognize how I have been using English translations and comparing them to one another. In virtually every problem passage so far, at least one of the main translations has done an excellent job in helping us arrive at a proper translation and interpretation.

Annotated Bibliography

Journals

Joseph A. Fitzmyer, "The Languages of Palestine in the First Century A.D." *Catholic Biblical Quarterly* 32 (1970): 501–31.
Fairly technical survey of Aramaic, Hebrew, Greek, and Latin as used in Palestine.
Porter, Stanley E. "Did Jesus Ever Teach in Greek?" *Tyndale Bulletin* 44, no. 2 (1993): 199–235.
Porter argues strongly that Jesus (at least occasionally) taught in Greek.

Blogs

Roberts, Mark D. "What Language Did Jesus Speak? Why Does It Matter?" *Patheos*. 2010. Accessed July 11, 2014. www.patheos.com/blogs/markdroberts/series/what-language-did-jesus-speak-why-does-it-matter.
Sanders, Seth. "Jesus' Language More Complicated than Experts Claim." *Religion Dispatches*. June 9, 2014. Accessed July 15, 2014. www.religiondispatches.org/jesus-language-more-complicated-than-experts-claim.

Sanders's article is carefully crafted and linguistically nuanced. It's a great response to the claim that Jesus spoke (primarily) Hebrew.

CHAPTER 21

The Gospel Is Dynamite

Romans 1:16

The Legendary Teaching on Romans 1:16

The gospel is dynamite, according to Romans 1:16: "For I am not ashamed of the gospel, because it is God's *power* for salvation to everyone who believes, first to the Jew, and also to the Greek" (emphasis added). The gospel is powerful. It can take a dead man and make him alive. It can take a sinner and make him holy. It can make a blind man see. It can take a lame man and make him walk. Who could deny the power of the gospel? In Romans 1:16, Paul declares God's power for salvation, and the Greek word he used for "power" is *dunamis*. This is where we get our English word *dynamite*. I looked up the word *dynamite* in a dictionary, and it said, "Any person or thing having a spectacular effect" or "to blow up, to shatter, or to destroy."[1] When God comes into your life, it is not peaceful. It is absolutely spectacular. He shatters your former life. He blows it up, totally obliterates who you were, and now you are a new creation. The gospel is truly dynamite.

Introduction: Unraveling the Legend

Two areas reveal some problems with this understanding of Romans 1:16. The first relates to the misuse of Greek, and the second has to do with that specific interpretation. The first question that comes to mind is this: does the English word *dynamite* come from the Greek word *dunamis*?

---

[1] "Dynamite," *Dictionary.com*, accessed May 21, 2014, www.dictionary.reference.com/browse/dynamite?s=t.

Dynamite was coined in 1867 by Alfred Nobel, the inventor of dynamite. The English word *dynamite* actually comes from the Swedish word *dynamit*. The Swedish word Nobel coined comes from the Greek word used in Romans 1:16. So technically, the English word *dynamite* comes from the Greek word *dunamis* through the Swedish word *dynamit*. The name Nobel should sound familiar because that is the same man behind the Nobel Peace Prize.

However, would Paul have been thinking about dynamite when he wrote Romans 1:16? Absolutely not! The main reason Paul *could not* have been thinking about dynamite is because Nobel had not invented it yet! In fact, it wasn't invented for about 1,800 years. Therefore, Paul did not have this specific explosive, destructive force in mind.

Dynamite and Romans 1:16: A Problem with the Greek

Is this the correct way to use Greek in interpreting Scripture? If I were to e-mail you and say, "Pastor Jeff is nice," what would you think? You would likely think I have a kind pastor, that he is pleasant and delightful. Those are the kinds of meanings that probably come to your mind when you hear the word *nice*. But what if someone were to study that e-mail 1,800 years from now? Perhaps he would think this: *Dave was speaking English, but he could have been familiar with Latin, so he was probably referring to the Latin background for the word. We derive the English word* nice *from the Latin* nescius, *which means "ignorant." So what Dave really meant was that Pastor Jeff was ignorant.* Hopefully you see how ridiculous that logic is! But interpreting *dunamis* as *dynamite* is worse. Though *nescius* existed before the English word *nice*, Paul apparently wrote that the gospel is "dynamite" about 1,800 years before dynamite was invented! Therefore, it is much more problematic for Paul to be thinking about dynamite in the first century than for someone to misinterpret my use of the word *nice*.

Dynamite Versus the Gospel: The Problem with the Interpretation

Dynamite is a wholly inappropriate analogy for the gospel. One scholar said: "Even to mention dynamite as a kind of analogy is singularly inappropriate. Dynamite blows things up, tears things down, rips out rock, gouges holes, and destroys things."[2] The gospel is not a destructive force that blows things up. The gospel reconciles us to God through Christ. The gospel gives us peace with God. It is the wonderful story of God lovingly creating us; and even through humanity's fall and continual rejection of Him, God initiated with us

---

[2] D. A. Carson, *Exegetical Fallacies*, 2nd ed. (Grand Rapids: Baker, 1996), 34.

through Christ, bringing his perfect Son to restore humanity into a right relationship with God himself.

Application: A Better Illustration of the Gospel's Power

Dynamite is used to paint a picture of the vast greatness of God's power. When we think about dynamite, we do think about an explosive power. But for Paul, God's great, vast, magnificent power is demonstrated by the empty tomb. In Ephesians 1:20, using the same Greek word for *power*, he wrote, "He demonstrated this *power* in the Messiah by raising Him from the dead and seating Him at His right hand in the heavens."[3] If you want a great illustration of the vastly magnificent power of God, you don't need to look further than the empty tomb. God's great power is wonderfully illustrated by his bringing someone who is dead to life.

Then what does the Greek word mean if not dynamite? This word means "to be able to accomplish something."[4] In the case of Jesus' resurrection, it means God had the ability to accomplish the resurrection. For the idea that the gospel is God's power for salvation in Romans 1:16, it means God is able to accomplish, through the gospel, what he intends to accomplish, which is here defined as salvation for those who believe.

Some people think the word *salvation* means, "I have a ticket to heaven." But salvation can be a broad term. It does include the concept of saving us from having God's wrath poured out upon us for eternity. However, especially in the context of Romans 1:16, it includes that *and* more. Salvation in Romans 1:16 is also the idea that the gospel is the power of God to conform us to the image of his Son, what some theologians call sanctification. But the gospel is also the power of God that will give us a new body, what theologians call glorification. Think about it this way: the same power at work in raising Christ from the dead is also at work in the gospel and in our lives if we believe in Christ. That power took us from being spiritually dead and made us spiritually alive. That is the power we are talking about in Romans 1:16, the power of the gospel. It is a power to change our hearts, to transform our lives. It includes being rescued from hell, but it's so much more than that. So we can be comforted when we read Romans 1:16 to know that God is a powerful God, a God who can take people who are dead and make them alive. That is the God we love, the God we serve, and that is the power of the gospel.

---

[3] See also 1 Corinthians 6:14.
[4] Cf. BDAG, 262–63.

Annotated Bibliography

Commentaries

Cranfield, C. E. B. *Romans*. 2 volumes. ICC. Edinburgh: T&T Clark, 1975.
  None of these commentaries directly addresses the problematic use of dynamite, but their interpretations of the verse demonstrate that it is a problematic illustration.
Morris, Leon. *The Epistle to the Romans*. PNTC. Grand Rapids: Eerdmans, 1988.
Schreiner, Thomas R. *Romans*. BECNT. Grand Rapids: Baker Academic, 1998.

Books

Carson, D. A. *Exegetical Fallacies*. 2nd edition. Grand Rapids: Baker, 1996.
  See page 34.
Baxter, Benjamin J. *"In the Original Text It Says:" Word Study Fallacies and How to Avoid Them*. Areopagus Critical Christian Issues. Gonzalez, FL: Energion, 2012.
  See pages 17–18.

Websites

Mounce, Bill. "Is a Moros a Moron (Matt 7:26)?" *Teknia*. January 18, 2009. Accessed June 23, 2014. www.teknia.com/blog/moros-moron-matt-7-26.
  Mounce mentions the dynamite issue but is focused on the same type of word study problem on a different word.

CHAPTER 22

Just Say You Believe in Jesus and You Will Be Saved

Romans 10:9–10

The Legendary Teaching on Romans 10:9–10

Some people today make salvation difficult. They even appear to get in the way of a sinner seeking Jesus, but Paul makes salvation so simple:

> On the contrary, what does it say? The message is near you, in your mouth and in your heart. This is the message of faith that we proclaim: If you confess with your mouth, "Jesus is Lord," and believe in your heart that God raised Him from the dead, you will be saved. One believes with the heart, resulting in righteousness, and one confesses with the mouth, resulting in salvation. (Rom 10:8–10)

It really is that simple. If you believe in Jesus and then you confess this belief with your mouth, you will be saved. I will say a prayer, and you just repeat the prayer after me, and that will be the belief you have coming out through your mouth, and you will be saved. Then you can know without a shadow of a doubt that you are saved. You never have to worry about your salvation again as long as you believe and you confess it through this prayer.

Introduction: Unraveling the Legend

Have you ever been confused by Paul's word order? He says "confess" and then "believe." How can you confess something you have not yet believed? Wouldn't it make sense to believe it and then confess it? Some people have said this verse is teaching two steps to salvation: If you only believe, but don't confess, then you are not saved. Is that true? If so, then believing in Jesus would not be enough for salvation because you would have to add confession.

129

Also, what does *confess* mean? Does "confess" refer to repeating a prayer? Does this verse justify the use of a sinner's prayer?

A Closer Look at Romans 10:9–10

In verse 8, Paul paraphrases Deuteronomy 30:14. In the verses leading up to this (Rom 10:6–7), Paul explains that God has not made salvation too difficult. We don't have to go up into heaven; we don't have to go down into the abyss. Instead the word of faith proclaimed by Paul is near to them. Paul copies the word order from Deuteronomy 30:14 in Romans 10:9. Deuteronomy 30:14 had "mouth" and then "heart," so Paul said, "confess with your mouth" and then "believe in your heart." However, verse 10 *reverses* the order. Paul said "heart" first and then "mouth."

Paul is building on the expression used in Deuteronomy 30:14. He is not giving an order by which these steps take place in salvation. Believing and confessing are the inward and outward aspects of the same thing; they are two sides of the same coin. If you are a Christian, you will believe in your heart. If you are a Christian, you will confess with your mouth. They will both be present if you are a Christian. Confession is a manifestation of belief, not a separate work you add on to be saved. It's what happens when you are a Christian.

The idea that you could have faith without confession, or vice versa, is totally foreign to Paul's thinking. One scholar says, "No distinction is to be drawn between the confession and the faith. The confession is believed and the faith confessed."[1] Therefore, this is not a two-step process for salvation.

However, does "confess" refer to a prayer? Paul uses the Greek word for *confess* only four times in all of his writings, two of which are in this passage. His use in Titus 1:16 is helpful: "They *profess* to know God, but they deny Him by their works. They are detestable, disobedient, and disqualified for any good work." I had a friend many years ago who was struggling with a drug addiction to crack. He was thirty-one years old at the time. We started talking about his salvation, and he said, "I know I'm saved. I got saved when I was sixteen years old." Then he explained how he went to a church and heard a sermon. At the end of the service, the preacher asked people to come down the aisle if they wanted to get saved. My friend walked the aisle, and the preacher led him in a prayer; he repeated the prayer. That was how he explained his conversion to Christ. Then I asked when he started using crack. Three months after he had this "believe-confession" experience, he started using crack. Fifteen years later, when I met him, he had never stopped using for more than one month. He had consistently been doing crack for the last fifteen years. As I got to

---

[1] C. K. Barrett, *The Epistle to the Romans*, Harper's New Testament Commentaries (New York: Harper and Brothers, 1957), 200.

know him better, I discovered that he was a compulsive liar and a thief. He wasn't involved in a body of believers and was sleeping with his girlfriend. I saw these things, and I heard him say that he professed to know God. Yet his life was detestable, disobedient, and disqualified for any good work. Paul was describing just such a man in Titus 1:16: people who say they know God, but in reality they don't.

What does the word *confess* mean? It doesn't mean to base your assurance of salvation on a prayer. Scripture never says a prayer is the basis for salvation. Assurance of salvation is given by the Holy Spirit as we live our lives in honor to God and submit to Christ's lordship. It's not based on a prayer prayed fifteen years prior. Faith is not merely an intellectual assent. The demons believe and are not saved. Our faith must manifest itself in our lives. We are saved by faith alone but not by a faith that is alone. Notice how this confession is tied to faith in Romans 10, but in Titus 1:16 the profession is tied to a lack of good works. The word for *confess* means "a profession of allegiance," or a declaration of loyalty.[2] To claim that repeating words someone else says automatically gets you saved is totally foreign to this passage. That's a "magical formula" view of salvation. Faith has to be present for salvation to take place. True saving faith will manifest itself in not being ashamed to confess Jesus as Lord and living a life in honor of him.

These verses are not presenting salvation as a two-step process. You don't have to confess first and then believe or believe first and then confess. Also, the word *confess* is not referencing the sinner's prayer. Paul is talking about a declaration of loyalty, a proclamation of allegiance.

Application

Salvation is by grace through faith. There is no other way to be saved but by placing your faith in the finished work of Jesus Christ on the cross. All other avenues are fruitless. You may have prayed the sinner's prayer, but it is not the prayer that saves. Faith can be expressed or manifested in a prayer; that could be saving faith. Don't look back and think: *I prayed a prayer, I repeated those words, and therefore I know I'm saved.* The question is this: Have you placed your faith in Jesus Christ and Him alone? And is that faith being manifested in your life?

Christians should have an urgency in evangelism. Proclaim the gospel like lives depend on it because lives do depend on it. But we need to be careful not to manipulate people into saying something they really don't believe or even

---

[2] BDAG, 708–9.

understand. Getting someone to repeat a prayer might ease *our* conscience; but if they don't have true, saving faith, they are still bound for hell.

When my daughter was six years old, she attended VBS at a local church. She came to me afterward and said: "Daddy, I got saved!"

I said, "Really? What happened?"

She said, "I prayed the prayer."

And I said: "Honey, I am so proud of you, and I love you so much. I know that you want to serve Jesus all your life." I affirmed her. I didn't understand what had happened, but I affirmed her. The next day I asked her a question: "Danielle, if you were to die, why do you think you would go to heaven?"

She thought about it and said: "Because I obey my parents."

Now part of me really loved the fact that my six-year-old daughter had elevated obedience to her mother and me to that level. The other part of me was sad. I can guarantee you I never taught my daughter that by obedience to me she earned her way to heaven. In fact, I am confident none of the churches we have ever attended in our entire lives ever taught her that. But somehow she had this concept in her mind that she could work her way to heaven. I responded: "So you obey your parents and then you get to go to heaven?"

Immediately a confused look crossed her face. She didn't know. She had prayed the prayer, but she didn't know. It took a long time to get that "works salvation" mentality out of her. Someone had manipulated my daughter into saying some words. She didn't understand the gospel. Let's make sure that when we present the gospel to people they understand what they are responding to.

If they express that they believe and are ready to give their lives to Christ, rather than telling them to *repeat* a prayer, have them *pray* the gospel to God. When I explain the gospel to someone and he or she is following along and seems to understand, I say, "Alright, explain it back to me." At that point I typically see that the person doesn't quite grasp it. Then we go back and forth, over and over again. I explain it and then I have the person explain it back to me. Once he or she can demonstrate having truly grasped it and can say, "Yes, I want to give my life to Christ," then I say, "What you have explained to me as the gospel, pray it to God."

Have *them* pray. I don't want them ever to think about me when it comes to their salvation. I want them to think of God; there is never danger in telling people to go before the throne of grace. If they have truly repented of their sins and turned to God in saving faith, then they should be able to articulate an acceptable form of the gospel in prayer to God. If they can't, maybe they have not understood enough to grasp the truth of the gospel. God has not called us to make converts. He has called us to make disciples. That discipleship can and should start as we are witnessing.

Annotated Bibliography

Commentaries

Morris, Leon. *The Epistle to the Romans.* PNTC. Grand Rapids: Eerdmans, 1988.
   Characteristically Morris, he writes at an accessible level.
Schreiner, Thomas R. *Romans.* BECNT. Grand Rapids: Baker Academic, 1998.
   At times technical, this is by far one of the best commentaries on Romans available.

Journals

Dunson, Ben C. "Faith in Romans: The Salvation of the Individual Life in Community?"
   Journal for the Study of the New Testament 34, no. 1 (2011): 19–46.
   The scope of Dunson's article extends to the issue of faith in communal and individual
terms; the argument is fairly technical, and knowledge of Greek is generally assumed throughout. He assumes the conclusion above.
Pedersen, Sigfred. "Paul's Understanding of the Biblical Law." *Novum Testamentum* 44, no.
   1 (2002): 1–34.
   Pedersen's discussion describes Paul's thought in terms of the Mosaic law. Romans
10:1–13 is discussed within that framework. Pedersen's discussion is technical and requires
close attention to his argument. He assumes the conclusion above.

Websites

Ross, Thomas. "Do Romans 10:9–10 or Romans 10:13 Teach the 'Sinner's Prayer'?" *Faith
   Saves.* Accessed July 12, 2014. www.faithsaves.net/exegesis-application-romans-109-
   14-soulwinning-churches-christians-passage-teach-sinners-prayer.
   While not agreeing with everything in this long online article (or several things from this
website), it makes some helpful points.

CHAPTER 23

Synagogues Had Men and Women Seated Separately

1 Corinthians 14:34–35

The Legendary Teaching on 1 Corinthians 14:34–35

One of the most offensive practices of the modern Christian church is based on a neglect to grasp background information pertinent to the correct interpretation of 1 Corinthians 14:34–35: "The women should be silent in the churches, for they are not permitted to speak, but should be submissive, as the law also says. And if they want to learn something, they should ask their own husbands at home, for it is disgraceful for a woman to speak in the church meeting." This verse should never be used to teach that women must be silent in the church today. The reason Paul gave this command is that the early churches were based on the structure of synagogues. Synagogues had men sit on one side and women on the other. So when a wife wanted to ask her husband a question, she would have to disrupt the service and yell across the room. The church at Corinth had a significant struggle with being disorderly (1 Cor 14:33). Therefore, do not prohibit women from speaking in church based on this passage.

Introduction: Unraveling the Legend

Some of the legends in this book are fairly easy to disprove, but coming to a firm interpretation, at times, can be difficult. That is the case with this text. This passage has many difficulties. Fortunately, clarifying the background information used is not a difficult issue.

In his widely read book, Emil Schürer says, "The congregation sat in an appointed order, the most distinguished members in the front seats, the younger behind; men and women probably apart."[1] Schürer then states in a footnote, "The separation of the sexes must be assumed as self-evident, although it does not happen to be mentioned in any of the more ancient authorities. For what is said in Pseudo-Philo . . . of the Therapeutae cannot be here taken into account. Nor is a special division for women mentioned in the Talmud."[2] This apparent "self-evident" assumption is highly problematic.

One of the leading experts on the ancient synagogue is Jewish rabbi Lee Levine, professor of Jewish history and archaeology at the Hebrew University of Jerusalem. Levine says[3] that until the last few decades, the conclusion that men and women sat separately in synagogues was universally assumed. This modern tradition reached back to the Middle Ages, and presumably back to the founding of synagogues. This assumption was shattered when challenged by S. Safrai in 1964.

Safrai argues against this seating arrangement based on two factors. First, the archaeological data that had been collected from the New Testament era until about AD 700 contained zero traces of evidence of this seating arrangement regardless of the location of the synagogue: in Israel or outside Israel. Further substantiating this claim is that plenty of synagogue inscriptions found from this time period name parts of the synagogue, but nothing has been found naming a place reserved for women. Second, Safrai says the rabbinic sources are silent on this supposed seating arrangement. There are many discussions on the parts of the synagogue but none about women sitting separately from the men. Levine concludes, "There can be little doubt that throughout Late Antiquity, Jews gathered in the synagogue for religious purposes without making any distinctions in seating arrangements between males and females."[4] If this text can't be explained by the legendary background information, what does it mean?

Interpreting 1 Corinthians 14:34–35

A recent publication by Philip Payne has argued that these verses were not originally part of Paul's letter.[5] While some scholars have been persuaded by

---

[1] Emil Schürer, *A History of the Jewish People in the Time of Jesus Christ*, 2nd division, vol. 2, trans. S. Taylor and P. Christie (Peabody, MA: Hendrickson, 2003; repr., Edinburgh: T&T Clark, 1890), 75.

[2] Ibid., 75–76 n. 109.

[3] The following summarizes the comments from Lee I. Levine, *The Ancient Synagogue: The First Thousand Years*, 2nd ed. (New Haven: Yale University Press, 2005), 503–4.

[4] Ibid., 505. Note the "striking example" of a woman sitting in the front row of an ancient synagogue (ibid.).

[5] See Philip B. Payne, *Man and Woman, One in Christ: An Exegetical and Theological Study of Paul's Letters* (Grand Rapids: Zondervan, 2009), 217–70.

Payne's theory, many are not.[6] One of the reasons for including these verses is that while a decision is not easy, none of the manuscripts Payne discusses have the verses missing. Therefore, a contextual interpretation of these difficult verses is in order.

Any interpretation of this text must consider that Paul affirms women praying and prophesying in the congregation (as long as they have a head covering) in 1 Corinthians 11:5. He also appears to affirm the ability of "all" to prophesy in 1 Corinthians 14:31, just a few verses earlier. While a survey of various interpretations would helpfully demonstrate the difficulties involved in this passage, the following summarized interpretation will suffice.[7]

Paul has explained that women can be involved in the speaking of prophecy (11:5). The current context is about the *evaluation* of prophecies in orderly worship (14:29–33). This prohibition is about women evaluating prophecies in the church gathering. Paul appeals to the "law" for support (cf. 14:21), without stating the passage he was depending on. While it could be Genesis 3:16, it is much more likely Genesis 2:20–23. Paul has already appealed to Genesis 2 in 11:8–9 (and again in 1 Tim 2:13). Paul uses Genesis 2 (in 1 Corinthians 11 and 1 Timothy 2) to argue that the roles of men and women were set based on creation order. If a man prophesied and a woman evaluated it, the roles set in creation order would not be preserved.[8]

This passage does not bar women from speaking at all in the assembly; it just prohibits a particular role: evaluating prophecy. These verses do not prohibit women from learning. In 1 Timothy 2:11, Paul similarly says, "A woman should learn in silence with full submission." Paul wants women to learn so he tells them to ask their husbands at home. The desire for women to learn is present in Paul's letters.

---

[6] Peter Head's fascinating presentation at SBL in New Orleans (2009) is helpfully summarized in the following blog articles: www.evangelicaltextualcriticism.blogspot.com/2009/11/sbl-new-orleans-2009-i-peter-head.html and www.evangelicaltextualcriticism.blogspot.com/2009/11/sbl-new-orleans-2009-i-peter-head_22.html.

[7] For more details on the following interpretation, see James B. Hurley, *Man and Woman in Biblical Perspective* (Grand Rapids: Zondervan, 1981), 185–94; W. J. Dumbrell, "The Role of Women—a Reconsideration of the Biblical Evidence," *Interchange* 21 (1977): 14–22; D. A. Carson, *Showing the Spirit: A Theological Exposition of 1 Corinthians 12–14* (Grand Rapids: Baker, 1987), 129–31; Wayne Grudem, *The Gift of Prophecy in 1 Corinthians* (Washington, D.C.: University Press of America, 1982), 245–55.

[8] It is possible, per David E. Garland, *1 Corinthians*, BECNT (Grand Rapids: Baker, 2003), 667–70, that Paul is only talking about a wife challenging her husband's prophecy since the Greek word for "woman" and "wife" are the same. See also David W. J. Gill, "1 Corinthians," in *Zondervan Illustrated Bible Backgrounds Commentary: Romans–Philemon* (Grand Rapids: Zondervan, 2002), 173–74.

Application

No ancient evidence supports the contention that ancient synagogues separated men and women in the assembly. Instead of relying on specious background information, interpreting the passage in its context leads to the conclusion that Paul was building on the gender role distinctions he found in Genesis 2:20–23. Distinction in *role* has no relationship to distinction in *value*. The members of the Trinity have *distinct* roles but *equal* value. Paul exhorted the congregation to orderly worship by recognizing the appropriate roles women and men should have in the public assembly. These roles are founded in creation, not culture, and therefore are timeless, not time bound.

Annotated Bibliography

Commentaries

Carson, D. A. *Showing the Spirit: A Theological Exposition of 1 Corinthians 12–14*. Grand Rapids: Baker, 1987.

Carson's exposition is readable. After surveying various interpretations to this passage, he explains a view similar to the one above. See especially pages 129–31.

Garland, David E. *1 Corinthians*. BECNT. Grand Rapids: Baker, 2003.

This commentary is fairly academic. He presents a slightly different interpretation from the one presented above, focusing on husbands and wives instead of the more general interpretation of men and women. See especially pages 667–70.

Books

Levine, Lee I. *The Ancient Synagogue: The First Thousand Years*. 2nd ed. New Haven: Yale University Press, 2005.

This is the best research available on ancient synagogues. Levine argues conclusively that there is no good evidence for men and women being seated separately in synagogue worship. See especially pages 499–505.

Websites

Safrai, Shmuel. "Were Women Segregated in the Ancient Synagogue?" *Bible Headquarters*. Accessed July 16, 2014. www.bibleheadquarters.org/WereWomenSegregatedintheAncientSynagogue.html.

Safrai was the scholar cited by Levine who began the shattering of the assumed separation. This article is helpful, though I would disagree with the interpretation of 1 Corinthians 14:34–35.

CHAPTER 24

Grace Is Unmerited Favor

Ephesians 2:8

The Legendary Teaching on Ephesians 2:8

In the short letter Paul wrote to the Ephesians, he mentioned "grace" twelve times in only six chapters. This is an important concept to Paul. He wrote in Ephesians 2:8, "For you are saved by grace through faith, and this is not from yourselves; it is God's gift." The Greek word translated *grace* is *charis*. It means "unmerited favor, or an undeserved gift." The first several times I heard the definition of *grace* as "unmerited favor," I had no idea what that meant. Let's examine that definition. The English word *merit* comes from a Latin word that means "to earn." It's used today when referring to the idea that you have done something to earn a reward, or maybe your actions deserve a reward. To say that grace is "unmerited" means it is unearned or undeserved. The word *favor* most commonly refers to a kind act, as in "I did him a favor." But in the expression "unmerited favor," it refers to a gift bestowed as a token of good will. We use it today in an expression like "party favors" (a gift given to someone for coming to a party). So the expression "unmerited favor" refers to a gift that was undeserved.

In Ephesians 2:8, the gift that is not deserved, that is unmerited, is salvation. Let's say a man dies, is lying in the street, and an ambulance pulls up to him. The medic hooks up the defibrillator, and he shocks the person lying on the ground and brings him back to life. The dead man did nothing to earn being made alive. He was just lying in the street dead. He didn't sign a release form saying, "Go ahead and bring me back to life." He didn't agree to it; he didn't consent to it; he did nothing to earn being made alive, nothing to earn being rescued or saved from death. This is what God has done for you in Christ Jesus, giving you life you did not deserve.

Introduction: What's Wrong with That?

Some of you right now are scratching your heads, thinking, *That is what I've always heard. What's wrong with that?* Remember, there are different types of urban legends. Most of the legends in this book are *mistaken legends:*[1] wrong interpretations. This legend is a little different because I actually agree with everything I just stated. So if you are a little relieved, that's good. You should be! This legend is an example of a teaching that is *incomplete* rather than *incorrect*. Grace truly is an undeserved gift, but it is *more* than that. Ephesians 2 might be the best passage to see the incompleteness of this definition.

Ephesians 2:8 in Context

Ephesians 2:8 is contained within a larger section: 2:1–10. Ephesians 2:1 explains that before Christ all Christians were dead in "trespasses and sins." That's how this passage begins. Verse 2 explains that sin characterized our life and that we aligned ourselves with the prince of the power of the air: Satan. Then in verse 3 Paul drives home our sinful behavior by referring to "our fleshly desires, carrying out the inclinations of our flesh and thoughts." At the end of verse 3, Paul declared that by nature, by our very being, we are a people automatically destined for God's wrath to be poured out on us. So these verses can be understood through two concepts: the idea of *by nature* and *by action*.

Sinful by Nature

We were not born with a good nature. In other words, because of Adam's sin, we have inherited a disposition toward sin. We did not enter the world in a sinless state, eager to glorify God with our lives. We might look at a new-born baby and say, "So innocent, so pure!" However, in reality, that baby has a corrupt nature. Everyone enters the world separated from God because of the sinful nature we inherited from Adam. This is a difficult concept for some people to handle, especially in the United States, where we are raised to think we are generally good people who only *sometimes* do bad things.

Paul describes this in Romans 5:12: "Therefore, just as sin entered the world through one man, and death through sin, in this way death spread to all men, because all sinned." Sin came into the world through one man, and that man is Adam.[2] Adam caused sin to enter the world, which caused death to enter the world, which caused death to spread to all men. Leon Morris summarizes it this way: "Adam was one man, and he did one act, but the result spread to all

---

[1] See the prologue for more explanation.
[2] See Romans 5:14 for this clarification.

his posterity."[3] The word *death* in verse 12 refers to the concepts of physical and spiritual death. This is why all humans are sinful by nature.

Sinful in Action

All humans also commit sin. John MacArthur said, "A person does not become a sinner by committing sins but rather commits sins because he is by nature a sinner."[4] Ephesians 2:1 describes our life before Christ as being characterized by "trespasses and sins." Paul uses these two words to talk about departing from God's standards. The reason he uses two terms is to communicate the heinousness of our life before we knew Christ. Before he mentioned grace in this passage, he needed to explain how despicable our actions were before Christ. He did the same thing, with exuberance, in Romans 3:10–18, Paul's description of humankind. Grace is not simply unearned. It is more than that.

Comparing Grace and Mercy

Comparing two similar theological terms will help refine the definition of grace: *grace* and *mercy*. Several years ago a couple explained to me their practice of spanking their children. They said that when their children did something wrong, they would take them aside and make sure that the child being punished understood that the action that brought on the discipline was wrong. If the child knew it was wrong and was in direct disobedience, then they explained to the child that they were going to get a spanking. They didn't do it in anger but calmly, and they would give the child a spanking. Sometimes the child would ask for grace, and the parent would sometimes say, "OK, I will give you grace, and I won't spank you this time." Whether you agree or disagree with this disciplining philosophy, I think it provides an interesting window into the terms *grace* and *mercy*. These terms are *not* interchangeable. Both seem to contain elements of God's bestowing or granting something not earned, but they are not the same. In Ephesians 2:4, Paul describes God as being abundant "in mercy." The word *mercy* is usually defined as "punishment withheld (or, wrath withheld)," but mercy means more than that in Ephesians 2. In Ephesians 2:4, Paul says God looked at our pitiful condition, looked at our life characterized by "trespasses and sins," and driven by his love, he withheld the punishment. So mercy in Ephesians 2 includes the ideas that God

---

3 Leon Morris, *The Epistle to the Romans*, Pillar New Testament Commentary (Grand Rapids: Eerdmans, 1988), 230.
4 John F. MacArthur Jr., *Romans*, MacArthur New Testament Commentary (Chicago: Moody, 1991), 295.

sees our pitiful condition, our misery and distress, that we were characterized by "trespasses and sins," and that He loves us. That is the emphasis of mercy. Grace is *not* the withholding of punishment; that is mercy.

Grace focuses on the forgiveness needed because of the current state we are in. It is a gift that is not earned, but it is more than that. We didn't simply live in a way not to earn salvation; we lived in a way characterized by fighting, kicking, and screaming against receiving the gift. That is how our lives were characterized. If I said to my daughter, "Danielle, I am going to buy you a bicycle for Christmas," and she responded by being completely disrespectful to me and my wife, picking on her brother, not doing her homework or chores, would I still give the bike to her? I never told her the gift was dependent on how she acted. I just said I was going to give her the bike. But if she decided to kick, scream, and insult my benevolence and graciousness to her, the gift is not just unearned; it is more than that. It is *de-earned*.[5] We did not simply receive salvation as a gift of God that we did nothing to receive, but we lived in such a way to warrant God's refusal to save us because our lives were so desperately characterized by trespasses and sins. Our entire existence before Christ was characterized as spitting in the face of the One who was reaching out to save us. This was who we were by nature before Christ. Grace is a *de-earned gift*. Grace emphasizes the unmerited or de-earned aspect, and mercy emphasizes the misery one is in before something is bestowed.

Back to the spanking illustration—picture the child directly disobeying his mother in a grocery store. The mother says, "Bobby, you directly disobeyed Mommy, and you are going to get a spanking." The child, in full contrition, says, "Mommy, I am so sorry. I was bad, and it was wrong of me to do that. May I have grace?" Now, the mother might say: "I think he has learned his lesson. I am not going to give him a spanking. I am going to withhold the punishment." That's what the child is asking for: the withholding of punishment. He is hoping that his mother sees his misery. Technically, then, he is not asking for grace; he is asking for mercy. Therefore, mercy is the *withholding* of punishment, and grace is the *giving* of forgiveness and favor.

In the context of Ephesians 2, we see that we were miserable, pitiful, sinful trespassers who lived a life in opposition to the God who loved us, that we were born destined to have God's wrath poured out on us, and then we get to verse 4: "*But God*" (emphasis added). God was driven by a great love, and he withheld his wrath. Instead, he poured out his mercy and bestowed grace, a gift that was de-earned. So while grace is truly unmerited favor, it is more than that. Defining grace as an unearned gift could be misleading since it is also *de-earned*.

---

[5] I'm intentionally avoiding the word "de-merit" so it isn't associated with *demerit* (when someone receives a penalty for misconduct).

Application

One area of application is praise and thanksgiving. This is the beauty and wonder of salvation: what God has done for us in Christ. It is incredible! Not only were we born apart from him and he reached out to us by initiating salvation, but the whole time we were fighting against him. This is the love of God on display, or as Ephesians 2:7 says, that God has saved us for this purpose, "so that in the coming ages He might display the immeasurable riches of His grace through His kindness to us in Christ Jesus." If we understand God's grace accurately, what he has done for us, this truth should lead us to worship and adoration.

Correct doctrine is a second area of application. When understood within this context, God's grace is absolutely overwhelming. The idea that we did anything to merit or earn salvation, the idea that we mustered up repentance or faith within ourselves, the idea that we worked *with* God in our salvation, is totally at odds with what grace truly is. And Paul drives this point home in Ephesians 2:9, saying, "Not from works, so that no one can boast." It's not of us; it's not by us; it's not for us! God is the initiator and the preserver of our salvation.

Annotated Bibliography

Beeke, Joel R. *Living for God's Glory: An Introduction to Calvinism*. Orlando: Reformation Trust, 2008.

Beeke's discussion on grace is what initially clued me in to the insights in this chapter. See especially pages 102–3.

Berkhof, Louis. *Systematic Theology*. Carlisle, PA: Banner of Truth Trust, 1958.

Berkhof's classic work has some helpful thoughts on mercy and grace. See especially pages 71–72.

CHAPTER 25

Good Works Are Optional for Christians

Ephesians 2:10

The Legendary Teaching on Ephesians 2:10

We can be comforted as Christians that once we are guaranteed of eternal salvation by accepting Jesus Christ as Savior, our eternal ticket has been punched. The Bible never says we need to grow in holiness. God never said we need to do good works. That would be salvation by works. While God desires for us to grow and become more like Jesus, it is not required. No verse actually says we have to become more like Christ. For example, Ephesians 2:10: "For we are His creation, created in Christ Jesus for good works, which God prepared ahead of time so that we should walk in them." Paul said that we *should* walk in good works, not that we *will* walk in good works. So we can be comforted that if good works are not a part of our lives, we will still go to heaven.

Introduction: Comparing Translations

Several things in the legendary teaching above are true. For example, we should never believe we earn our salvation by works. Also, the emphasis on Christ's atoning work on the cross should comfort us. However, something is wrong with the interpretation of Ephesians 2:10 above: is it appropriate to place the emphasis on the word *should*? Let's examine how other translations rendered the second part of that verse.

The HCSB says, "So that we should walk in them." I told my daughter a while ago, "You should walk the dog a little longer today because it might snow tomorrow." Do you think she walked the dog any longer? Nope. And when she didn't, what did she say? "You said I *should*, not that I *have to*." So the "should" understanding of my daughter and the presentation of the legendary teaching are pretty much the same. I call this the *optional understanding*. The HCSB, NKJV, RSV, ESV, and KJV say "should."

The NLT says, "So we can do the good things." This translation does not appear to present good works as optional. The word *can* seems to communicate the idea of having the *ability* to do good things. The NLT appears to say we now are able to do good things. This is the *ability understanding*.

The NET says, "So we may do them." This seems to communicate the idea of *permission*. Recently our family was sitting down for dinner, and my wife said to my son, "You may sit next to your father" (usually my daughter sits next to me). She was trying to encourage him to sit next to me without commanding him. He chose not to sit next to me. She said, "D. J., I told you to sit next to your father." He replied, "You said I *may* sit next to my father." He interpreted my wife as giving him permission. This is the *permission understanding* of Ephesians 2:10.

The NIV says, "For us to do." That appears to communicate the idea of purpose: the *purpose understanding*. So interpretations of Ephesians 2:10 include the *optional*, the *ability*, the *permission*, and the *purpose understandings*. What is Paul trying to communicate? Was he saying we have the option of walking in good works, the ability to walk in good works? Was he giving us permission to walk in good works, or did he say God saved us for the purpose of walking in good works?

Let's look at those translations again because they are all trying to communicate the same thing, but they don't communicate it through the verb *should* or *can* or *may*. They communicate it with the first word in that phrase. Each translation starts with either "so that" (HCSB), "that" (KJV, NKJV, RSV, ESV), "so" (NET, NLT), or "for" (NIV). All those words at the beginning of the phrases are trying to communicate *purpose*. Each translation is wrestling with how best to communicate the concept of purpose, which is in fact what the Greek is communicating as well.

Translation	Apparent View	Connecting Word
HCSB, NKJV, RSV, ESV, KJV	*optional understanding*	that
NLT	*ability understanding*	so
NET	*permission understanding*	so
NIV	*purpose understanding*	for

Purpose Clauses in the New Testament

Analyzing identical purpose clauses throughout the New Testament can help us understand more accurately what Paul means in Ephesians 2:10. In 2 Timothy 2:10, Paul says, "This is why I endure all things for the elect: *so that* they also may obtain salvation, which is in Christ Jesus, with eternal glory" (emphasis added). Is Paul trying to communicate that the elect *may* obtain salvation, but they *might* not? No, Paul is communicating the *purpose* for his endurance. This is why Paul is pushing on in his ministry. He is not communicating the idea that the elect may not actually be saved in the end.

In Luke 22:29–30, Jesus says to his disciples, "I bestow on you a kingdom, just as My Father bestowed one on Me, *so that* you may eat and drink at My table in My kingdom. And you will sit on thrones judging the 12 tribes of Israel." Jesus assigns a kingdom to his disciples so they *may* sit at his table. Is Jesus indicating that they *might not* sit at his table? Whether they eat and drink, they will definitely sit on the throne. So is Jesus saying they *will* sit on the throne, but they *might not* be able to eat at the table? No, Jesus is communicating the *purpose* for his bestowing of the kingdom.

One more example should suffice. John 3:16 says, "For God loved the world in this way: He gave His One and Only Son, *so that* everyone who believes in Him will not perish but have eternal life" (emphasis added). The idea of purpose is communicated at two places in John 3:16. First, God gave his Son *so that* everyone who believes will not perish. Second, God gave his son *so that* everyone who believes will have eternal life. The latter is the same type of purpose phrase used in Ephesians 2:10. What if John 3:16 was translated like Ephesians 2:10? "For God loved the world in this way: he gave his one and only Son, so that everyone who believes in him *might* not perish but *might* have eternal life." Do you like that translation? I haven't found it anywhere, but the idea of translating it that way is fairly offensive. It is extremely unlikely that John was trying to communicate that if you believe, then you *might* get eternal life. How about this translation: "So that everyone who believes in him *should* not perish, but they *should* have eternal life." Or this one: "Everyone who believes *may* not perish but *may* have eternal life." Again, many of us are not comfortable with those translations because they do not communicate the idea of purpose. They communicate the idea that it might or might not happen. They are not communicating the idea that if you believe, you *will* have eternal life. God's purpose was to give eternal life to those who place belief in his Son.

The Meaning of *Purpose*

In order to understand a purpose clause, we need to talk a little bit about English grammar. Look at this simple English sentence: I am going to the store in order to buy milk. So the purpose for going to the store is because I intend to buy milk. That is my purpose in going. Do I know that my purpose for going to the store will actually take place? No, because several things could happen that would prevent me from doing what I am purposing to do—that is, buying milk. For example, I could forget my wallet and leave it at home. Maybe I walked into the store, got a little distracted, shopped around, and forgot the whole reason I was there: to buy milk. Maybe I got there and I didn't have enough money. Maybe there was a threat of snow, and I got to the store, and they were sold out of milk. Many things could happen to prevent me from buying milk. So when I say I am going to the store to buy milk, I do not know if it is actually going to happen. I am just telling you that is the purpose for my going to the store.

Communicating that it *actually happened* is what a result clause communicates. For example, if I said, "I went to the store so that I bought milk," I am communicating the result of my action of going to the store. The result of my going to the store was that I got milk; it actually happened. When I communicate purpose, I can't know if it will actually be the result of my action because I can't guarantee anything. I am just a human being. There are no guarantees that any human can bring about the intended result of our actions. However, what about God?

When God purposes something to happen, it is going to happen. He sent his Son so that those who believe in him will have eternal life. If you believe, you *will* have eternal life.[1] That was the purpose, and those who have faith in Christ will have eternal life. If God says he is going to the store to buy milk, he is not going to forget his wallet, forget why he went, or run out of money. God can guarantee that what he purposes will happen.

A Closer Look at Ephesians 2:10

Ephesians 2:10 says God created us in Christ Jesus for the purpose of doing the good works he prepared for us to do. It is not presented as an option. Paul isn't saying we simply have the *ability* (though we do) or that we have permission to do good works. Good works are part of the purpose of our salvation. It is why God saved us—so that we will be changed and walk, that is, *live*, in the good works he prepared. God purposed it so it will come to pass. Our lives will be marked by good works.

However, this does not necessarily mean we have no option but to do every little detail that was predetermined for us to do.[2] Looking closely at the context

---

[1] The use of "will" is not intended to communicate a future aspect but definiteness.
[2] What some call "determinism."

of Ephesians 2:1–10 will clarify what Paul means by *walking* in these good works.

Paul begins this section in Ephesians 2:1–2 by stating that we previously walked in our sins (before being saved by grace through faith). Our pattern of life, our habit, was characterized by sin. It's not that everything we did was sin, but sin is what characterized our lives before Christ. Satan so impacted our lives that we habitually, consistently sinned. That is what *walk* means in Ephesians 2:2. Paul used the same word for *walk* in Ephesians 2:10. He basically bookends the passage with this verb. It is the same word in the Greek, and it refers to the conduct of our lives,[3] the sphere in which we live so as to be characterized by that sphere.[4] Previously our conduct was characterized by sinfulness. Now that we have been made alive, raised together with Christ, and seated in the heavenly places (Eph 2:5–6), our lives will be characterized by good works. This is similar to what James is talking about in James 2 about faith and works: faith in Christ saves, but it is never a faith unaccompanied by works. Paul is not talking about specific individual works. He is talking about the pattern of your life. He is not talking about perfectionism or sinlessness but explaining the purpose for God's saving us. He is saying Christians will do good works.

Application: Test Yourselves

What does it mean if our lives are not characterized by good works? I'm not talking about perfection or sinlessness. What does it mean if your life is consistently, habitually not characterized by good works? Reading through Ephesians 2 backward, it might mean you are not seated in the heavenly places, that you weren't raised with Christ, nor were you made alive. Maybe you are still dead in your "trespasses and sins." Paul said in 2 Corinthians 13:5: "Test yourselves to see if you are in the faith. Examine yourselves. Or do you yourselves not recognize that Jesus Christ is in you?—unless you fail the test." So, are good works optional for Christians? No. Our lives are to be characterized by good works.

Annotated Bibliography

Commentaries

Larkin, William J. *Ephesians: A Handbook on the Greek Text*. Waco: Baylor University Press, 2009.

---

3 Cf. BDAG, 803 (definition 2).
4 Cf. Louw and Nida, 41.11.

As with most commentaries, Larkin comments that Ephesians 2:10 is a purpose clause. This is a highly technical book with knowledge of Greek required. See especially page 35.

Greek Grammars

Wallace, Daniel B. *Greek Grammar Beyond the Basics: An Exegetical Syntax of the New Testament*. Grand Rapids: Zondervan, 1996.

Wallace is helpful for understanding purpose clauses in general, though he does not specifically comment on this one. See especially pages 473–74.

Websites

Mounce, Bill. "Is the Subjunctive 'Shall' or 'Might'? (John 3:16)." *Teknia*. May 19, 2013. Accessed July 22, 2014. www.tinyurl.com/MounceJn316.

Mounce makes some helpful comments on the purpose clause in John 3:16.

CHAPTER 26

Pastors Are Required to Do the Ministry of the Church

Ephesians 4:12

The Legendary Teaching on Ephesians 4:12

Some people think the responsibility for doing ministry rests in the local members of a congregation. Unfortunately for them, the Bible contradicts this statement. Ministry is the main task of the pastors of the church. Paul wrote in Ephesians 4:11–12 (KJV): "And he gave some, apostles; and some, prophets; and some, evangelists; and some, pastors and teachers; for the perfecting of the saints, for the work of the ministry, for the edifying of the body of Christ." The first task given to church leaders is the perfecting of the saints. The concept communicated in this phrase is the preparation, training, or equipping of Christians. Christians need to be trained; and it is the job, calling, and duty of the pastor to train them.

The third task given to church leaders by Paul is the command to edify the body of Christ. Pastors are to preach the Word of God, and this will cause Christians to be edified. Being edified is the idea of being spiritually strengthened through the ministry of the pastor. Now, does anyone really doubt that pastors are to train and edify Christians? No! So why do we have all these people saying pastors are not supposed to do the work of ministry? The second task given by Paul clearly teaches that pastors are to do the work of the ministry. This is why most pastors are paid, so they can do the ministry others are just too busy to do. That is why most pastors are hired, and ultimately that is what God has called them to do. Pastors are the most trained, most educated, most experienced, and most prepared to do the ministry. Why would God put pastors on the bench?

151

Introduction: Unraveling the Legend

The main issue here is the way the King James Version translated Ephesians 4:12. The KJV is a wonderful translation of Scripture. It captured the meaning of the Greek and Hebrew text in an extremely helpful way for the people it was translated for 400 years ago. The translations made available since then have incorporated advancements in scholarship made since the last revision of the KJV in 1769. In fact, the issue with the KJV and this verse has nothing to do with the actual *words* used. The words are fine. It has to do with one little item: a comma.

Translation Comparison on Ephesians 4:12

Let's compare the KJV to several other translations.

KJV: "For the perfecting of the saints, for the work of the ministry, for the edifying of the body of Christ."

NKJV: "For the equipping of the saints for the work of ministry, for the edifying of the body of Christ."

NASB: "For the equipping of the saints for the work of service, to the building up of the body of Christ."

ESV: "To equip the saints for the work of ministry, for building up the body of Christ."

HCSB: "For the training of the saints in the work of ministry, to build up the body of Christ."[1]

The KJV translates this verse in such a way that it appears to be a list of three tasks given to church leaders. However, notice what all the other translations have in common: none have the comma the KJV included. You might be wondering: *But what does the original Greek have? Did the original Greek have a comma?* The earliest Greek manuscripts we have access to did not have punctuation marks: no commas, no periods. They didn't even have spaces between the words. The punctuation marks and spaces between words were added later by people copying the manuscripts based on the context and how well they knew the Greek language.

---

[1] The NIV (2011), NIV (1984), NET, and NLT are more similar to the latter translations, not the KJV.

A Closer Look

So the main question we are asking is this: are two tasks delegated to church leaders in this list or three? And I agree with the more recent translations, like the HCSB, that Paul was not providing a list of three tasks. The main point is this: the context of Ephesians 4 itself argues for the participation of the saints in the work of ministry.

In Ephesians 4:11, Paul gives a list of different types of church leaders: apostles, prophets, evangelists, pastors, and teachers.[2] These church leaders are given the task to equip the saints. But according to the context of Ephesians 4, who is to do the work of ministry? Let's look at three verses around Ephesians 4:12 to see if context will aid in coming to a confident solution.

1. *Ephesians 4:7 emphasizes each individual Christian.* Paul says in Ephesians 4:7, "Now grace was given to each one of us according to the measure of the Messiah's gift." These ideas of "grace" and "gift" lead into a quote from the Old Testament that mentions the idea of gifts; this causes Paul to provide the list of church leaders. But does Paul say, "Grace was given to the church leaders"? No, that is not what he says! "Grace was given to each one of us," that is, all Christians. The emphasis in Ephesians 4:7 is on every single individual Christian in the church.

2. *Ephesians 4:15 exhorts every Christian to be involved in the maturing of the saints.* In Ephesians 4:15, Paul says, "But speaking the truth in love, let us grow in every way into Him who is the head—Christ." Again Paul emphasizes every Christian by saying, "Let us." This is an exhortation for every Christian to grow in every way into Christ. The concept is maturation, becoming more Christlike. But notice the phrase that comes before the "let us." "But speaking the truth in love." This is the same concept communicated by the author of Hebrews when he exhorts all Christians to "promote love and good works" (Heb 10:24). If we are speaking the truth in love to one another, we are promoting love and good works. Every Christian is being exhorted to grow in every way into him. And *each individual* is involved in this.

3. *Ephesians 4:16 emphasizes the importance of every part of the body, not just the leaders.* The clincher to this interpretation of Ephesians 4:12 is Paul's words in Ephesians 4:16: "From Him the whole body, fitted and knit together by every supporting ligament, promotes the growth of the body for building up itself in love by the proper working of each individual part." Paul says

---

[2]   There is considerable debate over the final two in the list: pastors and teachers. The question is whether this is describing one office (i.e. "pastor-teacher") or two offices (i.e. "pastors and teachers"). This is beyond the purpose of this chapter. However, see Daniel B. Wallace, *Greek Grammar Beyond the Basics: An Exegetical Syntax of the Greek New Testament* (Grand Rapids: Zondervan, 1996), 284, for some insightful thoughts on this.

"every supporting ligament" because everything in the body is important. And he doesn't say at the end "by the proper working of the church leaders" but "each individual part." Church leaders are not responsible for promoting the growth of the body but each individual part. So three times this passage has an emphasis on each one of us, each member. That is the context. You *don't* need to know Greek to see this. You *do* need to read Ephesians 4 over and over again so that you can see that the emphasis is on *each one of us*; that is the overarching context. So the context of the chapter indicates that church leaders are not required to do all the work of ministry, but they are required to equip the saints to do the work of ministry.

The Meaning of the Verse

Ephesians 4:12 has three phrases. How do they connect to one another?

1. *For the training of the saints.* Training or equipping the saints is what the church leaders from 4:11 are supposed to do. That is the task delegated to them by Paul.

2. *In the work of ministry.* This is the task of the saints, to do the work of ministry.

3. *To build up the body of Christ.* This is defining the work of the ministry; it finds its purpose in the building up, the edifying, the spiritually strengthening of the body of Christ. And interestingly, that is exactly how the NET Bible translates this: "To equip the saints for the work of ministry, that is, to build up the body of Christ." The phrase "that is" is added to explain that Paul is defining the phrase "work of ministry."

Addressing the Two Legends

Two legends have developed from this verse. The first relates to church leaders. Ephesians 4:12 says church leaders are to equip the saints for the work of ministry. It does not say "appoint people to positions of ministry." A pastor asked my wife to lead a Bible study. She was willing but wanted training. When she asked to be equipped, the pastor simply said she would be fine without any training. He *appointed her to a position.* He did *not* train her or equip her for anything and actually refused to do so.

This is not just an isolated incident. Why would a pastor reject giving training to someone? I am not going to judge that pastor's heart because I don't know what he was thinking. But I believe there are lots of reasons a pastor might do that. Maybe he is too busy. Maybe he is overworked and close to burnout. Maybe he really doesn't understand what it means to "equip." I think some pastors in churches I have attended are just trying to find a warm body to fill a spot. They are just desperate to get people to say they will fill particular ministry positions.

That is not, however, what Ephesians 4:12 tells them to do. It says *to equip the saints for ministry*. Equipping is a time-consuming investment in discipleship. And I think some pastors do not realize how underprepared many church members are to do anything in ministry, from singing in the choir to teaching a class to acting in a drama. Some pastors at times seem to think that if they can get a church member involved in doing something, it will work out all right. I have heard pastors say they see something in church members that these members don't see in themselves. These pastors believe that if such Christians would take a step in faith and try, they might succeed. But when a church member says, "OK, I will do it," sometimes he or she needs help to know how to approach a particular ministry or the tools needed to assume responsibility for the ministry. Lacking these can result in failure, burnout, or a counterproductive ministry. So one mistake some pastors make is to appoint a person to a position but not equip the person for ministry. This doesn't mean pastors have to be the one doing the actual equipping, but they have to make sure the person is equipped and trained for ministry. That is the first part of the legend.

The second part relates to all Christians, the church members who are not leaders or on staff. We are to do the ministry and not expect the church leaders to do all the work of the ministry of the church. This is what my colleague Larry Dixon calls "the myth of the omni-competent pastor." I am not saying pastors do nothing except train us to do ministry. They need to be doing ministry as well. But that is not what Ephesians 4:12 is about, and that is not mainly how the church should be structured. It should be that pastors equip, guide, and lead—then we are empowered to do the ministry. Think about a church of 1,000 members that might have eight full-time pastors. You have 1,000 Christians who could be doing ministry or eight full-time ministers. We should expect the pastors to train us or find someone to train us, but we shouldn't rely on them to be the ones actually doing all the ministry of the church.

A friend at a church I attended came to me and said he wanted to get involved in some sort of ministry in the church. I asked him what ministry he was interested in, and he said: "I don't even care. I just want to do something. I want someone to train me to do something." I asked if he had talked to any of the pastors because I was sure they had something that needed to be done. He replied that he had asked both his Sunday school teachers and some of the pastors, and they always said they'd get together and find somewhere for him to serve. But for years he never received training to do any ministry. He wanted to. He was willing. But he couldn't get equipped to do anything. In many churches the pastors are overworked. You have probably heard the number that 20 percent of the people do 80 percent of the work. While that is not the case in every single church, many people expect their pastors to do all the church ministry.

So if you know that someone is sick, maybe in the hospital, is your first thought, *I wonder if the pastor is going to visit them?* If the person is your friend, why don't *you* go visit? If you know the person is ill, you could always call or e-mail the pastor and say, "Hey, I am just letting you know I am going to go visit so-and-so in the hospital." That way the pastor knows your sick friend is being visited. You don't have to lean on the deacons or the pastors to do all the ministry. We can be doing that. Do you see how this fits together really well with promoting love and good works? We need to serve our pastors by relieving them of some of the ministry they are doing on a daily basis so they can spend more time in prayer, in studying God's Word, and in training. Maybe if they spent less time doing the actual ministry, they would have more time to do the training and equipping we want so we can do the ministry. Furthermore, by serving in the church, we can fulfill the exhortation to promote love and good works.

Annotated Bibliography

Commentaries

O'Brien, Peter T. *The Letter to the Ephesians*. PNTC. Grand Rapids: Eerdmans, 1999.
   O'Brien's discussion on this point is technical, and one needs to have a working understanding of Greek syntax and grammar.
Best, Ernest. *A Critical and Exegetical Commentary on Ephesians*. ICC. Edinburgh: T&T Clark, 1998.
   Best's discussion is fairly technical throughout, and a working knowledge of Greek syntax is needed for understanding Best's discussion.

Journal Articles

Davis, John Jefferson. "Ephesians 4:12 Once More: 'Equipping the Saints for the Work of Ministry?'" *Evangelical Review of Theology* 24, no. 2 (2000): 167–76.
   Davis's work draws on both historical exegesis and the Greek text itself. It may be inaccessible to those without a theological education.
Rojas, Juan Manuel Granados. "Ephesians 4,12: A Revised Reading." *Biblica: Commenatii Periodici Pontificii Insituti Biblici* 92, no. 1 (2011): 81–96.
   Rojas's analysis is highly technical and requires a working knowledge of Greek, an understanding of syntax, and a familiarity with structural analysis. Rojas's work is intended for scholars.

Websites

Piper, John. "Alone in a Big Church: A Call to Small Togetherness." *Desiring God*. September 20, 1981. Accessed June 4, 2014. www.desiringgod.org/sermons/ alone-in-a-big-church.

CHAPTER 27

Jesus Emptied Himself of the Glory of Heaven

Philippians 2:6–7

The *Legendary* Teaching on Philippians 2:6–7

Philippians 2:6–11 is an important passage for understanding the nature of Jesus. In verse 6, Paul explains that Jesus didn't think being equal with God was robbery; that is, Jesus wasn't guilty of taking something that didn't belong to him. If Jesus were pretending to be God, if he were a mere creation, then pretending to be God would be robbery. Verse 7 contains the phrase that has puzzled many: Jesus emptied himself. Of what? Some have said Jesus emptied himself of his deity, that he was no longer God. However, that would be heresy. Instead, Jesus emptied himself of the form of being God and now took the form of a human being. Rather than being clothed in the glories of heaven, he was clothed in the rags of humanity.

Introduction: Unraveling the Legend

The assortment of teachings on Philippians 2:6–7 ranges from rank heresy (Jesus emptying himself of his divine nature) to orthodox statements that do not take the text within its literary context. One of the difficulties with some legends is that while they teach sound, solid theology, they are still misinterpretations of the verses being discussed. While we can affirm the theology undergirding the interpretation above, the conclusion on this specific passage is problematic.

The Context of Philippians 2:6–7

Starting in Philippians 2:3 will provide sufficient information to understand the context for Paul's comments on Jesus in verses 6–7.[1] Verse 3 could serve as a heading for the following verses, as it summarizes Paul's main point: "Do nothing out of rivalry or conceit, but in humility consider others as more important than yourselves." The way to rid ourselves of selfishness is to busy ourselves with exhorting, consoling, partnering, and loving others (Phil 2:1–2). Paul is exhorting the Philippians to regard others as more important and to look out for the interests of others, not just their own (2:4). Then Paul provides an illustration to help the Philippians picture what it looks like to serve others by putting them first: be like Christ Jesus (2:5).

A Closer Look at Philippians 2:6–7

Paul says in verses 6–7, "Who, existing in the form of God, did not consider equality with God as something to be used for His own advantage. Instead He emptied Himself by assuming the form of a slave, taking on the likeness of men." The translation "form of God" could be misleading to those with a Western mind-set. Carson explains that the word *form* in verse 6 ("form of God") and verse 7 ("form of a slave") refers to the idea that Jesus began "in the mode of existence of God himself but took on the mode of existence of a servant. This 'mode of existence' of God embraces both essence and function: he enjoyed real equality with God, and he became a real servant."[2]

The key to understanding Paul's illustration is the phrase typically translated "a thing to be grasped" (ESV, NASB; similarly NET, NLT). The HCSB and NIV say: "something to be used for/to His own advantage" (see also the NRSV). The KJV and NKJV refer to "robbery."[3] What's going on with this phrase?

Work done by Jaeger (in 1915) and greatly refined by Hoover (in 1968, 1971) has provided ample evidence that the Greek phrase is part of an idiomatic expression.[4] It probably began in the conversations of common people meaning "a piece of good fortune." As it was adopted for use in literature, it developed to mean "to regard as something to use for his own advantage." Of

---

[1] N. T. Wright, "*Harpagmos* and the Meaning of Philippians 2:5–11," *Journal of Theological Studies* 37 (1986): 346–47, is one of the few interpreters to fit his interpretation into the context of Philippians 2:1–5.

[2] D. A. Carson, *Basics for Believers: An Exposition of Philippians* (Grand Rapids: Baker, 1996), 44.

[3] BDAG, 133–34, mentions that the translation "robbery" is "next to impossible" in Philippians 2:6.

[4] See R. W. Hoover, "The Harpagmos Enigma: A Philological Solution," *Harvard Theological Review* 64 (1971): 95–119, for this entire discussion.

course, in Philippians 2:6, it is preceded by the word "not," which provides the following translation: "did not consider equality with God as something to be used for His own advantage" (HCSB). Jesus did not consider the fact that he was God as something to exploit.[5]

This statement about how Jesus perceived himself is contrasted with what follows in verse 7: "Instead He emptied Himself by assuming the form of a slave." The NIV captures the contrast between the idiom of verse 6 with the concept of emptying in verse 7 perfectly: "Rather, *he made himself nothing* by taking the very nature of a servant" (emphasis added). Because Jesus was God, rather than viewing his deity as something to exploit, he took it as an opportunity to serve others unselfishly.

Paul uses a rather shocking term to describe Jesus in 2:7: *slave*. Paul had prepared the citizens at Philippi for this reference to Christ back in the first words he said to them: "Paul and Timothy, slaves of Christ Jesus" (1:1). We need to be careful about importing the modern American concept of slavery onto the term as used in the New Testament (for example, slavery in the ancient Near East was not based on ethnicity). When a Jewish believer heard Paul refer to himself and Timothy as "slaves," it probably brought up thoughts of Moses (see Num 12:7), associating it with honor. However, for the Gentile Christians in Philippi (probably most of the church), slavery was not viewed as relating to honor in any sense. Slaves did not have rights or privileges. Paul then proclaimed that rather than Christ using his deity as a reason to have others serve him, Jesus himself took the form of a lowly slave, humbly serving others.

Correlation in the New Testament

This is a radical statement about the humility of Christ and his desire to serve others. It correlates well with other verses in the New Testament. Jesus says, "For even the Son of Man did not come to be served, but to serve, and to give His life—a ransom for many" (Mark 10:45). Jesus came with the intention to serve others, as the foot washing in John 13 so poignantly illustrates.

Paul talks about Jesus similarly in two places. Romans 15:3 says, "For even the Messiah did not please Himself." Jesus' purpose was not to please himself. In 2 Corinthians 8:9, Paul explains the depth of Christ's sacrifice: "Though

---

[5] Two top New Testament scholars have made similar affirming comments about Hoover's conclusion. Moisés Silva, *Philippians*, 2nd ed., BECNT (Grand Rapids: Baker, 2005), 104, said, "This essay, which reflects thoroughness and a clear-headed method, must be regarded as having settled this particular question." Wright, *"Harpagmos,"* 339, says, "If Hoover is right [as Wright believes] . . . , the views of all the other scholars we have reviewed for the sake of clarity in the current debate are undercut at a stroke." See also N. T. Wright, *The Climax of the Covenant: Christ and the Law in Pauline Theology* (Minneapolis: Fortress, 1991), 78.

He was rich, for your sake He became poor, so that by His poverty you might become rich."

Placing Philippians 2:6–7 Back into the Context

Paul is not simply explaining the character of Christ; he is exhorting the Philippians to be like Christ in a particular way: serving others. Paul is commanding them to have the same mind-set toward service that Jesus had (2:5). Jesus is Paul's illustration for not using your status for exploitation but to serve others. Jesus, being fully God, was fully unselfish.

Philippians 2 is not primarily about Jesus divesting himself of the glories he had in heaven. It certainly is not communicating that Jesus poured out his deity and ceased to be God.[6] Paul is using Jesus as an illustration on how the Philippians are to conduct themselves in a manner worthy of the gospel (Phil 1:27).

Philippians 2:6–7 Illustrated

I accepted a position at Columbia International University (CIU) in December 2012. Danielle, my daughter, and I arrived on campus a few weeks before the rest of our family. For our first full day on campus, we decided to go to the gym to work out. After working out, we were both sweaty and exhausted. She walked out to the foyer while I got my wallet and keys from the locker room. When I walked out toward the foyer, I saw Danielle standing in the hallway with the president of CIU, Dr. Bill Jones, down on one knee talking with her. A small amount of fear shot through my body. I was new to CIU and didn't know Dr. Jones well. What could he be asking my daughter? What was *she* saying?

Dr. Jones was only trying to figure out who she was. Then he insisted we join him for his advisory council's year-end barbecue. Danielle and I sat at a table that was chest high with Dr. Jones's administrative assistant. Then he came over to join us, but there were only three chairs. I immediately got up to offer him my chair, but he insisted that he would stand. So the president of CIU was standing at the table while the rest of us were sitting. But the story doesn't end there. When my daughter's cup of water ran out, he refilled it for her. When we finished eating, he grabbed our plates and threw them away. He acted more like a waiter than the president of a university. Dr. Jones had every right to ask us to serve him; his position enabled him to ask me to give up my seat, refill his empty cup, and throw away his trash. He didn't view his position as an opportunity to exploit us but as an opportunity to serve us humbly. Dr. Jones has the

---

[6] For a wonderful survey (and critique) of these and several more views, see Wright, "*Harpagmos*," 321–44.

mind of Christ Jesus as explained in Philippians 2. He made himself nothing (2:7) and took the form of a servant (2:6).

This is what Philippians 2 looks like today: taking every opportunity to serve others rather than looking for opportunities to be served. How can you be like Jesus and Dr. Jones? Be careful that this is not just about appearing to look like Jesus but actually adopting the mind-set of Christ. Dr. Jones was not putting on a show. As I've discovered in my time at CIU, this is part of his DNA. He has been so transformed by his relationship with Christ that seeking to serve others is embedded in his character. That's what obedience to Philippians 2 looks like.

Annotated Bibliography

Commentaries

Carson, D. A. *Basics for Believers: An Exposition of Philippians*. Grand Rapids: Baker, 1996.

This is a nontechnical work that avoids much technical language and use of Greek. See especially pages 44–45.

Silva, Moisés. *Philippians*. 2nd ed. BECNT. Grand Rapids: Baker, 2005.

Silva's work is fairly accessible. Knowledge of Greek is helpful. See especially pages 102–5.

Journals

Hoover, R. W. "The Harpagmos Enigma: A Philological Solution." *Harvard Theological Review* 64 (1971): 95–119.

This is a brilliant, groundbreaking summary of Hoover's dissertation. A must read for anyone studying this text. It is written at a fairly high academic level.

Wright, N. T. "*Harpagmos* and the Meaning of Philippians 2:5–11." *Journal of Theological Studies* 37 (1986): 321–52.

A great survey of the history of interpretation, favoring the philological argument by Hoover and the theological understanding of Moule. Written at a highly technical level.

Blogs

Decker, Rodney J. "Philippians 2:5–11, The Kenosis." *NT Resources*. Accessed July 12, 2014. www.ntresources.com/blog/wp-content/uploads/2013/05/kenosis.pdf.

Decker does a good job of summarizing this complicated issue succinctly. Fairly technical.

CHAPTER 28

We Can Do Anything Through Christ Who Gives Us Strength

Philippians 4:13

The Legendary Teaching on Philippians 4:13

Scripture is filled with promises from God to his children. Philippians 4:13 contains one of the most popular and encouraging promises of all: "I am able to do all things through Him who strengthens me." All of us have goals in life. Some of you want to be professional athletes. Others may want to be famous musicians or actors. Some want to start their own businesses. Whatever you want to do, remember this verse and claim it daily. Put it on your mirror so you see it every morning and every evening. While apart from Christ you can do nothing, through him you can accomplish anything.

Introduction: Unraveling the Legend

This is one of the most popular verses in the entire Bible.[1] Walk into any Christian bookstore and you will see jewelry, coffee mugs, T-shirts, and bumper stickers with Philippians 4:13 on them. As my pastor, Jeff Philpott, says, "If you see a Bible verse on a mug, T-shirt, or bumper sticker, it's probably being taken out of context." The youngest Mixed Martial Arts (MMA) champion in UFC history, Jon Jones, has a Philippians 4:13 tattoo. Evander Holyfield, former heavyweight boxing champion of the world, had Philippians 4:13 on his boxing shorts. The July 27, 2009, cover of *Sports Illustrated*, with Tim Tebow's picture, clearly shows Philippians 4:13 written on his eye black. Is this how Paul intended for this verse to be understood?

---

[1] See chapter 8.

The Context of Philippians 4:13

Paul is thanking the Philippians for their generous gift (4:10). He explains that he has learned to be content in whatever circumstance he is in (4:11). Verse 12 provides the range of "circumstances" to which he was referring: having little, having much, being hungry, being full, having abundance, or being in need.

It is challenging to be content when having little or when in abundance. Many people might think having riches will lead to contentment. But the National Endowment for Financial Education estimates that as many as 70 percent of Americans who get a lot of money suddenly will lose all that money within a few years.[2] If you haven't learned the secret to being content when you have little, it won't be easy to learn it when you have an abundance. Many people are scared of going broke or suffering for Christ's name. Chris Gnanakan, executive director of Outreach to Asia Nationals, says, "Don't be scared of affliction, be scared of affluence."

A Closer Look at Philippians 4:13

I heard a preaching professor say, "All means all and that's all all means." Philippians 4:13 declares that Christians can do "all things" through Christ. Does "all" really mean anything without exception? No, sometimes, as in this verse, "all" is qualified in such a way as to limit its extent.

The translations are fairly consistent, stating that "I can" (or "am able") "to do all things." However, the NIV says, "I can do *all this* through him who gives me strength." Even though the Greek word is plural (hence most translations have "all things"), the NIV decided to translate it with the singular word "this." Why would they do this? Perhaps the translators were trying to get the reader to look closer at the context. The phrase "all things" seems to mean "anything," but the phrase "all this" makes me ask: what does the "this" refer back to? Once that question is asked, then the key to correctly interpreting this verse is unlocked. The "this" or "things" Paul was referring to were the various circumstances in 4:12.

But there is another problem. The Greek of Philippians 4:13 does not say Paul can "do" all things; it says "I am able" with the verb following it being implied. While most English translations have supplied "do," it probably is not the most appropriate word. Paul's thought from 4:11–12 is continuing, and

---

[2]   Matthew DeLuca, "What Could Happen to You: Tales of Big Lottery Winners," *NBC News* (May 17, 2013), accessed July 7, 2014, usnews.nbcnews.com/_news/2013/05/17/18323470-what-could-happen-to-you-tales-of-big-lottery-winners.

the idea is probably that of being "content" from verse 11.[3] Therefore, Paul is saying, "I am able to be content in all these circumstances by the One who gives me strength."

Ignoring the final phrase of Philippians 4:13 is what turns it into the "Superman" verse.[4] Paul is not claiming that he is able to look within himself and find the strength and ability to accomplish any task before him. He's not even saying that he, by himself, can attain contentment. It is only "through Him who strengthens me," that is, Christ himself is the One who does the empowering to enable contentment to thrive in all the circumstances Paul encounters.

This verse is not promising to make you a better athlete or the next president of the United States. Instead, Paul is declaring that God can help all Christians be content in every circumstance, whether persecution, poverty, or riches; if you live in a mansion or a prison; whether you are eating filet mignon or stale bread. Regardless of the circumstances you are currently in, God can help you be content. Another way to state this verse is this: God will give you strength to be content through whatever circumstances he assigns to your life.

Application

When I've explained the above interpretation of this verse, some people have stated that I've robbed the church of this Scripture. However, I believe a correct interpretation of this verse leads to a vast array of appropriate applications. As I write this chapter, I am struggling with pain from a kidney stone. It would be a misapplication of this verse to claim it in order to pass the stone immediately without pain. That doesn't mean the verse doesn't apply, for I can still depend on God to strengthen me and give me contentment in this situation.

If you are in a loveless marriage and you aren't sure if you can persevere another day, God can give you strength to be content. He can satisfy your needs and desires. If you are being tempted at work to be dishonest in order to gain that promotion, God can give you the strength to be content and do what is right. If you are being persecuted for your faith in Jesus Christ, God is able to empower you to be supernaturally meek and gentle and in prayer for your persecutors.

This verse explodes with relevance when it is understood within its literary context. Paul, who had been imprisoned many times, endured countless beatings (several times near death), received thirty-nine lashes five times, was

---

[3] See Peter T. O'Brien, *The Epistle to the Philippians*, NIGTC (Grand Rapids: Eerdmans, 1991), 526.

[4] See Ben Witherington, "The Superman Verse—Phil. 4.13 and What It Does Not Mean," *Patheos* (October 11, 2012), accessed July 9, 2014, www.patheos.com/blogs/bibleandculture/2012/10/11/the-superman-verse-phil-4-13-and-what-it-does-not-mean.

beaten with rods three times, stoned, and shipwrecked three times (see 2 Cor 11:23–26), learned how to be content through those situations. God has the ability to teach us contentment through difficult circumstances as well.

Annotated Bibliography

Commentaries

O'Brien, Peter T. *The Epistle to the Philippians*. NIGTC. Grand Rapids: Eerdmans, 1991.
Knowledge of Greek needed. Great commentary and precisely interprets this text. See especially page 526.

Websites

Mounce, William D. "When Does a Singular Better Translate a Plural? Phil 4:13." *Koinonia*. Accessed July 17, 2014. tinyurl.com/MouncePhil4.
Mounce does a great job showing how the NIV's translation seeks to avoid the legendary interpretation.
Witherington, Ben. "The Superman Verse—Phil. 4.13 and What It Does Not Mean." *Patheos*. October 11, 2012. Accessed July 9, 2014. www.patheos.com/blogs/ bibleandculture/2012/10/11/the-superman-verse-phil-4-13-and-what-it-does-not-mean.

CHAPTER 29

Abstain from All Appearance of Evil

1 Thessalonians 5:22

The Legendary Teaching on 1 Thessalonians 5:22

Christians need to consider many gray areas, to think long and hard before doing certain actions. We want to be careful about the places we go and the people we are with. What if someone who is a weaker brother in the faith, another Christian, saw us doing something that appeared sinful? Surely, as Christians, we are told to avoid sin. But what about things that may or may not be sin, but others *think* they are sin? Or that might *appear* to be sinful? Notice what Paul says in 1 Thessalonians 5:22: "Abstain from all appearance of evil" (KJV). Paul is unequivocally clear. If something appears to be evil, even if it isn't, you must abstain from it. You must not do it. Therefore, avoid the gray areas. Live a holy life to God. Put love of fellow brothers and sisters in Christ before love of self, and avoid areas that could *appear* to be sinful.

Introduction: Unraveling the Legend

When I was in seminary, a couple of guys were walking across the campus one day, and they were drinking nonalcoholic beer. Nonalcoholic beer has about .05 percent alcohol—you would have to drink a lot of it to get even a little drunk. It seemed as if they were trying to prove a point, like saying, "Hey, we're drinking beer, but it's not alcoholic beer," and they got in trouble.

When I was at work a few days later, I mentioned this to a friend who was a deacon in a local church, and he said, "Well good, I'm glad they got in trouble." I asked him why. He said, "Well, what did the bottle look like?"

And I said, "It looked like it was beer."

And he said, "So it looked like they were drinking beer, and 1 Thessalonians 5:22 says, 'Avoid the appearance of evil,' and since drinking beer is evil, they looked like they were drinking beer; that is evil."

Then I asked him, "Do you know what IBC root beer is?"

He said, "No."

I said, "It's root beer—not beer at all—0 percent alcohol, just soda; and it's in a brown bottle that kind of looks like an alcoholic beverage. You can easily confuse it with beer."

He said, "Well, Christians shouldn't be drinking that either because then someone might think you are drinking beer."

So I asked, "Drinking IBC root beer in a bottle would be sinful?"

He said, "Well, . . . yes."

I wanted to see how far I could take this, so I told him the following true story. "About a week ago I was on my way to work, and I looked in my rearview mirror, and I saw a minivan. Some kids were in the backseat, and I saw their mom taking a drink out of something I was sure was a bottle of beer. I thought: *What am I going to do? I can't just let her drive around drinking. Her kids are going to get killed!* So I slowed down to let her pass, and she quickly cut around me. As she drove by, I was looking over to see what she was drinking: it was Arizona iced tea. I was wrong!"

I asked him what he thought, and he replied, "That's sinful too."

I said, "Really? So I can't drink root beer or iced tea because someone somewhere might confuse the bottle for an alcoholic beverage, and therefore I am not avoiding the appearance of evil?"

He said, "I guess so." He didn't really like his conclusion, but he thought he had to believe that. He *felt* like he had to because that is what 1 Thessalonians 5:22 says and means . . . or so he thought.

A Closer Look

What would it look like if we had to avoid everything another Christian thought was sinful? Some Christians say women shouldn't wear pants. Does that mean that no Christian women anywhere should wear pants because some Christians think wearing pants is evil and therefore you are not avoiding the appearance of evil in some people's eyes? What about women wearing makeup, men with long hair, playing poker, watching a movie, watching TV, using the Internet, listening to any music that is not Christian music? Some would say you can't listen to contemporary Christian music either. How about having instruments in your worship service? Some Christians say it should be voices alone.

If we have to avoid everything some Christian somewhere thinks is sinful, then I don't want to leave my house! It's just impossible. We could not do so many things. But is that really what this verse is saying? Is this verse truly teaching the principle that we can't do anything that could *appear* evil?

Looking at the Context

In 1 Thessalonians 5, Paul gives a series of commands. In verse 16 he says, "Rejoice." In verse 17 he says, "Pray." In verse 18 he says, "Give thanks." Rejoice, pray, give thanks. He could have stopped right there, and that would have been hard enough. But then he gives two prohibitions, two things we are *not* to do. First, in verse 19, he says, "Don't stifle the Spirit" or "Do not quench the Spirit" (ESV). And in verse 20 he says, "Don't despise prophecies."

Verses 20–22 put this idea of avoiding the appearance of evil into context: "Don't despise prophesies, but test all things. Hold on to what is good. Stay away from every kind of evil." The word "despise" means to have no use for something because it is beneath one's consideration; it refers to something you discard.[1] It's like hearing the teaching of the Word of God and saying, "That is not even worth considering." So, when you are listening to spiritual instruction, Paul prohibits this dismissive attitude. Don't view spiritual instruction as unworthy to consider. That is the concept "despise" communicates.

How did I get from "prophecy" to "spiritual instruction"? When many people hear the word *prophecy*, they usually think of the idea of prediction. There were Christians in Thessalonica who were apparently speaking prophecies. In 1 Corinthians 14, Paul provides an extended discussion on his thoughts about prophecy. He says prophecy does not find its *main* purpose in predicting the future. The main purpose of prophecy is edification, encouragement, and consolation (1 Cor 14:3). In that same chapter, in verse 12, he makes clear that prophecy was intended for the edification of the church, the building up of the church. That is the purpose of prophecy. Further on in that section, in verse 29, Paul tells the Corinthians to evaluate the prophecies given in the church. So prophecy may have a predictive element, an exhortation element, or both. But the word *prophecy* itself does not necessitate that we are dealing with prediction. Since the purpose of prophecy is edification, I am going to use the phrase "spiritual instruction." That kind of encapsulates the purpose of prophecy, whether it is predictive or not.

---

[1] BDAG, 352.

In 1 Thessalonians 5:21, Paul says, "But test all things." That word *but* is extremely important. In *contrast* to viewing spiritual instruction as unworthy of consideration, Paul commands them to test all things. These two phrases should be understood in contrast with each other, not independently. One of the reasons verses 21 and 22 are taken out of context so often is that some translations, like the KJV, do not have the word *but* translated. The KJV does not say, "But prove all things," it just says, "Prove all things." The inclusion of the word "but" is important because it communicates a contrast between these two elements—the despising of spiritual instruction and the testing. Seeing that there is a contrast helps avoid interpreting verse 21 separately from verse 20.

What does Paul mean by "test all things"? He is not speaking generically or universally. He is not saying, "You want to make sure you test everything. So if you are going to buy a car, test-drive it." He is not speaking generically because this phrase is in a context, and it is contrasted with another phrase: "Don't despise prophecies." Instead, he means that when spiritual instruction occurs, rather than ignoring it, rather than despising it, test it. Test all of it. Notice what the NIV does. The NIV in verse 21 doesn't say, "Test all things," but it says, "But test them all." When I read that, I ask, "Well, all of *what*?" It makes me look back and analyze the context and conclude that the word *them* must refer to the prophecies. It refers to the *spiritual instruction*. When Paul says, "Test all things," he is referring to testing the spiritual instruction you are receiving.

The 1984 NIV had an unfortunate translation of 1 Thessalonians 5:21.[2] It said, "Test everything. Hold on to the good." Not only did the old NIV leave out the word *but* like the KJV did, but it also started a new sentence in the middle of the verse, as if a new thought was beginning. While that is possible, it misses the flow of the passage. Basically the old NIV seems to paint a picture of this passage as listing several unrelated commands. Notice, however, that the updated 2011 NIV has the word *but* and puts a semicolon in the middle of verse 21, indicating that holding on to what is good is related to "test them all." It includes the word *but* so you know there is a contrast. Rather than starting a new sentence with "hold on to what is good," it includes a semicolon, indicating that the thoughts are connected.

What does it mean to test? What are we to do when testing? There are two options: first, if the spiritual instruction passes the test, if the spiritual instruction is biblical, then we must hold on to it. What does it mean to hold on to

---

[2]   The NIV was updated in 2011. For information on this, see Douglas J. Moo, "The New International Version (NIV)," in *Which Bible Translation Should I Use? A Comparison of 4 Major Recent Versions*, ed. Andreas J. Köstenberger and David A. Croteau (Nashville: B&H, 2012), 78–80.

true spiritual instruction? Luke 8:15 provides a good example. It uses the same word for holding on. It says, "But the seed in the good ground—these are the ones who, having heard the word with an honest and good heart, hold on to it and by enduring, bear fruit." When the Word of God is proclaimed, we need to hold on to it; and when we do, there is going to be evidence of it: bearing fruit. The NET in Luke 8:15 doesn't translate it "Hold on," but says, "Cling to it," and the NIV says, "Retain it." When we hear spiritual instruction that is good, we need to cling to or retain that instruction. One Greek dictionary defines "hold on" this way: "to continue to believe, with the implication of acting in accordance with such belief."[3] This is not referring to mental assent to a truth and then moving on with your life. There should be change, there should be fruit, and we should be acting in accordance with that belief. We need to cling to the truths that are taught to us, not merely acknowledge them. That is what we do when we hear spiritual instruction and it is good, which raises another question. What do we do if it is bad? Now the context for the verse under consideration has been established.

The Twisted Text: Reject Bad Teaching

When you have tested spiritual instruction and it's good, cling to it. But if it's bad, Paul says *reject* it, *abstain* from it, *avoid* it, *stay away* from every kind of evil. So when Paul says to stay away from every kind of evil or every form of evil, what is he referring to? In the context it is fairly clear—false teaching, false spiritual instruction. The NIV translates it, "Reject." That is a helpful translation. "Reject every kind of evil." That last part, "every kind of evil," does not refer, then, to one's lifestyle but to false teaching.

Live Out the Good, Reject the Bad

Paul commands the Thessalonians to give heed to spiritual teaching and examine it. If it's good, if it is true and lines up with the teaching of the apostles, then cling to it, retain it, live it out in your life. If you find that it is false, reject it. This has absolutely nothing to do with harming the weaker brother or doing something another Christian might *think* is wrong. It has nothing to do with whether you have a beard or long hair, or women wearing pants. *It is not a passage about lifestyle. It is a passage about being able to discern true and false teaching.* The topic of how a Christian should live regarding gray areas is important, but that is not being addressed in this passage. This passage is commanding discernment in the teaching of the Word of God.

---

[3] Louw and Nida, 31.48.

So the first application is not to despise spiritual instruction. Sometimes our pride will get in the way. We will hear a sermon, and we won't like it—not because it's not true but because it confronts and rebukes us. We might have the tendency to despise the sermon, and sometimes we might even despise the preacher behind the sermon! But Paul says we need to be eager to be confronted by our sin when the Word of God is proclaimed. This applies to the proclaimer of the Word as well. A teacher is not to stand up and spout off the data they have learned. But they themselves should have spiritually wrestled with the passage, with the principles they are proclaiming. A powerful sermon is created when a preacher has been transformed by the message, confronted by the passage himself, changed through wrestling with it all week long, and then Sunday morning we hear the fruit of his wrestling and struggling with the principles in the passage. That is ideally what takes place when we hear someone proclaim the Word of God, when hearing spiritual instruction.

While for some the problem might be pride, others struggle with clinging to the good. We hear the sermon and exclaim, "Man, that was good! Wow, I never knew that about that passage. That is great! That just changes everything. I need to change the way I live." But do we change the way we live? We are not only to retain the information in our heads but to live it out in our lives. Like in Luke 8:15, when you have retained it, when you have clung to it, there should be fruit. Have you ever heard a sermon on Sunday morning and thought, *I need to change the way I do this or the way I do that?* You are convicted. The next question is: do you change? If not, you are not clinging to what is good.

I heard a sermon recently, and I was convicted by it. That whole week I was thinking about the thing I knew I needed to change, the thing I knew God wanted me to do differently. All week long I thought about it. Not once did I change, but I thought about it all week. You know what happened the next week? I thought about it. I kept thinking about it. And I kept getting more and more convicted, but I didn't change. Was I retaining it? Was I clinging to what is good? No, I was thinking about what was good, but I was not retaining it. I was not clinging to it because I wasn't doing it. It took about four weeks. It was in the front of my mind for four weeks, and I finally said, "That's it; this is the week." And I changed. The Lord granted me repentance. I was thinking about it the whole time, but I was rejecting it with my life. I finally put what I had heard into action. We need to cling to the good teachings, and we need to live them out.

Second, we need to learn to discern false teaching. When we hear someone teaching something false—maybe we are listening to a sermon on the radio or maybe we are watching someone preach a sermon on TV, and it is false—then we need to reject it. We need to be careful about *whom* we are listening to. It's easy to think you are rejecting false teaching. You hear something and you think, *Oh, this guy is crazy. This is not right at all.* But if you keep listening to it, you can be taking little bits and pieces of it and integrating it into your view of God, not even realizing you are doing it.

You want to know where a lot of our false beliefs come from? Television shows, the movies, and all the commercials we watch. They are immersed with false ideas, and we allow our brains to be immersed in these wrong things. They make you feel like your life is incomplete because you don't have their product. They are trying to persuade you that a one-night stand won't really have lasting consequences. Many movies are manipulating us so that we end up rooting for evil! All media have a message, a story to tell. It is trying to communicate something, and it is powerful. However, reject false teaching. Don't let it penetrate your mind and conform your way of thinking to the world's way. Instead, embrace and cling to the truth and be transformed by true spiritual instruction.

Annotated Bibliography

Commentaries

Green, Gene L. *The Letters to the Thessalonians*. PNTC. Grand Rapids: Eerdmans, 2002.
    Accessible to most; the Greek text is transliterated and set off in parentheses, and the discussions are written with a broad audience in mind.
Fee, Gordon D. *The First and Second Letters to the Thessalonians*. NICNT. Grand Rapids: Eerdmans, 2009.
    This work is fairly technical but accessible to the intelligent and interested layperson. It is intended for a fairly broad audience; the Greek text is integrated into the discussion, but it is transliterated.

Websites

Wallace, Daniel B. "1 Thessalonians 5:22—the Sin Sniffer's Catch-All Verse." *Bible.org*. June 30, 2004. Accessed June 14, 2014. www.tinyurl.com/SinSniffer.
    A great analysis of this legend.

CHAPTER 30

Hell Is the Absence of God

2 Thessalonians 1:9

The Legendary Teaching on 2 Thessalonians 1:9

God is loving. But some people have taken the biblical view of God's being loving to an unbiblical extreme; they say God would not send anyone to hell. It would be one thing to punish unrepentant humanity for a time period. But for eternity? How could anyone who did that be considered "loving" in any sense of the word? People who hold to that view are those who ignore (or at least downplay) the  holiness and justice of God. Yes, God is loving, but He is holy, righteous, and just. The consequences for not believing in Jesus Christ as Lord and Savior are explained in Scripture: eternal punishment in hell. Paul stated in 2 Thessalonians 1:9, "They will suffer the punishment of eternal destruction, away from the presence of the Lord and from the glory of his might" (ESV).

A few aspects of this verse need comment. First, the punishment is eternal, not temporary, destruction. Second, the punishment is isolation. It is *away* from God's presence. The NIV is even stronger: "shut out from the presence of the Lord." God is holy, and anything that is not holy must be ushered away from his presence. He can't allow impurity near him, so those who have not been cleansed by the blood of Jesus Christ must be moved outside of his presence. This is what hell is: aloneness, nothingness.

Have you ever been somewhere that is completely dark, completely silent? Maybe a deep, dark cave. At first you might think, *This is kind of peaceful and restful*. But after a short time it starts driving you crazy. Your mind starts playing tricks on you. That isolation is what hell is going to be like. That is the punishment. It is the absence of God, the absence of people, the absence of relationships, and the absence of everything.

Introduction: Misconceptions About Hell

There are many misconceptions about hell: Satan rules hell with his demons and a pitchfork; hell is a temporary place of punishment before the ultimate annihilation; everyone in hell is crying out in repentance hoping God will relent of the punishment. These misconceptions are not dealt with in this chapter. The misconception about hell from 2 Thessalonians 1:9 is that God is *absent* from hell. The verse says that those who don't know God will be sent "away from the presence of the Lord" (ESV). This phrase needs to be analyzed from a few different angles.

2 Thessalonians 1:9 and the Greek Preposition

The first issue to consider is the phrase "away from." Those two words translate a single Greek preposition. Prepositions in Greek, as in many languages, can be flexible and mean several different things. One of the meanings of this Greek preposition is "separation" or "away from." For example, Acts 15:33, "After they had spent time *there*, they were *sent away from* the brethren" (NASB, italics added). So this Greek preposition can communicate the concept of separation.

Another possible meaning of this Greek preposition is "cause," the concept of "coming from something." First Corinthians 6:19 illustrates this: "Or do you not know that your body is a temple of the Holy Spirit who is in you, whom you have *from* God?" (NASB, italics added). First Corinthians 6 says Christians have the Holy Spirit, and the Holy Spirit was from God. God *caused* the Holy Spirit to come to us, and that is why we have the Holy Spirit. Therefore, while this word can mean "separation," it can also communicate almost the (nearly) opposite idea, being a source and the cause of something.[1]

2 Thessalonians 1:9 and Bible Translations

Bible translations evidence some wrestling in their translations of this verse. The NIV takes a strong stand on the concept of separation ("shut out from the presence of the Lord"). The ESV also communicates separation: "away from the presence of the Lord" (exactly the same in the NASB and NET). Three other translations communicate separation differently: NLT, NRSV, and RSV. However, there are a few exceptions.

---

[1] Paul uses this preposition about 105 times in his writings; the meaning is divided nearly equally between these two options. The way Paul used it doesn't necessarily help us understand the text under discussion.

The ESV has a footnote that contains the opposite concept: "Or *destruction that comes from.*"[2] The HCSB originally (2005) said "away from," but now they have changed it (2009) to "eternal destruction from the Lord's presence." Several translations are similar to the HCSB in communicating the concept of cause or source: KJV, NKJV, ASV, and even the Tyndale New Testament (1526).

Analyzing "(Away) from the Presence of the Lord"

The phrase "(away) from the presence of the Lord" needs to be studied. It occurs many times in the Septuagint and six times in the New Testament.[3] There is no consensus on its meaning.

Sometimes it means "coming from the presence of the Lord" or "caused by the presence of the Lord," as in Jeremiah 4:26: "And all the cities were torn down by fire *from* the presence of the Lord."[4] The cities weren't torn down by fire because they were pushed away from the presence of the Lord. Instead, the fire *came from* the presence of the Lord and burned down the cities. Acts 3:19 is the clearest example in the New Testament: "Therefore repent and turn back, so that your sins may be wiped out, that seasons of refreshing may *come from* the presence of the Lord." God is the source and the cause of the seasons of refreshing. The phrase can refer to separation or away from,[5] or it can refer to coming from something as its origin and source, to cause something.

The Old Testament Background to 2 Thessalonians 1:9

Paul is probably relying on an Old Testament passage that uses similar terminology, words, and concepts: "From the presence of the fear of the Lord and from the glory of his power" (Isa. 2:10).[6] The only difference in Isaiah 2:10 is the phrase "of the fear." The Greek translation of Isaiah 2:10 and the Greek of 2 Thessalonians 1:9 are identical, letter for letter, word for word, except for the phrase "of the fear." Paul is likely leaning on Isaiah 2:10.

The context of Isaiah 2:10 appears to indicate that Isaiah did not mean "comes from" but "away from." The whole verse says, "Go into the rocks and hide in the dust from the terror of the LORD and from His majesty splendor."

---

[2] Thanks to Amber O'Brien for pointing this out to me.

[3] The six times are: Acts 3:20; 5:41; 7:45; 2 Thess 1:9; Rev 6:6; 12:14. Unfortunately, none of the other uses are Pauline, and they are all in a different genre. This should be kept in mind as the texts are examined.

[4] Author's translation of the Septuagint.

[5] Besides 2 Thessalonians 1:9 and Acts 3:20, the other four uses probably communicate the idea of separation. However, the only text that contained the exact phrase as in 2 Thessalonians was Acts 3:20.

[6] Author's translation of the Septuagint.

They are hiding from God, separating themselves from God, as much as they can because they are scared of the coming judgment. This is why some scholars have pointed to the parallel of Isaiah 2:10 as evidence that Paul was communicating the concept of separation.

However, the larger context of Isaiah 2 makes clear why they are separating from the presence of the Lord. Three times the chapter says they separated themselves from the presence of the Lord (verses 10, 19, and 21). But why are they doing that? The Lord's majestic splendor is the source and cause of their coming destruction. Isaiah 2 explains that we do not want to be near the Lord's majestic splendor because it will destroy us. So the punishment in Isaiah 2 is not that they are separated from the Lord but that the Lord's presence and his majestic splendor are going to destroy them. Paul references the context of Isaiah 2 to say that the power and the presence of God destroy the unconverted.[7] They are not being cast away from God's presence; they are hiding from Him.

The Context of 2 Thessalonians 1:9

The same conclusion could be arrived at by paying close attention to the context of 2 Thessalonians 1:9. Verses 7–8 say, "This will take place at the revelation of the Lord Jesus from heaven with His powerful angels, taking vengeance with flaming fire on those who don't know God and on those who don't obey the gospel of our Lord Jesus." Paul says (in verse 8) that the revelation of Jesus (his presence) is going to deal out vengeance or punishment to those who do not follow him. This is the context leading up to verse 9: Jesus is going to punish. It would be easy to mistake verse 9 as a new sentence and a new thought because most of the translations have put a period at the end of verse 8. However, the Greek text only has a comma, indicating that the editors take this as a continuing thought.[8] Jesus is still the one doing the action, and Jesus is actively punishing the persecutors of the Christians at Thessalonica. That idea fits much better with the presence and power of God being the source of the punishment rather than the removal of God's presence and power. If the whole context is about Jesus coming to punish, it doesn't fit well contextually to say that the punishment is "removal." Instead, it makes more sense to say Jesus is coming to punish, and when He comes, *that coming* will be the punishment.

In 2 Thessalonians 2:8 (only a few sentences later), Paul is still discussing the return of the Lord (like 1:9) and the impact of that on the wicked. The main difference is that the identity of the wicked has changed from 1:9 to 2:8, from persecutors of Thessalonians (1:9) to the man of lawlessness (2:8): "And then

---

[7]   A study of the phrase "the glory of his power" also shows a connection between the Hebrew word for "glory" in Isaiah 2:10 and coming judgment.

[8]   This is closer to the Tyndale New Testament (no separator) and the KJV (a colon).

the lawless one will be revealed. The Lord Jesus will destroy him with the breath of His mouth and will bring him to nothing with the brightness of His coming." While the words are not identical, the concepts are the same. Both refer to the idea of destruction; the concept of the appearance of his coming and his glorious strength are also somewhat similar. But more importantly, Paul communicates that the destruction in 2:8 comes with or by the breath of God's mouth. The presence of God in 2:8 is the cause and source of the destruction. It's not because of the absence of God but his presence. In 2:8 Paul is communicating the same concept as in 1:9: the presence of God causes destruction upon the wicked.

Conclusion

The common understanding of hell as the absence of God[9] sounds appealing because it seems to clean God's hands of being directly involved in punishing the wicked. Many Christians like the idea that God is loving, but the idea that He is actively involved in punishing people in hell can make some uncomfortable. That is why they propose that God would never be "in" hell. Psalm 139:7–8 says, "Where can I go to escape Your Spirit? Where can I flee from Your presence? If I go up to heaven, You are there; if I make my bed in Sheol, You are there." There is nowhere you can go and be outside of God's presence; there is no place where God is absent; so God cannot be absent in hell. While hell is not separation from an omnipresent God, it is "the negation of fellowship with the Lord."[10]

We must be careful not to downplay God's holiness and justice. God does love, but his love is a holy, righteous, and just love. It would be accurate to say that God is *not* a loving God, a holy God, or a just God—he is love, he is holiness, he is justice. These are not attributes that merely *describe* him; they flow *from* him.

Hell is a horrible place. One reason to avoid hell is because God *is there*. We do not want to be in the place where he is pouring out his wrath upon the wicked. It isn't the absence of God that makes hell so hellish; it is the presence of a just, holy, and jealous God. While it may be valid to say that hell is the separation from God's love, it is not biblical to say it is the absence of God.

---

[9] Other verses that could be used to advocate an "absence from God" view of hell that cannot be covered here include Matthew 8:12; 22:13; 25:30.

[10] J. I. Packer, "What Is Hell?" (video) *Between Two Worlds* (June 23, 2014), accessed June 23, 2014, www.thegospelcoalition.org/blogs/justintaylor/2014/06/23/what-is-hell.

Annotated Bibliography

Commentaries

Green, Gene L. *The Letters to the Thessalonians*. PNTC. Grand Rapids: Eerdmans, 2002.
    This is a fairly accessible work, though technical language is used at points, and a general knowledge of Greek is assumed.

Journals

Quarles, Charles L. "The ΑΠΟ of 2 Thessalonians 1:9 and the Nature of Eternal Punishment." *Westminster Theological Journal* 59 (1997): 201–11.
    This is the best work on this topic hands down. It is fairly academic, but it is a vital read for anyone wanting to know more about this *legend*.

CHAPTER 31

A Divorced Man Cannot Be a Pastor

1 Timothy 3:2

The Legendary Teaching on 1 Timothy 3:2

When Paul lists the qualifications for someone to be a pastor, he says something that is offensive to American culture today. Paul wrote in 1 Timothy 3:2, "An overseer, therefore, must be above reproach, the husband of one wife." If a man has been divorced and then gets remarried, he is the husband of two wives: the first wife he divorced and now the second wife. God has strict requirements for  those who are going to be his full-time ministers. God wants only the best to be serving him in this role. This is the pattern from the Old Testament as well. Priests had many qualifications thrust upon them if they wanted to serve at the temple. Leviticus 21 says a priest could not shave his head or the edges of his beard. It says he cannot marry a prostitute or a nonvirgin, and it says he can't even marry a woman who has been divorced. Regardless of the circumstance of the person who was divorced, a priest was not allowed to marry her. The closest thing we have to a pastor in the Old Testament is the priest. In the same way God had higher standards for priests in the Old Testament, he has a higher standard for pastors in the New Testament. Pastors cannot ever have been divorced.

Introduction

While I was attending a church in North Carolina, a man applied for the position of associate pastor. Many years prior he got married while he was not a Christian, but then he turned from his sins and gave his life to Christ. His wife was displeased with this change in his life, and she started having multiple affairs; she eventually left him. He begged her to stay, but she left. He raised their kids by himself. About five years after she left him, he met someone else, and they got married. About two decades later he was applying for the position of associate pastor. He was a man who had an unbelieving wife have an affair while married to him and then abandon him. He married his second wife and had been faithful to her for over twenty years. Is he disqualified from being a pastor based on the phrase "the husband of one wife"? That is the question we are now asking.

A Closer Look

What is the meaning of the phrase "husband of one wife"? While there are many different interpretations, I think the best way to approach this text is to give six observations that summarize what the phrase *does* mean. At the same time these observations will respond to other interpretations. All six will be positive observations, and then at the end we will see how these six observations are responses to other interpretations.

1. *The qualification is about the present state, not the past.* Look at the list of qualifications for an elder in 1 Timothy 3: above reproach, husband of one wife, self-controlled, sensible, respectable, hospitable, able to teach, not addicted to wine, not a bully, gentle, not quarrelsome, not greedy, manages his household well, has his children under control, not a new convert, a good reputation. The verb that introduces this list says that he "must" meet these qualifications, and the Greek verb is in the present tense. While that most naturally leads to the thought that this list is talking about the present, that isn't the required understanding. In fact, it probably means it is simply a general command (as opposed to a specific command given for a specific context). But the list *itself* seems to indicate that it is a "here and now" list. Let's take a closer look at two examples to demonstrate that this is not talking about "have you ever" done something but about the present. The third qualification says an elder must be self-controlled. This word for *self-controlled* means "restrained in conduct" or "level-headed."[1] Does this mean a man seeking the office of elder who was known for being out of control in his college days is therefore disqualified ten, twenty, thirty, or forty years later? "Well, you were out of control when you were twenty. I know you are sixty now, but you *were* out of control back then!" What if he was unrestrained when he was seven or eight years old? Have you ever met a seven-year-old boy who was unrestrained? Better yet, have you ever met a seven-year-old boy who was self-controlled? That would be the shocker. Many seven- to ten-year-old boys have self-control issues. Does that mean

---

[1] BDAG, 672.

they are disqualified from ever being pastors? No, I don't think that was Paul's meaning because Paul was referring to the character during the time period the person is seeking the office of elder.

One more example: not a new convert. I think this qualification kind of "seals the deal" regarding Paul's talking about the present time period. Every Christian at some point was a new convert. Are all Christians therefore disqualified because at some point in their past they were new converts? No. Paul is talking about during the time period they are seeking the office of elder, not at a previous time. Go through the entire list and apply this same logic. The descriptions are all talking about the present state, not necessarily the past.

2. *Nearly all of the descriptions are about character qualities.* This list, for the most part, is describing a characteristic of the man seeking the office of elder. A few could be taken differently. The seventh qualification says, "an able teacher" (HCSB) or "able to teach" (ESV). I think that is the right way to translate the word. However, the ISV says "teachable." While that makes sense in this context, I am still convinced it means "able to teach" and that it is an exception on the list. The reason Paul included this noncharacter qualification is because of the role of someone serving as a pastor: they will frequently be teaching. Therefore, this is a skill or gift he wants to make sure all pastors have.

The fifteenth qualification is not exactly a character quality: not a new convert. However, Paul provides the reason for this qualification of an elder not being a new convert. He says in verse 6, "Or he might become conceited and fall into the condemnation of the Devil." The reason he does not want them to be new converts has to do with the idea of conceit or pride, which is connected to the concept of character.

While these two don't quite fit the character quality description, the other thirteen do. That leads me to conclude that the "husband of one wife" description would also most likely refer to the idea of character quality, a habit of someone's life, not necessarily something he did once or twice.

3. *All of the descriptions in 1 Timothy 3:2 are positive.* "An overseer, therefore, must be above reproach, the husband of one wife, self-controlled, sensible, respectable, hospitable, an able teacher." Those who understand the phrase "husband of one wife" as an expression that means "cannot have been divorced" understand it as a prohibition. But everything else in verse 2 is a positive characteristic required for those seeking the office of elder. Verse 2 has no prohibitions. So understanding the husband of one wife as a prohibition for divorce would be taking the phrase differently from all the other characteristics and qualifications in verse 2. It would be a little unnatural in the context of the verse.

4. *Prohibitions in this list are preceded by the word "not."* Paul did provide some prohibitions. He said in the following verse, "Not addicted to wine, not

a bully but gentle, not quarrelsome, not greedy" (1 Tim 3:3). Notice that each time a description is something negative, something an elder *can't* be, it is preceded by the word *not*. And the pattern continues throughout the passage. Further down Paul adds, "Not . . . a new convert" (v. 6). So the pattern in this context indicates that if Paul were going to say an elder can't be divorced, he would have said "not divorced."

5. *The parallel with 1 Timothy 5:9 should be instructive for how we interpret the phrase in 1 Timothy 3:2.* First Timothy 5:9 is helpful in determining the meaning of "husband of one wife" in 1 Timothy 3:2. The literal translation of "husband of one wife" is "one-woman man," and in 1 Timothy 5:9 Paul says that a widow who wants to be put on the list to receive support from the church must be a "one-man woman." The same three Greek words are used in the phrases. So whatever the phrase means in 5:9, it is going to have basically the same meaning in 3:2, except one is talking about a wife, and the other is talking about a husband. One of the ways this phrase has been understood is that an elder cannot remarry after his wife dies because then he will have been the husband of two wives. However, notice what Paul says in 1 Timothy 5:14: "Therefore, I want younger women to marry, have children." Why would Paul tell younger widows to marry, to do something that was possibly going to disqualify them from ever receiving aid from the church if they became a widow again later in life? If there is something inherently wrong or sinful about remarrying after your spouse dies, why would Paul tell younger widows to do it? That interpretation does not make sense in the context of 1 Timothy. This leads right into observation 6.

6. *Polyandry was uncommon.* Polygamy is having more than one wife at one time. Polyandry is having more than one husband at one time. Some people think the phrase "husband of one wife" refers to a prohibition against polygamy. But that would mean the phrase "wife of one husband" in 1 Timothy 5:9 is a prohibition against polyandry. Polyandry was uncommon in the first century both in the Jewish and Greco-Roman societies.[2] Why would Paul put on this list for widows a qualification that was so rare people might not have known anyone who would have been disqualified by it? It would be an odd thing to have on the list. Therefore, the phrase "husband of one wife" is probably not intended to be a prohibition against polygamy as its primary meaning.

The Meaning of the Phrase

Those are the six observations about the phrase "husband of one wife," but what is the actual meaning of the phrase? Let's talk about idioms. An idiom

---

[2] For example, see Craig Keener, *And Marries Another* (Grand Rapids: Baker, 1991), 90.

is a combination of words forming a meaning that is distinct from the literal meaning of the words and instead forms a figurative meaning of the words. A few years ago I took my family to a Chinese restaurant, and my daughter opened a fortune cookie with these words: "Keep your feet on the ground even though friends flatter you." My daughter was about six years old at the time. She read it and got a puzzled look on her face. Then she looked at me and said, "What does this mean?" I told her, as best I could in six-year-old terminology, that it meant she should have a realistic understanding of herself. And she said, "But I have to keep my feet on the ground, right?" She was looking for the literal meaning, the literal sense. She thought it was saying it was wrong to get on an airplane, or to jump, or to sleep on her bunk bed. She thought she literally needed to *keep her feet on the ground*. She didn't understand the idea of an idiom.

Sometimes you will hear a preacher do this when trying to explain a passage of Scripture. He will say, "This is an idiom," explain the idiom, and then say, "But the literal meaning is . . ." Then he will go through the words and tear apart the idiom. Imagine doing this to the idiom: "It's raining cats and dogs." Do you understand the idiom better by analyzing every single word and interpreting it literally? Or do you understand it better as a phrase that means it is raining hard? The phrase "husband of one wife" is an idiom. So what we are looking for is an interpretation of this phrase that refers to the present, has to do with the idea of character, is a positive description, not a prohibition, and that can match up with the parallel in 1 Timothy 5:9. The interpretation should match up with *all* those observations.

One of the common understandings of this phrase is that a pastor must be married. But being married is not a character quality. So that's not what this phrase is talking about. Other interpreters have suggested it means a widower can't get remarried. But this is not a character quality. It is not a positive description but a prohibition. A more common interpretation is that it means an elder can only be married once with no divorce before his conversion to Christ. But that would be a reference to the past, not the present, and it is not a character quality. Also, it would be a prohibition, not a positive description. Another common interpretation is that an elder can only be married once with no divorce after his conversion to Christ. But this has the same problems as the previous interpretation. Another popular understanding is that an elder cannot be a polygamist. But not being polygamous is not necessarily a character quality. It is also a prohibition, not a positive description, and it does not parallel 1 Timothy 5:9 at all. So what is left?

The faithful spouse view. This view states that the husband in 1 Timothy 3:2 must be a faithful spouse. Faithfulness is an important characteristic in ministry, and Paul is stating that being an unfaithful spouse means you are disqualified. This view refers to the present and is a reference to character. It is positive, not a prohibition, and it parallels 1 Timothy 5:9 perfectly, the idea that if a widow wanted to be put on the list she must have been a faithful spouse to her husband.

Some people have objected that this is a lowering of the qualification for a pastor. If the phrase means "never divorced," then realize that a man who struggles with lust or pornography, or someone who has even had an affair, would not be disqualified because of the phrase "husband of one wife" if the phrase means "never been divorced." But if it is a reference to "faithful character," then if someone's character is defined by lustful thinking or indulging in pornography, that person would be disqualified even if he never acted on it in an affair. If a man decides to divorce his wife because he just wants another spouse, then he is unfaithful. He would be disqualified not because he has been divorced but because he was unfaithful to his spouse.

In brief, I believe Scripture teaches two acceptable reasons for divorce: adultery (sexual unfaithfulness) and abandonment. Those are the two reasons that could render someone the innocent party, and they could still be considered a faithful spouse even though they've been divorced. The adulterer or the one who abandoned the innocent person is the unfaithful spouse. So the specifics of the situation are important.[3]

What if someone was the guilty party twenty years ago, but for the last fifteen years has been faithful. Then what do you do? The question is: does he have the character of being a faithful spouse, not has he *always* had that character trait. The question is does he *now*? So let's return to the man that I mentioned earlier. His wife was unfaithful to him, she abandoned him, he remarried five years later and had a twenty-year track record of faithfulness. Everything I saw in that man's life showed me he was a faithful spouse. He demonstrated it for over two decades. Whether he was or wasn't faithful twenty years earlier is not the most relevant issue. The question is this: is this man's life characterized by faithfulness to his wife or not? In this situation, yes, he has been faithful for many years so I believe he is qualified to be a pastor.

Application

We can apply this teaching in three relevant ways. First, do not treat those who have been divorced like they have committed the unpardonable sin. The evangelical church in America has been guilty of this from time to time. I have

---

[3] This is obviously a complicated issue with many differing interpretations. For a great brief overview of the debate, see Andreas J. Köstenberger, with David W. Jones, "Separating What God Has Joined Together," in *God, Family, and Marriage: Rebuilding the Biblical Foundation*, 2nd ed. (Wheaton: Crossway, 2010), 223–38.

heard some horrific stories of people who have been divorced and the way they were treated. They may have been the innocent party, but even if they were not, it is *not* the unpardonable sin. Second, do not limit the office of pastor to those who have never been divorced—at least not based on the phrase "husband of one wife." You may have some other arguments, but as far as this phrase goes, it does not limit the office of pastor to someone who has not been divorced. A divorced man could be a pastor if he has the present characteristic of faithfulness to his spouse according to 1 Timothy 3:2. Third, make sure a pastoral candidate meets the qualification of faithfulness. I have known men who have had affairs for years and continue to serve as pastor, even though the church knows. They have been unfaithful to their wives continually, but people in the congregation don't realize he has been disqualified. So make sure that if someone desires to become a pastor he meets this qualification, that he is faithful to his spouse.

Annotated Bibliography

Commentaries

Lea, Thomas D., and Hayne P. Griffin Jr. *1, 2 Timothy, Titus*. NAC. Vol. 34. Nashville: B&H, 1992.

This is an accessible work written with both pastors and teachers in mind. The approach of this volume is to treat the exegetical issues within an intentionally theologically conservative framework.

Mounce, William. *Pastoral Epistles*. WBC. Nashville: Thomas Nelson, 2000.

As with the rest in the Word Biblical Commentary series, this book is highly technical and comprehensive and written with the scholar in mind.

Journals

Doriani, Daniel M. "The Profile of a Pastor: A Sermon Based on 1 Timothy 3:1–7." *Presbyterion* 19, no. 2 (1993): 67–76.

As the title suggests, it is written for a broad audience and footnotes are few. The Greek text is set in parentheses without transliteration.

Glasscock, Ed. "'The Husband of One Wife' Requirement in 1 Timothy 3:2." *Bibliotheca Sacra* 140 (1983): 244–58.

Glasscock provides an academic yet accessible survey of the interpretations of this passage. He treats the Greek as if the reader has a fundamental grasp of it; aside from this the article is accessible to most audiences.

Owens, Mark D. "Should Churches Ordain the Divorced and Remarried? An Examination of Μιᾶς Γυναικὸς Ἀνήρ in the Pastoral Epistles." *Faith & Mission* 22, no. 3 (2005): 42–50.

Owens assumes a working knowledge of Greek.

Books

Köstenberger, Andreas J., with David W. Jones. "Faithful Husbands: Qualifications for Church Leadership." Pages 239–48 in *God, Family, and Marriage: Rebuilding the Biblical Foundation*. 2nd ed. Wheaton: Crossway, 2010.

Websites

Anyabwile, Thabiti. "Finding Reliable Men: One Woman Man." *Pure Church*. October 8, 2007. Accessed June 23, 2014. www.thegospelcoalition.org/blogs/thabitianyabwile/2007/10/08/finding-reliable-men-one-woman-man.

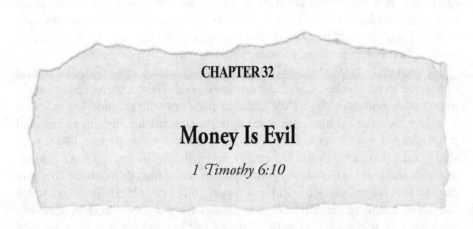

CHAPTER 32

Money Is Evil

1 Timothy 6:10

The Legendary Teaching on 1 Timothy 6:10

We live in a society obsessed with money and material possessions. Idolatry for money is not new, but society has taken it to new heights. The apostle Paul, being aware of the danger of money, told Timothy that "money is . . . evil" (1 Tim 6:10). Jesus himself said you cannot serve God and money (Matt 6:24). Money is put in contrast to God because God is holy and money is evil. So we need to avoid this danger at all costs as Christians, or we will suffer the perils associated with it.

Introduction: A Balanced View on Money

Evidence that this misquotation of Paul made its way into American culture can be seen in the song by the Andrews Sisters called "Money Is the Root of All Evil."[1] Christians need a balanced view of money. When thinking about money, we should avoid two polar extremes. The first extreme is that those who are truly spiritual and live holy lives will be rich. This teaching has manifested itself in a bold way today through the "prosperity gospel."[2] Teachers of the prosperity gospel believe God wants all of his children to be rich and healthy. Any problems with money or health can be traced to sin. This is horrible heresy. Nowhere does Scripture say God wants all his children to be rich. The Bible even has warnings to the rich (see 1 Tim 6:17–19). The second

---

[1] Released in 1946 and featured in the film *High Time* starring Bing Crosby. Thanks to Bob Rencher for pointing this out to me.

[2] For a great refutation of this heresy, see David W. Jones and Russell S. Woodbridge, *Health, Wealth and Happiness: Has the Prosperity Gospel Overshadowed the Gospel of Christ?* (Grand Rapids: Kregel, 2011).

extreme is that those who are truly spiritual and live holy lives will be poor, selling all they have and giving it to the poor. Christian ascetics are an example of this. There may not be many around today, but throughout Christian history some believers have refused to accumulate any worldly possessions.

Between these two extremes is the Bible. God allows some Christians to be rich, some to be middle class, and some to be poor. The concern of Scripture is not whether you are rich, middle class, or poor but your attitude toward what you have. Scripture is also concerned with the stewardship of your money and possessions. I read a sermon by a British preacher from the late 1800s who said good Christian stewardship entails doing the following: take out a piece of paper and make a list of everything you own and then think about how you can use that for the glory of God and serving other people. He gave examples like using a sewing machine to make clothes for the poor. Good stewardship is viewing your possessions at the disposal of God and not just for your own selfish desires and pleasures. The rich, middle class, and poor can all have a bad attitude about wealth, viewing their money and possessions selfishly. People from any economic status can have a sinful love of money that leads to their spiritual destruction. Within this theological context of money and possessions, we encounter 1 Timothy 6:10.

What Does 1 Timothy 6:10 Actually Say?

When someone quotes or paraphrases Scripture and it sounds different than what you remember, make sure you look it up in the Bible. I had a friend say to me that money is evil: "Even Paul said so!"

I replied, "You should probably look up that verse before citing it again." He had no idea where the verse was! The next day we were talking, and he said, "You're right, it doesn't say 'money is evil'; it says 'the love of money is evil.'"

I said, "Are you sure?" He said he was, but he was *surely* wrong.

The difference between "money is evil" and "the love of money is evil" is significant. When people say, "The love of money is evil," they are communicating that loving money is a sin in and of itself. They are declaring that we should not place our affections in something like money. Instead, our affections should be directed toward God. Those are good thoughts. But that is still not what the verse says. Paul did not say the love of money is evil, but, "For the love of money is a root of all kinds of evil, and by craving it, some have wandered away from the faith and pierced themselves with many pains" (1 Timothy 6:10). The text says that the love of money is a *root* of different kinds of evils.

The word *root* can refer to the part of a plant that is underground. However, this use is a figurative extension of the literal meaning. It refers to the reason or cause of something.³ When people have a love of money, it can be a reason or cause for sin. The basic idea is that many kinds of evils can be motivated by a love for money.⁴

The word *for* begins the verse because Paul is explaining in verse 10 something he said in verse 9: "But those who want to be rich fall into temptation, a trap, and many foolish and harmful desires, which plunge people into ruin and destruction." He doesn't say, "Those who are rich are sinful," or "Those who are rich will be destroyed." Instead Paul focuses on the *desire* to be rich. Being rich is not condemned. Paul is talking about the desire for riches because it leads to many different kinds of temptations: the desire to be rich leads to the desire for money. That is the connection between these two verses.

If you desire to be rich, that is going to lead to a love for money, and that is going to motivate all kinds of evils in your life. What kind of danger lies ahead for those who love money? Paul says some have abandoned Christianity because of their love for money. The main point in this passage is that many kinds of sins will be connected to someone who loves money.⁵

Application

The love for money can be connected to different sins. One of the main things that causes discord in marriages is money. For example, couples may have difficulty communicating about money, or they might have different priorities in spending money. Money conflict is one of the biggest destroyers of marriage. If one partner loves money more than he or she loves the other partner, that is going to create a huge problem. A love for money will drive injustice in our society. Prostitution and sex trafficking in the United States is (at least partly) driven by a love for money. One of the reasons the entertainment industry puts so much sexual immorality in movies is because sex sells tickets. The love of money is driving immorality in movies.

The main issue to focus on when it comes to the love of money is the sin of stinginess. I was listening to a radio show and a financial advisor was taking phone calls. A man, about fifty years old, called up and said, "I have been following the principles you teach for years. Before you were on the radio, I was doing these things. And my wife and I are very frugal. We put away just about everything we can."

The radio host asked him, "How much money do you make a year?"

---

³ See Louw and Nida, 89.17.

⁴ See Daniel B. Wallace, *Greek Grammar Beyond the Basics: An Exegetical Syntax of the Greek New Testament* (Grand Rapids: Zondervan, 1996), 265.

⁵ Similar thoughts concerning the love of money can be seen in Hebrews 13:5 and Ecclesiastes 5:10.

He said, "About fifty thousand dollars."

"Well how much money does your wife make?"

He said, "She stays at home." The radio host then asked how much they had saved. The man said, "About 1.5 million dollars." The radio host thought that was great. But the man said: "The problem is that we are having a hard time giving. We don't want to be generous with the church or with our children or with anyone. We have this mentality of hoarding money, and now we can't be generous with it."

The radio host ignored his concern and said, "But you saved 1.5 million! Great job!" This man was in the midst of confessing his love for money, and he was being praised for it! His love for money was preventing him from obeying Scripture's commands on giving, and he was confessing this on the radio. So much more money could be given to missions if we were released from the love of money and were more generous in giving. We cannot truly say that we love God with all our heart, soul, strength, and mind, but have a love for money that usurps God himself.

Be warned that just because someone has a lot of money doesn't mean they love it. Some people have a knack for making money easily. Some people are rich because they love money, and some are poor because they love money. Don't look at people's financial situation and judge them. That reflects more on your heart and probably your desire for riches than anything else.

Avoid the love for money. Stay away from that temptation. One of the best ways to flee from the temptation to love money is to be generous in giving, which can be freeing as it fights back against the love for money and a desire to have security through money.

Annotated Bibliography

Commentaries

Köstenberger, Andreas J. "1 Timothy." In *Ephesians–Philemon*. EBC. Revised ed. Edited by Tremper Longman III and David E. Garland. Grand Rapids: Zondervan, 2006.

An easy-to-read commentary, briefly giving insights on the biblical text. See especially pages 554–55.

Books

Blomberg, Craig L. *Christians in an Age of Wealth*. Biblical Theology for Life. Grand Rapids: Zondervan, 2013.

Blomberg briefly summarizes the issues involved in interpreting this verse, explicitly pointing out that the legendary understanding is wrong. See page 92.

Websites

Armstrong, John H. "Can Money Buy Happiness? The Real Answer Might Surprise You." *Act 3 Network*. March 3, 2014. Accessed July 12, 2014. www.johnharmstrong. com/?p=6195.
Some interesting and helpful thoughts on this verse.

CHAPTER 33

A Pastor's Children Must Be Saved

Titus 1:6

The Legendary Teaching on Titus 1:6

We have a huge problem in our churches: men who are clearly unqualified to serve as pastors. First Timothy 3 and Titus 1 both list the qualifications for being a pastor. And if someone does not meet these qualifications, it is improper and unbiblical for them to serve in this way. One verse in particular illustrates the dire situation our churches are in with these unqualified men leading them: "If anyone is above reproach, the husband of one wife, and his children are believers and not open to the charge of debauchery or insubordination" (Titus 1:6 ESV). This verse has five requirements to be a pastor, but I want to focus on one: "his children are believers." This phrase automatically disqualifies anyone from being a pastor if they have a child who is not a Christian. Why would Paul say you can't be a pastor if your children aren't saved? Because pastors are supposed to lead by example. If you put a man in the position of leading a church and his children are not saved, then you are communicating that evangelizing your children must not be that important because it's not that important to him. Also, if this man truly did meet all the other qualifications listed in Titus 1 and 1 Timothy 3, why are his children not saved? Maybe he is actually a different person in his home than he is in public. Maybe when the doors to his house are closed, he is quick to be angry. Paul put this qualification here for a reason, and as Bible-believing Christians we need to obey the Scripture and all its commands.

Introduction: Unraveling the Legend

Several Bible translations besides the ESV indicate that a pastor's children must be saved (see below). Trying to follow all of Scripture's teachings is admirable; I fully commend that attempt. I know of a church that included in their constitution a clause that stated if a pastor's child turned thirteen and they had not made a profession of faith, then the pastor must step down from his office. I was at the church when one of the pastor's kids turned thirteen and had not made a profession of faith. He quietly stepped down from his position. His daughter, who was not a Christian at that point, had no clue that her father was stepping down from being a pastor because she wasn't saved. It was low-key. About one year after that happened, she did make a profession of faith and experienced an amazing transformation. It was a great testimony of someone trying to live out what they thought was the correct interpretation of Titus 1:6. I heartily commend living out the commands we see in Scripture. However, I believe this particular application was a misinterpretation of Titus 1:6.

NASB	"having children who believe"
NIV	"a man whose children believe"
NLT	"his children must be believers"

The Parallel Passage to Titus 1:6: 1 Timothy 3:4–5

Before we dig deeper into Titus 1:6, read the parallel passage in 1 Timothy 3:4–5: "One who manages his own household competently, having his children under control with all dignity. (If anyone does not know how to manage his own household, how will he take care of God's church?)" Verse 4 begins by explaining the underlying principle to a man's relationship with his children and how it relates to being qualified as a pastor: he must manage his household well. The verb translated as *manage* means "to so influence others as to cause them to follow a recommended course of action" and "to guide, to direct, to lead."[1] It can be easy to stand up and tell others what they should do. But an effective leader is successful in exhorting others to do what they think is right, wise, and biblical—in other words, an effective leader. When he exhorts his followers to do something, they typically do it. He doesn't have to be perfect but competent, which here means a "high standard of excellence."[2]

That is what happens with good leadership. You give advice, you exhort, and followers give heed to it—not every time but characteristically. Notice the rhetorical question in verse 5, "If anyone does not know how to manage his own household, how will he take care of God's church?" Paul is expecting his readers to recognize that if someone is a poor leader in his house, he will be a

---

[1] Louw and Nida, 36.1.
[2] BDAG, 505.

poor leader in God's house. Being a good leader in the home is the "training ground"[3] for being a good leader in the church.

In the description of children in this passage, Paul tells Timothy that a pastor's children must be under control with all dignity. "Under control" translates a phrase that means "in submission" or "in obedience."[4] The idea is that they should be generally submissive, obedient children. Again, this is not a call for perfection; it does not mean a man is not qualified to be a pastor if his child is periodically rebellious. The question is: what is the pattern of the child's life? Are his children characteristically obedient and submissive, or are they typically challenging the authority of their father, and are they disobedient? The idea of "with all dignity" is that the father takes the task of leading his family seriously.[5] When you analyze some of these qualifications, it is a pretty high standard. Many fathers might have their children under control, but that doesn't necessarily mean it is because of the father, does it? Another parent is involved in the process: the mother. If the father does not take the task of parenting seriously, that is a problem. And many men could have wonderful children because their wives are spectacular. That does not mean they are necessarily qualified if they don't take the task of parenting seriously.

Nothing in Paul's letter to Timothy about the qualifications of an elder states that the children must be saved. Now let's return to Titus 1:6.

Titus 1:6 Examined

The ESV says, "His children are believers," but a footnote in the ESV says, "Or *are faithful*." In other words, this is another way this verse could be translated. That would change the meaning significantly! So the translators of the ESV recognized that this phrase could be understood in two ways. Notice some other translations of Titus 1:6. I mentioned above three translations that agree with the main text of the ESV, but the KJV, NKJV, and HCSB translate this as "having faithful children," and the NET Bible is similar: "with faithful children." The translations are fairly divided. The HCSB also has a footnote saying, "Or *believing*." They basically did the opposite of the ESV. They put "faithful" in the text and in the footnote put "believing," while the ESV put "believers" in the text and in the footnote put "are faithful." Why have some translations gone with "faithful" rather than "believers"?

---

[3] John R. W. Stott, *Guard the Truth: The Message of 1 Timothy and Titus* (Downers Grove: InterVarsity, 1996), 98.

[4] Cf. Louw and Nida, 36.18

[5] See Thomas D. Lea and Hayne P. Griffin, *1, 2 Timothy, Titus*, NAC (Nashville: B&H, 1992), 112.

The Greek word translated in this verse has two primary meanings: (1) trust-worthy or faithful, and (2) trusting or one who trusts, like a believer.[6] A few verses later Paul uses the same Greek word to mean "faithful" or "trustworthy": "Holding to the *faithful* message as taught" (Titus 1:9, emphasis added). Also in 1 Timothy 3:11, in another passage dealing with qualifications, this same Greek word is used, and it means "faithful:" "*faithful* in everything" (1 Tim 3:11, emphasis added). Finally, in 1 Timothy 6 that same word means "believ-ing": "Those who have *believing* masters" (1 Tim 6:2, emphasis added). The word can have either meaning, and that is why the translations are wrestling with how to translate it. The question is not, what *can* it mean? The question is, what *does* it mean in Titus 1:6? The Greek provides these two options, but other factors are going to have to help us reach a confident decision.

The context in Titus 1 is fairly ambiguous because it is simply a list of quali-fications. It's not a story being told that can help us know whether the descrip-tion is of those who are Christians or those who are faithful. We don't have enough of a context when we have only a list of descriptions since it is an *ambiguous context*, we need to rely on something else beside the immediate literary context to figure out what the word means.

Returning to the Parallel: A Closer Look

Therefore, let's compare Titus 1:6 to 1 Timothy 3:4, because they contain similar statements. The literal translations of the opening of each of these phrases is essentially the same because they contain the same Greek words: "having children" (the same verb for "having" and the same word for "chil-dren"). Since these two passages are similar, with the qualifications and the same Greek words introducing the clauses, it would be odd for the qualifica-tions to be significantly different. Think of it this way: why would Paul have a radically strict standard for Titus's context but then have a little more lenient standard for Timothy's context? Would anything in either Titus or 1 Timothy justify Paul's putting a different standard for Titus's church than the church addressed in 1 Timothy? I haven't found anything; I haven't seen any good arguments that have tried to answer that question.

Paul says the pastor's children must be submissive or obedient, under con-trol, and it gives no other clarification about the children in 1 Timothy 3:4. But in Titus 1:6, he uses a term that is admittedly vague, meaning either "faithful" or "believers." It is a term he uses with various meanings in different contexts. Therefore, since Paul used an ambiguous term in Titus 1:6, he clarified what he was looking for in pastors' children at the end of verse 6: "Children not

---

[6]   The Greek word is *pistos*; cf. BDAG, 820–21.

accused of wildness or rebellion." He wants to make sure the children are not involved in reckless behavior, a word typically translated as *debauchery* or *wildness*. The second description of the pastor's children is even more interesting. It referred to someone who was unable to be controlled.[7] It is usually translated with the words *rebellious* or *disobedient*. Does the idea of control sound familiar? Remember 1 Timothy 3:4: "Having his children under control"? It is not the same word, but it communicates the same concept.

If Paul were trying to say to Titus that pastors' children needed to be saved, I would have expected him to clarify this ambiguous Greek word differently, something like, "those who have experienced the washing of regeneration and renewal by the Holy Spirit." That is what Titus 3:5 says when it describes those who are saved. Instead, he describes rebellious, disobedient children clarifying what he meant by that ambiguous Greek word.

Application

One of the interesting things about the lists in Titus 1 and in 1 Timothy 3 is that the characteristics mentioned do not constitute what I would call a "super Christian." The lists actually describe what any Christian man should be with only one exception: the qualification of being "able to teach."[8] Even though the main intent of these passages is to explain the qualifications to be a pastor, it is still a great list for every man to look at and ask, "Do I meet these qualifications?" And if not, then maybe you need to work on that area some more.

Second, the main point of this passage is that pastors must meet these qualifications. One of the stereotypes in America of pastors' kids is that they are the worst children in the church. When I started going to church in high school, I learned quickly that pastors' kids had that reputation. This is a horrible stereotype! If a pastor has a child and that child is under his authority and is rebellious against the father's authority, some hard questions need to be asked of this man. I do recognize something could be physically or mentally wrong with a child that makes behavior appear rebellious. Many different aspects of the particular situation need to be considered. That is why *questions* need to be asked. But the questions, as hard, as awkward, and as painful as they may be, need to be addressed. Is this man qualified or not? The underlying principle Paul is getting at is about being a good leader people can follow. So if a man can't get his children to follow him, we should ask what is going on in the home that has caused this. We want to be careful that we don't quickly adopt a judgmental attitude, but we also want to be careful that we don't just ignore what this passage is teaching.

---

[7]   Cf. Louw and Nida, 37.32.

[8]   For more on this, see chapter 31.

Annotated Bibliography

Commentaries

Knight, George W., III. *The Pastoral Epistles: A Commentary on the Greek Text*. NIGTC. Grand Rapids: Eerdmans, 1992.

As with all commentaries in this series, this is a technical work focusing on the Greek text, and it assumes a working knowledge of the language.

Hendriksen, William, and Simon J. Kistemaker. *Exposition of Thessalonians, the Pastorals, and Hebrews*. New Testament Commentary. Grand Rapids: Baker, 2002.

This volume is accessible to a broad audience, from the educated layperson to the interested scholar. The Greek text is set off in parentheses so knowledge of Greek is not necessary for understanding the work.

Journal Articles

Grubbs, Norris. "The Truth About Elders and Their Children: Believing or Behaving in Titus 1:6?" *Faith & Mission* 22, no. 2 (2005): 3–15.

Grubbs reviews the evidence for both primary positions. This article assumes a working knowledge of the Greek language and evaluates the evidence in a technical manner; the article is therefore accessible to anyone with a basic knowledge of Greek.

Websites

Taylor, Justin. "Unbelief in an Elder's Children." *Desiring God*. February 1, 2007. Accessed June 23, 2014. www.desiringgod.org/articles/unbelief-in-an-elders-children.

_____. "You Asked: Does an Unbelieving Child Disqualify an Elder?" *The Gospel Coalition: Bible and Theology*. November 2, 2011. Accessed June 23, 2014. www. thegospelcoalition.org/article/you-asked-does-an-unbelieving-child-disqualify-an-elder.

CHAPTER 34

Christians Are Commanded to Tithe

Hebrews 7:1–10

The Legendary Teaching on Hebrews 7:1–10

Some Christians are living in disobedience because of their selfishness. They refuse to give God what is required. They refuse to meet the biblical standard of giving: a tithe. The word *tithe* means 10 percent, so Christians are required to give 10 percent of their income to the local church. Some people use the excuse that to require tithing is legalistic, but tithing actually began before the Mosaic law was given in Genesis 14:18–20. Furthermore, the author of the letter to the Hebrews used the Genesis passage to advocate tithing. He retells the story of Abraham giving Melchizedek 10 percent "of everything" (Heb 7:2). Then he reminds his readers that the people of Israel were required to give a tithe to the descendants of Levi. The key verse is 7:8: "In the one case tithes are received by mortal men, but in the other case, by one of whom it is testified that he lives" (ESV). The "mortal men" who received tithes were the Levites. The phrase "he lives" (7:8) is a direct reference to Christians giving their tithes to Jesus Christ.

Introduction: Unraveling the Legend

I was talking with a friend who had two master's degrees from seminary, and the issue of tithing came up. When I mentioned that tithing referred to giving 10 percent, he objected: "No, *tithing* just means 'to give.'" After several minutes he calmed down and realized that he was mistaken: *tithe* means "10 percent."[1] Determining whether Christians are required to tithe is not the exact purpose of this chapter. Rather, the question is whether Hebrews 7 requires Christians to tithe.

The Context of Hebrews 7

Hebrews 7:1–10 is a great text to practice sound principles of biblical interpretation. First, seeking the author's intent must always precede attempting to apply a passage. Second, the primary meaning of a passage needs to be the focus of interpretation. While secondary or tertiary meanings can be identified and interesting, they should not be the focus of the interpretation. Third, the interpreter must remember that only primary meanings build doctrine. If a text has an implication (a secondary meaning) that appears to support a certain doctrine, a separate text should be located that has that doctrine as its primary meaning. Then the secondary meaning can be used to validate the text that has that doctrine as its primary meaning.

Placing Hebrews 7:1–10 into the context of the argument of the entire letter will greatly benefit the interpretation process. The author of Hebrews explained that Jesus' sacrifice is superior to the sacrifices of the Mosaic covenant. Because of this, the Jews should not turn back to their former ways. The argument of Hebrews has several aspects to it.[2] After demonstrating that Jesus is superior to the angels (even though He was temporarily made lower than them [2:7]), the author then shows that Jesus' priesthood was superior to the Levitical priesthood. Based on Psalm 110:4, Jesus' and Melchizedek's priesthood are shown to be of the same kind. Since Melchizedek's priesthood was already demonstrated to be superior to the Levitical priesthood, Jesus' priesthood must also be superior to the Levitical priesthood. *Hebrews 7:1–10 demonstrates that Melchizedek's priesthood is superior to the Levitical priesthood*. That is the main point.

A Closer Look at Hebrews 7:1–10

Hebrews 7:1–10 can be broken into two sections: verses 1–3 say that Melchizedek remains a priest forever; verses 4–10 provide the proof of his superior priesthood. Three proofs are offered. First, Melchizedek is greater than Abraham because Abraham gave him an offering (v. 4). This is the central argument of the three. Second, Melchizedek is greater because he blessed Abraham (v. 7). The

---

[1] Note that just because the English word *tithe* means "10 percent" does not mean Scripture defines a *tithe* as "10 percent of income." Analyzing Scripture on tithing yields a different definition of this concept.

[2] This analysis is somewhat dependent on G. H. Guthrie, *The Structure of Hebrews: A Text-Linguistic Analysis* (New York: Brill, 1994).

third argument needs a little historical background. Levitical priests typically served only after they reached a certain age (twenty, twenty-five, or thirty— depending on the source consulted). After a certain age they stopped ministering. Eventually, of course, they would die. Now for the third argument: while Abraham's descendants paid tithes to priests who would die, Abraham paid his tithe to a priest who lives on—Melchizedek (v. 8). Therefore, since Melchizedek was able to perform the functions of a priest without having Levitical lineage, Jesus is also able to be a priest without the necessary lineage.

The one theological truth the author intended is this: *Melchizedek was greater than Abraham and thus greater than the Levitical priests*. Hebrews 7:1–10 is a stepping stone to 8:1–2, which proclaims that Jesus, a superior high priest, rendered a superior sacrifice. This is the author's primary meaning and what he intended to communicate.

Responding to the Legend

The argument for tithing from this passage usually focuses on Hebrews 7:8. Is the "he" in 7:8 a reference to Jesus? Some people have claimed that, concluding that Jesus is proclaimed to have received tithes. However, the word *he* does not occur in the Greek. It is implied in the Greek but *not* stated. Furthermore, the implied "he" (or "one") is not a reference to Christ but to Melchizedek. The author did not turn his attention to Jesus until verse 11. Everything before that is about Melchizedek. The contrast in verse 8 is between Levitical priests who received tithes and died and Melchizedek who received tithes but never died.

A second argument states that since Melchizedek's priesthood is greater than the Levitical priesthood, and Melchizedek is a picture of Christ, then Abraham must be a picture of Christians giving tithes to Christ. Typically neglected in this line of argumentation are the inconsistencies between Abraham's actions in tithing and what these advocates teach today. First, Abraham gave voluntarily while many preachers today claim the tithe is mandatory. Nothing in Scripture states that Abraham was commanded to tithe. Second, Abraham's tithe (of the spoils) was a response of thanksgiving to God for victory in war. The requirement for giving on the spoils of war in the Mosaic law was different (see Num 31:27–29). Finally, and primarily, the author of Hebrews was not arguing for the continuation of tithing in the new covenant. Whether tithing was required for Christians is completely irrelevant to the argument the author is making. Hebrews 7 functions as an illustration to demonstrate the superiority of Melchizedek's priesthood over the Levitical priesthood. New Testament scholar Paul Ellingworth concludes, "Abraham's action is unrelated to the later

Mosaic legislation on tithes . . . and this is not Hebrews' concern."[3] To prove tithing from the New Testament, a passage must be produced that has as its *primary* purpose to advocate tithing.

Application

Christians should give generously and sacrificially to their local churches. Many principles in Scripture support this claim. However, a mandated 10 percent cannot be proved from Hebrews 7.

Hebrews 7:1–10 provides the theological undergirding to demonstrate the superiority of Christ's sacrifice over the Mosaic law sacrifices. Jesus died for our sins, once and for all. We have no way to receive forgiveness apart from Christ. All other avenues to God are dead ends that provide no hope for forgiveness. Don't turn away from Christ; don't take your eye off the finish line. As Elvina Hall wrote in the nineteenth century:

> Jesus paid it all,
> All to Him I owe;
> Sin had left a crimson stain,
> He washed it white as snow.

Annotated Bibliography

Commentaries

Ellingworth, Paul. *The Epistle to the Hebrews: A Commentary on the Greek Text*. NIGTC. Grand Rapids: Eerdmans, 1993.

Though not the focus of his comments to any extent, he provides a solid (though technical) discussion on the passage. See especially page 361.

Journals

Köstenberger, Andreas J., and David A. Croteau. "'Will a Man Rob God?' (Malachi 3:8): A Study of Tithing in the Old and New Testaments." *Bulletin of Biblical Research* 26, no. 1 (2006): 53–77.

The article addresses the larger issue of the biblical arguments for tithing, as well as the legend above. See especially pages 20–25. Available online at www.biblicalfoundations.org/wp-content/uploads/2012/01/32-Tithing1.pdf.

Websites

Kelly, Russell Earl. "19. Hebrews 7: Extremely Important." Accessed July 17, 2014. www.tithing-russkelly.com/id8.html.

This is a chapter from Kelly's book that he has made available online. It is a detailed treatment of this issue.

---

[3] Paul Ellingworth, *The Epistle to the Hebrews: A Commentary on the Greek Text*, NIGTC (Grand Rapids: Eerdmans, 1993), 361.

CHAPTER 35

Christians Are Commanded to Go to Church

Hebrews 10:25

The Legendary Teaching on Hebrews 10:25

Church attendance is down across America. People aren't committed to going to church. A couple came to me and said they were having marital problems. My first question, as always, was, "Are you faithfully attending church?"

And since they are having marital problems, the usual response I get back is, "Well, you know, we have been missing some recently."

They are not in church! That is a big red flag indicating the genesis of the problems in their relationship. Why is it that people that are having all these issues are not in church? The answer is simple. It has to do with Hebrews 10:25: "Not giving up meeting together" (NIV). This command of gathering together for church in Hebrews 10:25 has not given us an option. It is a *command*! Therefore if we are not meeting together, we are in disobedience and sinning. The consequences of sin in our life will manifest itself many different ways. You need to be in church. You need to be here on Sunday morning, Sunday nights, and Wednesday nights. If you are not here, how are you going to learn from the pastors and teachers? How can we help you if you are not here? I know you have a lot of things going on in your life, a lot of things you have to get done. Many things can get in the way of going to church, and some of them can be legitimate. Church needs to be more important. You need to be here not because I am saying it, but because God's Word is saying it. You need to get your priorities straight, obey the Word of God, and get to church.

Introduction

Am I really challenging the idea that you should go to church? Yes and no. Think about this question: why do we go to church? Do you ever go to church and it feels a little monotonous, a little bit dry or stale? You wake up in the morning and you think, *I am really tired, and I don't want to go today.* You might go anyway, but you really don't want to go. Sometimes you don't feel like going to church. Do you ever go to church simply because you are *supposed* to go?

Keeping the Main Point the Main Point

When studying Hebrews 10:25, one of the questions we want to ask is: what's the main point the author of Hebrews is trying to communicate? Is the author's main point a command to go to church? This passage provides a good example of how paying close attention to context can help us understand more clearly and precisely what the author is and is not saying.

In this case we need to study 10:19–25 to more fully appreciate the context.

> Therefore, brothers, since we have boldness to enter the sanctuary through the blood of Jesus, by a new and living way He has opened for us through the curtain (that is, His flesh), and since we have a great high priest over the house of God, let us draw near with a true heart in full assurance of faith, our hearts sprinkled clean from an evil conscience and our bodies washed in pure water. Let us hold on to the confession of our hope without wavering, for He who promised is faithful. And let us be concerned about one another in order to promote love and good works, not staying away from our worship meetings, as some habitually do, but encouraging each other, and all the more as you see the day drawing near.

This passage has a series of three exhortations. Understanding all three together will greatly aid in comprehending what the author is trying to communicate. I'm going to touch briefly on the first two and then dwell on the third exhortation a little longer. The author and his audience have been meditating on Christ's sacrificial work for about ten chapters, and then, in Hebrews 10:19, he says, "Therefore." This sustained meditation on the work of Christ should compel us to action: draw near to God, continue in the faith, and promote love and good works.

Exhortation 1: Draw Near to God

Why would anyone lack confidence or boldness when approaching God? Thinking about some of the Old Testament stories used to illustrate God's holiness can help explain why some people would be intimidated to enter into God's presence. One in particular that comes to mind is from Leviticus 10:2,[1] the story of Nadab and Abihu. This is the story of two men offering up strange or unauthorized fire, and then God kills them (ironically) with fire. It is one of many stories that would be going through the mind of someone who was thinking about approaching God. You can see why it might make some people hesitate.

That is why Hebrews 10 mentions boldness in tandem with entering the sanctuary. We don't enter boldly because we are so wonderful but through the blood of Jesus. The "holy place" is no longer a literal, physical place; but on the basis of Jesus' blood, we can now approach God with confidence and boldness. We can enter the presence of God through the veil, which this verse defines as Christ's flesh. By Christ's flesh being torn on the cross, the way to God was opened to all without a human mediator. The curtain was split, and as that curtain was split, so Christ's body was broken for us to give us access into God's presence. This leads right into verses 21–22, which declare Jesus as the great high priest offering a greater sacrifice than anything Judaism had to offer; based on that we can draw near to God. Why? Because we are clean, both our hearts and our bodies. This is the first of the three exhortations: let us draw near.

Exhortation 2: Continue in the Faith

His second exhortation is to hold on to the confession of our hope. Why does he mention hope here? He previously mentioned hope in chapters 6 and 7, and Hebrews 6:19 is important to understand if we will understand why he brings up hope in the context of chapter 10. Hebrews 6:19 says, "We have this hope as an anchor for our lives, safe and secure. It enters the inner sanctuary behind the curtain." There are many connections between Hebrews 6 and 10. The words *hope*, *sanctuary*, and *curtain* are referenced in both chapters. But the key is that hope is our anchor. Hope is appropriate because we rely on Christ. He makes a promise, and he will keep the promise. Theologians refer to this as perseverance or preservation of the saints. The idea of holding on to our confession of hope is the idea of continuing in the faith.

Exhortation 3: Promote Love and Good Works

The third exhortation brings us to our main point: consider how to promote love and good works (Heb 10:24). He began by exhorting us to come into the presence of God. Do you believe that drawing near to God is an important

---

[1] Another appropriate story is 1 Chronicles 13:10–11.

thing for a Christian to do? Would you ever say to a Christian: "Coming into the presence of God is a good thing, but don't worry about it if you can't get around to it. It's kind of an optional thing for you to do. It's good but not vital." Of course not, because coming into His presence is absolutely vital! What about continuing in the faith? Can you imagine going up to a young believer and saying, "Look, you made a profession of hope. You say you are a Christian; now live like the devil! Don't worry about it! Your eternal ticket has been punched!" Would you ever say that to someone? No! Because perseverance, continuing in the faith, is essential. You want them to persevere so you urge them to do that. Those two exhortations are essential for Christians.

Then we arrive at the third exhortation, promoting love and good works. I believe many Christians think *this* is the optional part. If drawing near isn't optional and perseverance isn't optional, then why would promoting love and good works be optional? The reason for discussing the first two exhortations is to communicate that those two are vital, but so is the third. We need to think about this idea of promoting love and good works. We need to encourage one another. Sniping comments, gossip, and individualism prevent us from promoting love and good works. You are not promoting love and good works when you are slandering someone or telling lies about a person. You are not promoting love and good works when you isolate yourself from the body of Christ. Do you make a habit of promoting love and good works in the Christians around you? One commentator said, "The well-being of each believer is bound up with the well-being of the whole body."[2] For American individualists, this is an American heresy deep in the DNA of our culture. Most of us don't want our well-being bound up with the well-being of others around us. We want to stand on our own, be self-sufficient, and be a rogue Christian who can live out the Christian faith alone.

This word *promote* means "to rouse to activity,"[3] "to stimulate a change in motivation or attitude."[4] We are to motivate our brothers and sisters in Christ to be loving and doing good works. Notice that this is not a command given to pastors or the "superspiritual" only. This is a command given to *everyone*. All of us are to do this. All of us are to provoke one another to love and good works.

My wife is wonderfully Christ centered, and she has been known to ask people in our church: "What are you reading in God's Word? How is God challenging you this week?" She is not being critical; she really wants to know. Some people get offended by her question, and some get convicted. My wife is

---

[2] Brooke Foss Westcott, *The Epistle to the Hebrews: Notes and Essays on the Greek Text*, 3rd ed., Classic Commentaries on the Greek New Testament (London: Macmillan, 1909), 326.

[3] Cf. BDAG, 780.

[4] Louw and Nida, 90.55.

trying to provoke them to love and good works by getting them to share what they've learned. By that sharing, she may be provoked to love and good works as well.

The Arrival of the Legend

The verse that supposedly commands church attendance, verse 25, has now been placed in its context: "Not staying away from our worship meetings, as some habitually do, but encouraging each other, and all the more as you see the day drawing near." This verse is important for promoting love and good works. How are we going to spur one another to love and good works if we aren't spending time together? We can't! Relationships need to be intentional. Imagine we only said hello to our spouses twice a week for six months. How close do you think we would feel to them? We wouldn't know them at all! And that is what church is like to many of us. We have filled our lives with so many things. We are so busy with activities that we don't have time for one another, and because I don't have time for you, and you don't have time for me, we never hang out. We hardly see one another beside Sundays. In reality we don't know one another. And if I don't know you, how can I know you well enough to promote love and good works in your life?

If you think you are obeying this exhortation by attending church on Sunday, then you have totally missed what this text is about. The "not staying away from our worship meetings" is specifically put in contrast to encourage. This is not the first time he used the word for *encourage*. Hebrews 3:13 says, "But encourage each other daily," not only on Sundays and Wednesdays, maybe breakfast on a Friday once a month, as well. Daily encourage each other "so that none of you is hardened by sin's deception."

Application

Some people are asking today: why not listen to sermons at home rather than go to church? We can answer that questions in many ways, but this passage answers it in a specific way. After worshipping through music and the preached Word, we have the opportunity to talk to one another about how the sermon convicted us. The service could end, and we could walk out of the sanctuary and talk about the football game or the baseball game, or we could talk about where we are going to eat. We could talk about life and pop culture. Or we could ask one another: "What did you think of that message? How did the truth in that message impact your life? How are you going to be different this week? How are you going to apply that?" The job of the preacher is to preach what the Word of God says. His job is not to live it out in our lives.

A friend of mine says: "Information does not lead to transformation. But the application of information can lead to transformation." The preacher can't apply it to our lives. Only we can do that. That is our job.

We should be meeting together often enough to know one another in a way that enables us to encourage one another appropriately. Just showing up on Sunday morning is not going to do this. Leaving right after the teaching with no time of fellowship is not going to do this. We need to spend time together to spur one another on to love and good works. Please recognize that persevering in the faith and drawing near to God are both in parallel to promoting love and good works. Don't neglect this exhortation.

So, what is the urban legend here? Hebrews 10:25 is not really commanding church attendance as much as it is *exhorting the church body to promote love and good works in one another*. This is to be done in the context of meeting together. So, should we attend church? Yes, absolutely we need to go to church. We need a *context* for promoting love and good works. But that is not the essence of what this passage is about.

Annotated Bibliography

Commentaries

Allen, David. *Hebrews*. NAC. Nashville: B&H, 2010.

Allen's commentary is fairly accessible for the educated layperson, though technical language is found at times.

O'Brien, Peter T. *The Letter to the Hebrews*. PNTC. Grand Rapids: Eerdmans, 2010.

O'Brien's treatment of these issues is somewhat technical, though perhaps not beyond the expectations of an educated staff member or educated layperson.

Journals

Decker, Rodney J. "The Exhortations of Hebrews 10:19–25." *The Journal of Ministry and Theology* 6, no. 1 (2002): 44–62.

Decker's treatment is somewhat technical and focuses on the structure and other technical details of the text and the language.

Websites

Piper, John. "Consider How to Stir Up One Another to Love." *Desiring God*. September 18, 2005. Accessed July 20, 2014. www.desiringgod.org/sermons/consider-how-to-stir-up-one-another-to-love.

CHAPTER 36

Women Should Not Wear Jewelry

1 Peter 3:3

The Legendary Teaching on 1 Peter 3:3

Some teachings in Scripture confront us because they are so clear. I admit some verses are hard to understand. I empathize with those who read one of those verses and hesitate before making a radical change in their lives. However, some verses in Scripture are so plain, so clear, it is inconceivable to make excuses. Stated bluntly: women should not wear jewelry, expensive clothes, or makeup. If they do, they are living in disobedience to Scripture. First Peter 3:3 says, "Your beauty should not consist of outward things like elaborate hairstyles and the wearing of gold ornaments or fine clothes." Paul communicates the same concepts in 1 Timothy 2:9. These verses are clear, and there are two of them, so it is doubly clear. A woman's outward appearance should not consist of wearing gold or elaborate hairstyles or expensive clothing. Women are not to dress themselves with gold and pearls, no braided hair. Peter and Paul did not mince words. Women need to refrain from these sinful practices because they are explicitly condemned in God's Holy Word.

Introduction: Unraveling the Legend

I was on a flight from California to North Carolina. A woman sat next to me, and a man was in the window seat. About fifteen minutes into the flight, it became obvious what the next five hours were going to be like: the man flirting with the girl to try to get her phone number. I have to admit that while I tried not to be interested in what was happening, it was entertaining. He was clearly not going to get her number. As I listened, the conversation turned to the topic of clothing. He asked her how much the jeans cost that she was wearing. She said $500! I interrupted: "Excuse me? Did you say those jeans cost $500?"

She answered, "Oh, that's nothing. I have a friend who paid $1,000 for jeans." A thousand dollars! Do they walk for her? A pair of jeans could never do anything to make me spend $1,000 on them. That conversation gave me a context for the idea of "expensive apparel." The verses referenced above definitely appear to teach that women should not wear jewelry, have braided hair, or wear expensive clothes. Are these verses really as clear as they seem?

A Closer Look at 1 Peter 3:3

First Peter 3:3 is in the context of Peter's explaining to wives how to win over their unbelieving husbands. Notice that the HCSB says, "Your beauty should not consist of." Examining different Bible translations reveals that they are wrestling with that opening phrase. The ESV says, "Do not let your adorning be external." That sounds like a prohibition on any external adornment whatsoever. The NIV says, "Your beauty should not come from outward adornment." That seems to be a little softer. The NASB says, "Your adornment must not be *merely* external." The NASB sounds like it *can* be external, but it shouldn't *only* be external. Many people who read the NASB see words in italics and think those words should be emphasized. That is why reading the introduction to your Bible is important. In the NASB a word in italics means it is *not* present in the Greek text, almost the opposite of emphasizing it! Is Peter telling women to avoid having *any* external beauty? Is he saying a woman should not *solely* have external beauty? Is something inherently wrong with being externally beautiful?

This command is primarily focused on a specific group of women within the church, namely, wealthy women. Poor and slave women would not have had much (or any) choice in what they would wear. They were content if they had one nice dress. Wealthy women would have a choice, having many dresses.

The idea of not wearing expensive or elaborate dresses was a common admonition in the Greco-Roman culture. Peter echoed many writers before him.[1] When these Greco-Roman writers said, "Women, don't have braided hair or elaborate hairstyles, don't wear pearls or gold, and don't wear expensive clothing," they gave two types of warnings regarding how women were to dress. First, don't be ostentatious. Ostentatiousness refers to trying to impress others by one's appearance or dress. In other words, they were to avoid impressing others through externals. First Peter 3:4 says, "Instead, it should consist of what is inside the heart with the imperishable quality of a gentle and quiet spirit, which is very valuable in God's eyes." Peter is contrasting the concepts

---

[1] For references to such writers, see Peter Davids, "1 Peter," in *Zondervan Illustrated Bible Backgrounds Commentary: Hebrews to Revelation*, ed. Clinton E. Arnold (Grand Rapids: Zondervan, 2002), 136.

in verses 3–4, so comparing them will aid interpretation. Instead of focusing on impressing others with your appearance, women should focus on certain internal characteristics. The contrast between verses 3 and 4 is important. The descriptions in verse 3 are not bad in and of themselves, but such externals should not be the emphasis in a woman's life. Verse 4 explains what should be emphasized.

The second warning typically given by Greco-Roman authors was against dressing seductively. In other words, avoid enticing or alluring with externals. Did women dress in such a way that they exposed a lot of skin? Seneca, a Roman philosopher in the first century, was extolling the virtues of his mother in a letter he wrote to her. He was trying to comfort her in his exile, and he described her exceedingly virtuous character. He said, "You never liked clothes which showed the figure as plainly as though it were naked."[2] In the context he was contrasting his mother with women of the time. It used to be that high-class prostitutes were the only women to wear clothing that was see-through. But by the time of the dawn of Christianity, wealthy women were dressing that way, just like prostitutes. They would wear transparent clothing, jewelry, and their hair the same way as prostitutes. This is what Seneca's mother avoided and why he praised her.

Peter desires women to avoid drawing attention to themselves with externals, whether trying to impress people, making sure people realize how rich they were, or trying to seduce men. Peter gave his explicit reason for this in the opening verses of the chapter: "In the same way, wives, submit yourselves to your own husbands so that, even if some disobey the Christian message, they may be won over without a message by the way their wives live when they observe your pure, reverent lives" (1 Pet 3:1–2). Many Greco-Roman husbands were fine with their wives attending synagogues, and the same was basically true of their attending churches. Husbands would surely be impressed if their wives were to follow Peter's words. Husbands did not want their wives dressing like high-class prostitutes, even though wealthy women wanted to dress that way. If they changed the way they were dressing when they started following Christ, dressing the way their husbands wanted them to, the husbands would be impressed with the morality of their wives. The general purpose of this passage is a call for wives to live in such a way as to make the Christian life appealing to their pagan, unbelieving husbands.

Peter wanted women to avoid dressing seductively. He said this for the purpose of unbelieving, pagan husbands to be attracted to Christianity through the purity of their wives. He did not prohibit women from adorning themselves

---

[2]   Seneca, *Of Consolation: To Helvia* 16:4.

with jewelry or making themselves look beautiful. The real issue is a matter of stressing the right things, a matter of emphasis, and the intentions of the heart.

Application

Women, if you want to impress others, don't do it by putting an emphasis on outward beauty, but spend time refining your character. That doesn't mean you should ignore outer beauty. It doesn't have to be an either/or situation. Take a good, hard look at how much time and money you spend on external appearances and evaluate what your motives might be in the time and money you spend. Are you spending ten times more effort on your external beauty than inner beauty? In your heart, are you attempting to impress others by your external beauty?

Here is a quick warning. Don't judge other women whom you believe are spending too much time on the externals. Just because another woman looks beautiful does not mean she is emphasizing external beauty to the neglect of her inner beauty. My wife is a great example of this. She is absolutely beautiful, and she doesn't have to spend two or three hours getting ready to go out. Just a few minutes of preparation and she looks great. She doesn't need to wear makeup at all (that's a wonderful blessing for me). Be careful of a judgmental attitude. This passage is directed for women to look at themselves, not to look at other women.

Men should value inner beauty more than external beauty. The society we live in teaches every man to value external beauty as the most important quality in a woman. I remember in high school guys having debates about how good-looking a girl would have to be before they would consider marrying her. Pathetic! When men don't value holiness in women, women have difficulty valuing holiness in themselves. Men teach them about how they are valued by the comments they make. Most women probably want to be complimented on looking pretty, but that is not the only thing they want to be complimented on! As men, we need to emphasize in our wives and daughters the internal characteristics Peter talks about in verse 4. If men emphasize them, it will be much easier for women to avoid putting an overemphasis on the externals and place more value on internal beauty.

Annotated Bibliography

Commentaries

Davids, Peter H. "1 Peter." In *Zondervan Illustrated Bible Backgrounds Commentary: Hebrews to Revelation*. Grand Rapids: Zondervan, 2002.

Davids provides pertinent background information helpful for correctly interpreting this passage. See especially pages 135–36.

Jobes, Karen H. *1 Peter*. BECNT. Grand Rapids: Baker, 2005.

Jobes does a fine job explaining the meaning of this passage. The commentary does use Greek at times and can be somewhat technical. See especially pages 204–5.

Websites

Rochford, James. "(1 Pet. 3:3) Does This Mean that Women Should Not Wear Makeup and Jewelry?" *Evidence Unseen*. Accessed July 14, 2014. www.tinyurl.com/makeupjewelry.

This is a brief summary supporting of the main point of 1 Peter 3:3.

CHAPTER 37

First John 1:9 Is a Formula for Salvation

1 John 1:9

The Legendary Teaching on 1 John 1:9

Salvation is simple in the New Testament. Some people seem to want to complicate the matter. But John gives a clear verse explaining how to be saved: "If we confess our sins, He is faithful and righteous to forgive us our sins and to cleanse us from all unrighteousness." Confession is the way to salvation. John declares that when we confess our sins, God will then forgive us and cleanse us from our sins. Simply admit to God you are wrong, and salvation is yours.

Introduction: Unraveling the Legend

Two distinct legends arise from this verse. The legend above has fascinated me because those who use this verse as a formula for salvation nearly always use it in the area of Christian growth as well. I've heard preachers go back and forth between this being a formula for salvation and a statement on Christian growth in the same sermon! This verse has also been used to enslave Christians into *confessionism*: the belief that a Christian must confess every sin to God, big or small, in order to be in a right relationship with him.[1] Both of these legends will be clarified by the interpretation to follow.

---

[1] I'm indebted to Jim Elliff for this term and definition: "Confessionism: The Misuse of 1 John 1:9," *Christian Communicators Worldwide* (2013), accessed July 15, 2014, www.ccw-today.org/article/confessionism-the-misuse-of-1-john-19.

The Audience of 1 John

The purpose of this section (1:5–2:2) is explicitly declared in 2:1: "I am writing you these things so that you may not sin." John is not writing evangelistically but for their edification.[2] In a few places throughout this section, John reminds his readers of their salvation (cf. 1:7). He clearly believes the readers are Christians in 2:12: "Your sins have been forgiven because of Jesus' name" (cf. 5:13).

Unbelievers are addressed (indirectly) in 1 John, but they are not his audience. The opponents, those who have left the fellowship, are the unbelievers. First John 2:19 states this: "They went out from us, but they did not belong to us; for if they had belonged to us, they would have remained with us. However, they went out so that it might be made clear that none of them belongs to us." Leaving the community and forsaking Christ without returning was evidence that they were never truly part of the church in the first place.

The Context of 1 John 1:9

The structure of this section of John's letter has John using the phrase "if we say" as a way to cite his opponents (1:6, 8, 10) followed by a verse beginning with "if" which presents the correct view on the issue (1:7, 9; 2:1b). In 1:6, John explains that his opponents believed claiming fellowship with God while habitually walking in darkness was acceptable. John calls this a lie. In 1:7, John's response, he says walking in the light is the evidence that "we have fellowship with one another." Furthermore, Jesus then "cleanses us from all sin." John is not claiming that "if" they walk in the light, "then" they will be cleansed from sin but that those who have been cleansed are characterized by walking in the light.

In 1:8, most translations say something like, "If we say we have no sin," which seems to indicate that the opponents claimed to live a perfectly sinless life. While that is possible (and probably the meaning of 1:10), the specific Greek construction appears to indicate a state is involved, meaning, the state of sin. Four times the Greek word for *have* (*echō*) is paired with the noun for *sin* (*hamartia*) in John's Gospel: John 9:41; 15:22, 24; 19:11. In reading each of those passages, the same concept is being communicated. Take John 9:41 for example: "'If you were blind,' Jesus told them, 'you wouldn't have sin.'" Jesus isn't saying they would be living perfect, sinless lives but that they would

---

[2] Regarding the "we" in this passage, Wallace says that if the "we" in 1 John 1:9 refers to unbelievers, it "would be to take the pronominal referent to mean 'you, but not me.' Such is not impossible, of course, but it is highly unlikely and apparently otherwise unexampled in the NT" (Daniel B. Wallace, *Greek Grammar Beyond the Basics: An Exegetical Syntax of the Greek New Testament* [Grand Rapids: Zondervan, 1996], 698).

not be in a state of being guilty in sin.[3] The same interpretation applies to the other three verses. This makes all the more likely that John is saying the same thing in 1 John 1:8, as the NET says: "If we say we do not *bear the guilt of sin*, we are deceiving ourselves and the truth is not in us." The opponents were declaring that they do not bear the guilt of sin. John denies that they have any relationship with God; he even denies that they ever had one (cf. 1 John 2:19 above). This is the context for 1 John 1:9.

Confessing in 1 John 1:9

John begins verse 9 by discussing *confession*, the same Greek word discussed in Romans 10:9–10. John uses it in his writings eleven times. In the Gospel of John, the first two occurrences are John the Baptist confessing that he is not the Christ (John 1:20). The other two references discuss people confessing (or not confessing) Jesus as Christ (John 9:22; 12:42). The other four uses of this verb in 1 John all refer to confessing something about Jesus (1 John 2:23; 4:2, 3, 15). The use in 2 John 7 refers to people who will not confess that Jesus came in the flesh. Finally, Revelation 3:5 says the Spirit says to the church at Sardis that He will confess "his name," probably a reference to those in Sardis who are victors and are dressed in white clothes. First John 1:9 is the only time *sin* is the object of this verb for confession in John's writings or the rest of the New Testament.[4] This verb, connected with *sin* as its object, refers to admitting to wrongdoing.[5]

The verb for *confess* probably indicates the habit or ongoing practice of confessing. While some believe public confession is indicated, Akin's acute observation is worth noting: "While confession of sin could be made either publicly or privately, the context of 1:7 and 1:9, with God being the One to whom one confesses, makes it unlikely that John is referring to a public confession."[6]

Telling people that confessing their sin will lead to their forgiveness and cleansing is an incomplete gospel. The reason 1 John 1:9 doesn't present the complete gospel is because it's not intended to be a complete gospel presentation. Just as in the Gospel of John, when the author wants to describe what characterizes a Christian, he uses the verb *believe*. While several verses could illustrate this (e.g. 1 John 3:23; 5:10, 13), 1 John 5:1 should suffice: "Everyone who believes that Jesus is the Messiah has been born of God." The word John

---

[3] Cf. Colin G. Kruse, *The Letters of John*, PNTC (Grand Rapids: Eerdmans, 2010), 66.

[4] If you include a search with the verb ἐξομολογέω and not just ὁμολογέω, this would not be the case.

[5] Cf. BDAG, 708.

[6] Daniel Akin, *1, 2, 3 John*, NAC (Nashville: B&H, 2001), 74n132. This was the view of Augustine as well (see Raymond E. Brown, *The Epistles of John*, AB [New York: Doubleday, 1982], 208).

characteristically uses to describe the correct response to the gospel is *believe*. Admitting wrongdoing is not the same as believing. However, someone who has believed has admitted to wrongdoing.[7]

John is also not claiming that if someone forgets to confess a sin, then it isn't forgiven. Just as verse 7 describes those who walk in the light as those who have been cleansed, verse 9 says those who confess their sins to God have been forgiven and cleansed. Christians have no fear of coming to God (cf. John 3:21) and confessing their sins. John's Gospel describes an unbeliever as one who "hates the light and avoids it, so that his deeds may not be exposed" (John 3:20). Confessing sin is characteristic of a Christian. You don't have to spend an inordinate amount of time soul-searching to make sure you've confessed every sin to God out of fear that if you've forgotten something you'll be out of fellowship with Him.

Sin and the Christian

I do not believe this verse provides a formula for salvation, nor does it command the confession of every sin in order to be in fellowship with God. The main purpose of this verse is to communicate that Christians confess their sins to God. Those who characteristically do this can know they have been forgiven of sin and cleansed of unrighteousness. Therefore, verse 9 is probably not directly addressing the issue of the impact of sin on a Christian.

The sins Christians commit hurt their relationship with God and put it in tension. Sinning is saying to God that what I want is better than what he wants for me. It's saying no to God and is idolatry. The relationship isn't severed, but a relational wall can be built (compare 1 Pet 3:7 and prayers being hindered).

Application

John MacArthur wonderfully summarizes the point of confessing in 1 John 1:9: "If we are the ones continually confessing our sins then that is indicative of the marvelous work of the Spirit of God in our lives that has cleansed us from sin and given us a holy hatred of sin which causes us to be confessors."[8] Therefore, go to God with the confidence that you have been forgiven and cleansed; confess your sins to Him and make that a pattern of your life.

Our response to God saving us should be a life characterized by walking in the light. Admitting we struggle with sin and being willing to confess our sins

---

[7] Much more could be said on the relationship between confessing sin (admitting wrongdoing) and repentance. In order to repent one must admit wrongdoing. However, it is possible to admit wrongdoing and never turn from the sin.

[8] John MacArthur, "The Certainty of Sin, Part 3," *Grace to You* (July 21, 2002), accessed July 16, 2014, www.gty.org/resources/sermons/62-7.

to God is the characteristic of someone who has been saved by grace through faith. God does not desire for you to live in fear that you may have overlooked confessing a singular sin and thus cripple any chance for Christlikeness. Likewise, this verse is not about coming to faith, about "getting saved."

Annotated Bibliography

Commentaries

Kruse, Colin G. *The Letters of John*. PNTC. Grand Rapids: Eerdmans, 2010.

Kruse's commentary is fairly accessible with some helpful comments on this verse. See especially page 66.

Akin, Daniel. *1, 2, 3 John*. NAC. Nashville: B&H, 2001.

Akin's comments are particularly helpful regarding the character of the confession envisioned in this verse. See especially page 74.

Websites

Elliff, Jim. "Confessionism: The Misuse of 1 John 1:9." *Christian Communicators Worldwide*. 2013. Accessed July 15, 2014. www.ccwtoday.org/article/confessionism-the-misuse-of-1-john-19.

Elliff's rebuke of confessionism should provide relief to those who have been burdened under it.

Harris, W. Hall, III. "Exegetical Commentary on 1 John 1:5–2:2." *Bible.org*. July 28, 2004. Accessed July 15, 2014. www.bible.org/seriespage/exegetical-commentary-1-john-15-22.

Harris's discussion requires a knowledge of Greek. He has some keen insights into this text.

CHAPTER 38

Christians Should Not Allow Cults into Their Homes

2 John 10

The Legendary Teaching on 2 John 10

The home is a tender and personal place. As much as we might love to invite a Jehovah's Witness or Mormon missionary inside to talk more with them, we cannot. We might desire deeply to share the love of Jesus with them, but we are forbidden from doing this in our homes. The apostle John said in 2 John 10: "If anyone comes to you and does not bring this teaching, do not receive him into your home, and don't say, 'Welcome,' to him." Find other ways and opportunities to witness to them, but never let them into your home. Why? One of your children could hear the false teaching and be persuaded by it, or a weaker Christian might be swayed by their words.

Introduction: Unraveling the Legend

Some sage advice is given in this legendary teaching. A few other verses from the New Testament warn about false teachers. Galatians 1:8 says regarding those who preach a false gospel, "A curse be on him!" False teachers are described by Jesus as ravenous wolves, and we are to beware of them (Matt 7:15). Romans 16:17–18 says to "avoid" those who are divisive and teach contrary to Paul because they "deceive the hearts of the unsuspecting with smooth talk and flattering words." Surely inviting a false teacher into your life is dangerous. All these cautions are valid.

But is it disobedience to Scripture to invite false teachers into your home to witness to them? What if you are knowledgeable and informed about the cult? What if you are having acquaintances from work over for dinner, and you find out they are members of a cult? Must you cancel dinner? Is that the point of 2 John 10?

A Closer Look at 2 John 10

Second John was written by the apostle John "to the elect lady" (v. 1), whose identity is unclear. After the greeting John exhorts her to love one another and walk in love (vv. 5–6). Then John arrives at what is probably the main point of the letter: a warning. False teachers are going around proclaiming that Jesus Christ did not come in the flesh (v. 7). He warns her and encourages her to continue in the teaching of Jesus (v. 8). This provides the context for 2 John 10.

Two things are prohibited. First, do not receive them into your home. Second, do not say "welcome" to them. Verse 11 explains that when you say "welcome," you share "in his evil works." Have you ever wondered how saying "welcome" is sharing in his evil works? On the surface that really doesn't make much sense! And that is a contextual clue that something else might be happening in this verse. Akin incisively declares, "This verse, perhaps more than any in the epistles of John, is open to abuse and misunderstanding if removed from its immediate context."[1]

Elsewhere in the New Testament, Christians are encouraged to provide for preachers of the gospel. First Corinthians 9, Galatians 6:6, and Titus 3:13 are examples of this (cf. Luke 9:1–6; 10:1–12). Loving one another and walking in love include the idea of helping Christian leaders who have come to your town to have a base from which to do their ministry.

There is a difference between having a conversation in your home with a false teacher and "receiving" them into your home. The idea of receiving them and welcoming them is the idea of giving them a home base from which to do ministry. Christians are prohibited from providing any kind of support to someone spreading a false gospel. John gives these prohibitions right after the exhortation to love, which fits perfectly in context: it is not loving to anyone to give support to someone spreading heresy. Some people in your community could likely be deceived by him and think you agree with the false teaching because of the support you're giving. It's also not loving to the false teacher, for your goal should not be to support his false teaching but to share the truth with him.

Home in verse 10 has two possible meanings. While it could well refer to the place where the elect lady lives, in the context of first-century church life, her "home" was probably the meeting place for the local church. If the elect lady's home was the meeting place for the church, then the confusion in the

---

[1] Daniel Akin, *1, 2, 3 John*, NAC (Nashville: B&H, 2001), 233.

community would be exacerbated: *the church* would be giving a home base for the spread of heresy.[2]

Verse 11 supports this overall conclusion. The word for *shares* in verse 11 is the Greek word *koinōneō*, which is normally translated *fellowship*. While the modern concept of fellowship might relate to church potlucks, in biblical times *koinōneō* referred to partnering with someone. It was used to refer to people who went into business together, who had partnered together to accomplish a certain goal.[3] Simply saying the word *welcome* to people does not make you a partner in their ministry. However, inviting them into your home to set up a base from which to spread their false teaching is partnering with them in their evil works.

Second John 10 does not prohibit conversing with false teachers in your home. It also does not prohibit saying hello or the word *welcome* to a false teacher. It does prohibit a Christian from supporting the false teacher in spreading heresy. John was most likely referring to false teachers who wanted to use a local church as their base for ministry, not people visiting our homes.

Application

The warnings given at the beginning of this chapter still apply. False teachers are dangerous. Be careful in conversing with them and generally avoid them. If people knocked on my door from a cult I've never heard of, I'm not sure I would invite them into my house. However, I've studied several cults. If members of a cult I'm familiar with knocked on my door, I would absolutely invite them in and try to share the gospel with them. I've done this several times. But that doesn't mean caution isn't necessary. Consider others in your household. If a child is home, be all the more careful as you don't want the false teacher to persuade or influence your child. Of course, depending on the age of the child, it could be a great opportunity for discipleship.

If the word *home* is understood to be a reference to the church, then this verse is an exhortation to church leaders to be cautious about who is supported in ministry. For example, don't allow a false teacher to preach in your pulpit. This would be a quick and deadly way to poison the spiritual life of your congregation. New Testament scholar Peter Davids concludes:

> It is wise for leaders to be assured of the orthodoxy of visitors before giving them a platform from which they can spread their views, even the platform of an official welcome as a visiting Christian leader.

---

[2] For this latter understanding, cf. Peter H. Davids, *More Hard Sayings of the New Testament* (Downers Grove: InterVarsity, 1991), 228.

[3] For a helpful discussion on the meaning of fellowship, see D. A. Carson, *Basics for Believers: An Exposition of Philippians* (Grand Rapids: Baker, 1996), 16–17.

> Christian hospitality stops where danger to the well-being of the church begins; love does not go to the extent of endangering one's fellow Christians nor of allowing those who deny the Lord one loves to peddle their wares in that Lord's church.[4]

Christians should be loving to everyone. Our lives should be characterized by love. The way love manifests itself depends on the situation, however. Just as it's not loving to allow other Christians to continue in sin without confronting them, it's not loving to give false teachers support in spreading their false teachings.

Annotated Bibliography

Commentaries

Akin, Daniel. *1, 2, 3 John*. NAC. Nashville: B&H, 2001.

Akin has a clear explanation of this text, addressing the legend explicitly. See especially page 233.

Books

Davids, Peter H. *More Hard Sayings of the New Testament*. Downers Grove: InterVarsity, 1991.

Brief and nontechnical, Davids's chapter wonderfully interprets this verse and addresses the legend associated with it. See pages 227–30.

Journals

Polhill, John. "The Setting of 2 John and 3 John." *Southern Baptist Journal of Theology* 10, no. 3 (2006): 28–39.

Polhill provides the historical setting and briefly interprets the entire epistle, providing a great example of contextual interpretation at a nontechnical level. See especially page 33.

Websites

Johnson, Eric. "Should Christians Open Their Homes to Witness to Mormons?" *Mormonism Research Ministry*. Accessed July 16, 2014. www.mrm.org/witnessing-inside-home.

Johnson's article does a great job of researching this legend and coming to a sound conclusion.

---

[4] Davids, *More Hard Sayings*, 229–30.

CHAPTER 39

God Would Rather You Be Cold Toward Him than Lukewarm

Revelation 3:16

The Legendary Teaching on Revelation 3:16

The state of the church in America is appalling. One of the reasons the church isn't doing well is because those who call themselves Christians don't live much differently than unbelievers in society. In fact, one of the top reasons unbelievers give for not attending church is that there are too many hypocrites in the church. And I think they have a point. Many of us are hypocrites. The church has many who say they are Christian but don't really follow Christ. For example, look at divorce statistics. The divorce rate among those who call themselves Christians and those who do not are fairly similar. This problem is addressed in Revelation 3:14–19, which is a chilling passage for those who call themselves Christians in America today:

> Write to the angel of the church in Laodicea:

> The Amen, the faithful and true Witness, the Originator of God's creation says: I know your works, that you are neither cold nor hot. I wish that you were cold or hot. So, because you are lukewarm, and neither hot nor cold, I am going to vomit you out of My mouth. Because you say, "I'm rich; I have become wealthy and need nothing," and you don't know that you are wretched, pitiful, poor, blind, and naked, I advise you to buy from Me gold refined in the fire so that you may be rich, white clothes so that you may be dressed and your shameful nakedness not be exposed, and ointment to spread on your eyes so that you may see. As many as I love, I rebuke and discipline. So be committed and repent.

Being cold toward God means you are against him; you have no feeling or sentiment for him. You don't have a desire for holiness. If you asked me,

227

"How do you feel about your wife?" and I said, "Oh, I am cold toward her," you wouldn't view that as good. Being hot toward God means you are on fire for the Lord; you are motivated to live a holy life. Your life is a demonstration of God's grace at work in changing you.

But this text includes a third category: lukewarm. These are the fence-sitters. These are the people who profess to be Christians, but they have no excitement for God. They have a halfhearted condition of love and loyalty. They are not reading their Bibles, they aren't praying, and they aren't growing in Christ-likeness.

Do you ever wonder why God would rather you be cold toward Him than lukewarm? What is so bad about being lukewarm? Don't you think being against God would be worse than being a fence-sitter? When you declare yourself an enemy of God, people understand that you hate him. But when you say you are a Christian but you don't have any joy for him, your life slanders his name. You aren't demonstrating to unbelievers the abundant Christian life. You are hypocritical, and people hate hypocrites. That is why he says he will vomit you out of his mouth if you are lukewarm. So repent! Repent of your lukewarmness, turn to God, and bring glory to his name with your life.

Introduction: Unraveling the Legend

Some great thoughts are expressed in what is written above; and when this passage is preached this way, much truth is being communicated. Without some helpful background information, it is completely understandable that some preachers would get those concepts from this passage, and they would miss some of the contextual clues that will help us see what John is saying with the terms *hot*, *cold*, and *lukewarm*. This legendary interpretation has two main problems: (1) the definitions of the terms *hot*, *cold*, and *lukewarm*; and (2) helpful background information that was not used in the interpretation.

Questioning Definitions of *Hot, Cold,* and *Lukewarm*

People today might refer to someone being cold as lacking passion or affection. The word was never used that way in the New Testament; however, it appears to have occurred (infrequently) with this use in the first century outside the New Testament.[1] The word *cold* doesn't occur that much in the Bible. When it does occur outside of Revelation 3, it refers to something being physically cold. Could *cold* in this passage refer to something positive?

If I said someone was "hot," what could I mean? I could mean they are angry, that it is summertime and they are physically getting hot, or that they

---

[1] See BDAG, 1100.

are on fire for God. Is there any parallel to *hot* meaning "on fire for the Lord" in the early church? I couldn't find any references to *hot* meaning that. One Greek dictionary states that *hot* never referred to a favorable attitude toward someone.[2] How do we know *hot* means something positive?

The Greek word for *lukewarm* means "between cold and hot."[3] The context makes clear that lukewarm is something negative by saying the lukewarm person will be vomited out of God's mouth. But why is it defined as a "fence-sitter"? These people are described as fence-sitters because they are not on fire, nor are they cold; they are in the middle. But could the context provide a different definition of this word?

Background Information to the Rescue

A key to unlocking the correct interpretation to this passage relates to the background information about the aqueduct system in Laodicea. Laodicea was a city formed because it was at the center of trade routes going through that region. It did not have a natural water supply. Therefore, they had to pipe water in from a nearby city, what is known today as the modern city of Denizli. Denizli had hot springs and was located about six miles south of Laodicea. The Laodiceans constructed an aqueduct that ran from Denizli to Laodicea providing water for the citizens.

Other nearby cities had their own water sources. For example, six miles north of Laodicea was the city of Hierapolis, which was known for its hot springs. The springs at Hierapolis were famous for their healing qualities, similar to a Jacuzzi: it was used to relax and help sore muscles. The city eventually became a major health center, kind of like John's Hopkins or the Mayo Clinic today. People would travel to Hierapolis and sit in the hot springs to get physical healing. In fact, standing in Laodicea, you could look out toward Hierapolis and see the mineral deposits from the hot springs.[4]

Twelve miles east of Laodicea lay Colossae. This city was known for its cold, pure, and refreshing drinking water. The water came down from the snowy caps of Mount Cadmus, and the cold, life-giving water at Colossae explains why people originally settled there. It was the only place in the region that had this water. Someone could stand in Laodicea and look toward Colossae and see the mountain that provided the cold drinking water. The mountain fed the Lycus River that contained the cold, refreshing water.

---

2   See Louw and Nida, 79.71.
3   See ibid., 79.74.
4   See Michael Martin, *New Testament Maps and Artifacts*, accessed May 15, 2014, www .ntimages.net/Turkey/Laodicia/laod2hier.jpg.

When I was about fourteen years old, my parents dropped me off to watch a softball game a friend of mine was playing in nearby Sacramento, California. They were supposed to come back in about an hour when the game was over. One hour turned into two hours, which turned into three hours, and if you know anything about Sacramento, it can get tremendously hot. It was over 110 degrees that day. I was parched. I remember lying underneath a picnic table to find some shade. An ice cream truck came by, but I had no money. I was looking at the ice cream truck going by, and I was so thirsty that I wanted to lick the outside of the truck, thinking it might be cold and I could get some refreshment. That's how thirsty I was. When my parents showed up, they gave me a bottle of water. I don't know if water had ever tasted that good before or since. They handed me that water with the moisture on the outside dripping down, and I was looking at the water, and I thought, *This looks so good.* I drank down that bottle of water, and it was so refreshing. That was life-giving, refreshing water. Cold does not automatically mean bad. When those in Laodicea read Revelation 3, they knew exactly what John meant when he referred to hot and cold water.

The reference to vomiting or spitting out of His mouth demonstrates that John is talking about water. The traditional interpretation says that this is about spiritual fervor or your relationship with God. You don't spit spiritual fervor out of your mouth, and you don't spit your relationship with God out of your mouth, but you spit water out of your mouth.

I love coffee, and I can be fairly particular about it too. I even watched a video recently that said coffee tastes best when it is brewed between 195 and 200 degrees. I love *hot* coffee. I also like *iced* coffee. If I'm drinking a cup of coffee during the summer and it gets tepid, I will blend the coffee with some ice cubes to make an iced coffee. But do you know what I don't like? Lukewarm coffee! When my coffee gets lukewarm, I will either put ice in it or put it in the microwave.

When the people in Laodicea heard "hot" or "cold," the hot water of Hierapolis and the cold water of Colossae would have come to their minds. Both of these were good! In Revelation 3, *hot* doesn't refer to being on fire for the Lord but to being spiritually healing as Hierapolis's springs were physically healing. *Cold* doesn't refer to being against God. Instead, *cold* refers to being spiritually refreshing, to being a life-giving church. Both of these are good and are what churches should be. We should be a life-giving body; we should be a spiritually healing family.

But what about lukewarm? When the water from the hot springs of Denizli reached Laodicea, it was no longer hot but lukewarm. The citizens would take the water from the aqueduct and put it in jars in the shade to let it cool off because it was still a little bit on the warm side. Sometimes visitors would come to Laodicea, and they might not know about the water situation. They would pour a cup of water, drink it, and sometimes they would spit out the water because they weren't prepared for the taste or the temperature. Some visitors would swallow the water, and because of all the minerals and the calcium carbonate that was in the water, it would give them an upset stomach, and they would vomit the water out.

Contextual Clues to the Meaning of *Hot*, *Cold*, and *Lukewarm*

This is how the ancient aqueduct system in Laodicea provides the background for the meanings of *hot* and *cold*. The context will help us figure out the meaning of *lukewarm*. If we read this passage carefully without knowing the background information, John provided a clue in the passage itself to what these things mean. The passage begins with, "I know your works." That is the contextual clue that indicates this passage is *not directly about the attitude* of the people toward God. In other words it is not about their faith, whether they are cold to God or on fire for God. This is a letter written to a church *about the actions* of Christians. These actions, then, are evidence about their attitude. It is directly about the works of Christians. So *hot*, *cold*, and *lukewarm* are terms describing water that represent their works metaphorically. *Cold* and *hot* are good descriptions while *lukewarm* is a negative description. The reversing of the word order of "hot" and "cold" also suggests this. *Hot* and *cold* refer to good water and therefore good deeds—the spiritually refreshing, spiritually healing, life-giving works these local churches were known for. Lukewarm water was bad and refers to a lack of deeds, a barrenness of works. The Laodiceans viewed themselves as self-sufficient and needing nothing. The hot/cold/lukewarm metaphor challenges this idea of self-sufficiency. In 3:19, John gives the cure to a life of barren works: be committed and repent. *Lukewarm* refers to a lack of good works.

The traditional interpretation says that *hot* meant on fire for the Lord, *cold* meant against him, and *lukewarm* was the fence-sitter. But this passage is not set in the context of spirituality per se. He starts off with, "I know your works." It is about works being a reflection of our spirituality. If we have a good relationship with Christ, then that will be reflected in our works.

Through paying close attention to context (the opening phrase) and having a knowledge of the background information (the Laodicean aqueduct system), we discover that Denizli was the source of the lukewarm water for Laodiceans. Hierapolis was a few miles to the north and had hot springs, and Colossae was a few miles to the east and had cold water. The hot water stands for spiritually healing, the cold water refers to those who are spiritually refreshing or life giving, and the lukewarm water refers to those with a lack of good works.

Application

Our churches need to be places of spiritual refreshment and healing. Sometimes churches are known for shooting their wounded. We need to be known as a place that embraces those who are wounded. We are not called to be a social club. Gathering together does not satisfy the requirements of the church in the New Testament. God wants us to be known for being healing and refreshing; meeting together doesn't make you automatically healing and refreshing. Showing up on Sunday doesn't cause anyone to be spiritually healed or refreshed by you. We have to have some interaction. Don't be Christian in name only. If you find yourself barren of good works, repent. Be zealous for God, be zealous for good works, and let your love for Him overflow into your life.

Annotated Bibliography

Commentaries

Beale, G. K. *The Book of Revelation*. NIGTC. Grand Rapids: Eerdmans, 1999.
    While this commentary is technical and requires competence with the Greek language, Beale's discussion on this point is accessible and largely nontechnical.
Osborne, Grant R. *Revelation*. BECNT. Grand Rapids: Baker Academic, 2002.
    Osborne's discussion on this point is relatively accessible to most interested laypersons.

Journals

Porter, Stanley E. "Why the Laodiceans Received Lukewarm Water (Revelation 3:15–18)." *Tyndale Bulletin* 38 (1987): 143–49.
    Porter provides a great overview. Not overly technical.
Rudwick, M. J. S. "The Laodicean Lukewarmness." *The Expository Times* 69 (1958): 176–78.

Websites

Carson, D. A. "The Church in an Affluent Society (Rev. 3:14–22)." *The Banner of Truth*. 1979. Accessed July 15, 2014. www.tinyurl.com/CarsonAffluent.
Martin, Michael. *New Testament Maps and Artifacts*. Accessed May 15, 2014. www.ntimages.net/Turkey/Laodicia/laod2hier.jpg.
    Pictures of the mineral deposits at Hierapolis from Laodicea.
Martin, Michael. *New Testament Maps and Artifacts*. Accessed May 15, 2014. www.ntimages.net/Hierapolis-travertines-tns.htm.
    Close-up pictures of the mineral deposits at Hierapolis.

CHAPTER 40

Accept Jesus into Your Heart to Be Saved

Revelation 3:20

The Legendary Teaching on Revelation 3:20

Rufus McDaniel, an Ohio pastor who lost his son Herschel to an untimely death in 1913, penned a beautiful hymn the following year. The song's popularity quickly took off as Billy Sunday incorporated it into his evangelistic campaigns in 1915. "Since Jesus Came into My Heart" has captured many truths of Scripture but none more important than the reality of how one is saved: by accepting Jesus into your heart. If you are separated from Christ, you feel an emptiness deep inside your heart. You may not want to admit it, but you know something is missing. You have a Christ-shaped hole in your heart, and only Jesus can make you feel complete. Today you can alleviate those lonely feelings by praying to accept Jesus into your heart. Jesus is calling to you: "Listen! I stand at the door and knock. If anyone hears My voice and opens the door, I will come in to him and have dinner with him, and he with Me" (Rev 3:20). Jesus desires to come into your heart, and all you have to do is ask him.

Introduction: Unraveling the Legend

A student came into my office several years ago struggling with a pornography addiction. During the course of our conversation, I asked him when he became a Christian and to tell me the story. He said: "When I was about five or six, I went into my mother's bedroom crying. I told her I was ready to have surgery. She was confused and asked me what I was talking about. I told her I was ready to have the doctor cut open my chest so they could place Jesus in my heart. She explained that no surgery was involved, just a simple prayer of asking Jesus to come into my heart. I repeated her prayer, and that's how I got saved."

Do you hear what's missing from that "testimony"? He said nothing about sin, faith, repentance, the cross, or the resurrection. Almost every element necessary for a gospel presentation is missing! While Revelation 3:20 has been used time and again by evangelists to compel people to accept Jesus into their hearts, one other verse, though less frequently, is also used: Ephesians 3:17.[1] We will examine both to decide if this concept is biblical or a good way to explain salvation to those who are in desperate need of Christ.

A Closer Look at Revelation 3:20

The previous chapter discussed the problem in Laodicea: a lack of good works. The apostle John is addressing the church in Laodicea (see Rev 3:14), not unbelievers in the community. This is the first, and most important, contextual clue that Revelation 3:20 is not truly discussing the topic of salvation.

Against the previous point that John is addressing the church, someone might object that the church in Laodicea could have had unbelievers present. The cure for the illness of lukewarm works is prescribed in 3:19: "As many as I love, I rebuke and discipline. So be committed and repent." The Greek word for *love* used in 3:19 is *phileō*, "a term that is *never* used of God/Jesus loving unbelievers in the" New Testament.[2] The Old Testament text being alluded to, Proverbs 3:12, is in the context of God's loving those in his covenant community: Israel.[3] Grant Osborne concludes: "They are addressed as a valid church, have a guardian angel, and are the focus of divine love and discipline. There is no hint at all that they are not Christians."[4]

What exactly does Jesus say to the believers in his church? The common interpretation seems to claim that the text says Jesus "will come *into* him." However, virtually every major Bible translation is clear on this point: Jesus will come "in to" him (HCSB, ESV, NASB, KJV, NKJV, NRSV). Two translations say come "in" (NIV, NLT). But no translation is attempting to communicate the concept that Jesus is going to enter a person.

The Greek preposition used to communicate "to" (in the phrase "come in to him") does not refer to spatially moving into or penetrating something (the preposition *eis*). Instead John used a preposition (*pros*) that means "toward."

---

[1]   Sometimes Colossians 3:15 is used ("And let the peace of Christ rule in your hearts" [ESV]) in this discussion. However, not much in that verse could be used to advocate the above view since what is "in" the heart is "peace," not Christ (in Col 3:15).

[2]   Daniel Wallace, "Inviting Jesus into Your Heart," *Parchment and Pen Blog* (September 23, 2010), accessed on June 19, 2014, www.reclaimingthemind.org/blog/2010/09/inviting-jesus-into-your-heart. There are five examples of God/Jesus having *phileō* for someone; and four were directed toward believers (John 11:3, 36; 16:27; 20:2), and one describes the Father's love for the Son (John 5:20).

[3]   It is interesting to note that Proverbs 3:12 uses *agapaō* in the Septuagint.

[4]   Grant R. Osborne, *Revelation*, BECNT (Grand Rapids: Baker, 2002), 212n24.

The phrase "come in to" is used eight times in the New Testament, and it never refers to one person physically entering another person. For example, Mark 15:43 says that Joseph of Arimathea "came and boldly *went in to* Pilate." No one has suggested that Joseph physically entered the body of Pilate. All the other occurrences are similar to this one.[5] This verse has nothing to do with the offer of salvation.

Revelation 3:20 refers to the offer of fellowship with the living Christ once people have repented of their lack of zeal. While being a foretaste of the final messianic banquet, "the promise here is of acceptance, sharing, and blessing, a deep fellowship with the one offering forgiveness and reconciliation with God."[6] Christ should reign supreme in the assembly of believers. He is not only Lord of our lives but Lord over his church. We must keep ourselves connected to the Vine in order to be sustained.

A Closer Look at Ephesians 3:17

Ephesians 3:17 says, "And that the Messiah may dwell in your hearts through faith." While this verse may appear to promote the idea that when people get saved Jesus comes into their heart, an examination of the context will lead to a different conclusion. While there is some ambiguity and confusion regarding the structure of Paul's words in Ephesians 3:14–17, enough can be firmly established to rule out the legend being appropriately derived from this text.

Paul begins this section explaining that the following words are his prayer (3:14). Similar to Revelation 3, Paul's prayer in Ephesians 3 is for Christians; of this there is no doubt. He first explains his request that God grant the Ephesians strength in the inner man; this strength comes through God's Spirit (3:16). Verse 17 either functions as a separate request or, more likely, is the result of the first request. So the result of being strengthened by God's Spirit is that Christ will dwell in their hearts through faith (3:17). Christ dwelling in their hearts is the result of being strengthened, not coming to salvation. It's not that Christ wasn't already dwelling in their hearts, but, as Thielman explains, they were lacking "the inner strength and encouragement they should draw from" this truth.[7] Because the heart is the center of attitude and conduct, Christ's dwelling there means he is more deeply rooted in the life of the believer. This occurs "through faith" (3:17), not through a literal indwelling of Jesus in the heart.

---

[5] The eight occurrences, not including Revelation 3:20, are: Mark 6:25; 15:43; Luke 1:28; Acts 10:3; 11:3; 16:40; 17:2; 28:8. For more analysis on this, see Wallace, *Beyond the Basics*, 380–81, especially n. 70.

[6] Osborne, *Revelation*, 213.

[7] Frank Thielman, *Ephesians*, BECNT (Grand Rapids: Baker, 2010), 231.

Christ's being at the center of our lives is the result of the strengthening work of the Spirit. Jesus is in our hearts "through faith." This passage has nothing to do with the concept of salvation, but it does affirm that, in some way, Christ is in our hearts.

Is Jesus *in* Our Hearts?

Does Jesus indwell the heart of a Christian? A verse that addresses this issue directly is Galatians 4:6: "And because you are sons, God has sent the Spirit of His Son into our hearts." Therefore, the Holy Spirit indwells the heart of every Christian, but Jesus does not directly dwell in the heart of a Christian. Is this just a "theological technicality"? Yes and no.

This could simply be considered an issue of "Trinitarian confusion," that is, the different roles of the godhead being confused. There are certain roles for the Father, Son, and Holy Spirit. Sometimes they overlap; sometimes they don't. In this situation it is actually the Spirit who indwells.

However, this issue becomes serious, a first-order gospel issue, when someone is led to believe that salvation comes by asking Jesus to come into their heart. The proper response to the message of the gospel is not to ask Jesus into your heart but repentance and faith. The idea that people must ask Jesus to come into their hearts could be construed as something *they must do* in order to be saved. That is a distortion of the gospel. If this legend is taught in a way that explains that repentance and faith are the proper responses and then that is evidenced by asking Jesus into your heart, it becomes less problematic. But it does raise another issue.

Should we be incorporating such nonbiblical terminology into the gospel message? The wisest route would be to adopt biblical terminology when we present the gospel to avoid any confusion. There is no good reason to refer to the concept of asking Jesus into your heart during a gospel presentation. It can be confusing and is nonbiblical. This does not mean, however, that if the gospel was explained to you with that terminology that you are not saved. The issue of assurance in salvation comes down to a living faith and a transformed life.[8] Your salvation is not entirely dependent on the one who presented the gospel to you. We don't want to give false assurance to those we are witnessing to. The questions to ask are: Have you responded in faith? Is your faith persevering? Have you seen a change in your life since you professed faith in Christ? It is healthy to reevaluate our standing before God from time to time (see 2 Cor 13:5).

---

[8] On the topic of assurance in salvation, I highly recommend Mike McKinley, *Am I Really a Christian?* 9Marks (Wheaton: Crossway, 2011).

Annotated Bibliography

Commentaries

Osborne, Grant R. *Revelation*. BECNT. Grand Rapids: Baker, 2002.

Osborne's somewhat technical commentary is helpful in understanding what John is communicating in this verse. See pages 212–13.

Thielman, Frank. *Ephesians*. BECNT. Grand Rapids: Baker, 2010.

He does a good job of navigating this complicated structure, especially in developing an appropriate meaning to the verse above. See especially page 231.

Websites

Wallace, Daniel. "Inviting Jesus into Your Heart." *Parchment & Pen Blog*. September 23, 2010. Accessed June 19, 2014. www.reclaimingthemind.org/blog/2010/09/inviting-jesus-into-your-heart.

Wallace's contribution is absolutely excellent, directly countering the legend in this chapter.

Wax, Trevin. "Is It Biblical to Ask Jesus into Your Heart?" *The Gospel Coalition*. May 15, 2002. Accessed July 17, 2014. www.thegospelcoalition.org/blogs/trevinwax/2012/05/15/is-it-biblical-to-ask-jesus-into-your-heart.

Wax gently addressed the larger issue: the problem that could arise when using this phrase in evangelism. The danger is one of giving false assurance.

Epilogue

The Cause of Legends

I have isolated three issues that give rise to the different legends. Many times legends arise from two or three of these issues. We need first to diagnose the problem before we can implement solutions.

1. *Context.* By context I mean the literary context: the words, verses, paragraphs, and chapters around the legend being studied. Sometimes the context is simply not studied enough. Sometimes it's ignored. Other times it's analyzed incorrectly.

2. *Greek.* The original language of the New Testament was Koine Greek. There is a danger in studying Greek just a little, like taking one or two semesters in seminary. Some pastors have a vague knowledge of the language, but they don't know how to use it effectively and correctly in exegesis. Others have no knowledge of Greek and simply ignore it altogether.

3. *Backgrounds.* This refers to the historical context of the passage: events, culture, society, and items relevant to the original biblical audience. While many times we simply don't have access to background information that would be helpful in interpreting certain passages, the greater problem is using poor background information.

What's the Solution?

1. *Context.* Read the passage you are interpreting carefully! Read it over and over again. Sometimes I have to read through a passage thirty or forty times before I notice something that should have been obvious.

2. *Greek.* Learn Greek and use the best, up-to-date resources. I know: easier said than done! But now some great online and self-teaching resources are available. You can take online Greek courses at many different seminaries. The school where I teach has an online Greek program. Otherwise, you can learn through some other helpful resources like those found on Bill Mounce's website[1] or from David Alan Black.[2]

3. *Backgrounds.* Study the background and use the best background resources. Sources used by previous generations include Alfred Edersheim and Emil Schürer. While Keener's backgrounds commentary is a significant advancement,[3] the new "go to" source is the *Zondervan Illustrated Bible Backgrounds Commentary*. This set provides the background information necessary to interpret every verse in Scripture. The principle I apply for using background information is this: when in doubt over whether the information was relevant to the text being interpreted, use caution. I virtually always endeavor to verify the background information myself.

Where Is the Main Problem?

After mapping out the forty legends, I've found that, for the most part, the problem is not paying attention to the context. Knowing Greek and background information can be extremely helpful, but most of the legends analyzed could have been avoided or fixed if context was studied more carefully. At least thirty of the legends could have been resolved through a careful analysis of context without any knowledge of Greek or background information. This is encouraging because carefully reading the context is something that can be taught much easier than learning another language or becoming an expert in an ancient culture.

Misleading Versus Mistaken

In the prologue I discussed two types of legends. A *mistaken legend* is a *legend* that contains wrong information; it is incorrect. A *misleading legend* is not

---

[1] See www.teknia.com/classes.

[2] See www.newtestamentgreekportal.blogspot.com. Black has an introductory Greek book, a workbook, and DVDs of him teaching through the material. He also has an intermediate Greek book.

[3] Craig S. Keener, *The IVP Bible Background Commentary: New Testament*, 2nd ed. (Downers Grove: InterVarsity, 2014).

necessarily incorrect but incomplete, containing some truth but not the whole story. The majority of legends in this book are *mistaken legends*, but several qualify as *misleading*.

The seven *misleading legends* are those that need clarification in order to better grasp what's being said. Jesus was a carpenter, but He was more than that, being a builder. Carpentry is part of what He did. Jesus absolutely was flogged once, but He was flogged a second time as well. Repentance involves a change of mind, but it is much more than that, including changed behavior. Paul, being a leather worker, probably would have made tents, maybe even primarily made tents, but he was more than just a tent maker. A proper definition of grace includes more than just "unmerited favor," including the concept that the gift was "de-earned." Pastors should be involved in the ministry of the local church, but that is not their primary function: training others to do the ministry. Finally, Christians should be attending church, not for the purpose of showing up, but in order to promote love and good works in one another.

Addressing Legends

Now that you have read this book, how should you respond to someone who teaches a legend? Please be gracious and not judgmental or vexatious. Just because someone teaches something that is not what the text may be saying doesn't necessarily indicate bad intentions or motives. Furthermore, if the theology is right but the interpretation is wrong, it's less of a problem. Ideally what should take place in a sermon is the synergistic effect of a transformed life preaching the text with true theology. However, that doesn't always take place.

Remember that in edifying one another, Paul wants us not only to speak the truth but to speak it in love (Eph 4:15). Holding back truth is not loving, but speaking the truth harshly makes you a resounding gong or clanging symbol (1 Cor 13:1). Sometimes it might be better not to address the issue if it is small. Pray and ask God for wisdom before addressing legendary teachings in someone else's ministry. One of my hopes is that this book will help you avoid falling into the traps and motivate you toward paying better attention to context.

Conclusion

In the end our goal should be to interpret Scripture as accurately as possible, to apply that interpretation to our own lives, and to be transformed by God's Word so that our lives may bring glory to the One who rescued us from an eternal destiny in hell. May God give us the passion, focus, and desire to see His Word understood correctly and lived out in our lives that He might receive glory.

Name Index

Akin, Daniel *xii, 219, 221, 224, 226*
Allen, David *12, 210*
Anyabwile, Thabiti *188*
Armstrong, John H. *193*
Arndt, W. F. *23*
Arnold, Clinton E. *102, 106, 113, 122, 212*

Bailey, Kenneth E. *8, 13*
Bailey, Lloyd R. *50–53*
Barnett, P. W. *113, 115*
Barrett, C. K. *130*
Barrick, Audrey *43*
Baxter, Benjamin J. *128*
Beale, G. K. *232*
Beasley-Murray, G. R. *52–53*
Beeke, Joel R. *143*
Bell, Rob *49, 52*
Berkhof, Louis *143*
Best, Ernest *156*
Billerbeck, Paul *16*
Bing, Charles C. *57*
Blomberg, Craig *11, 13, 34–36, 52, 62, 65, 94, 104, 192*
Blue, J. Ronald *95*
Bock, Darrell L. *19, 30, 77, 107–8*

Bolen, Todd *53*
Borchert, Gerald L. *83*
Brand, Chad *12*
Brooks, James A. *26, 62*
Brown, Raymond E. *219*
Bruce, F. F. *28, 65, 84*
Butler, Trent C. *16*

Campbell, Ken M. *24, 26*
Carlson, Stephen C. *8*
Carr, Authur *62*
Carroll, John *77*
Carson, D. A. *37, 39–41, 47, 83, 89, 101, 103, 126, 128, 137–38, 158, 161, 225, 232*
Chafer, Lewis Sperry *55*
Chaffey, Tim *41*
Chan, Francis *52, 53*
Cranfield, C. E. B. *128*
Croteau, David A. *36, 57, 59, 104, 204*

Davids, Peter *65, 212, 214–15, 225–26*
Davis, John J. *156*
Decker, Rodney J. *161, 210*
DeLuca, Matthew *164*
Doriani, Daniel M. *187*

243

Douglas, J. D.   *84*
Dumbrell, W. J.   *137*
Dunson, Ben C.   *133*

Edwards, William D.   *74, 77*
Elliff, Jim   *217, 221*
Ellingworth, Paul   *203–4*
Eng, Steve   *44*
Erickson, Millard   *109*

Farrar, F. W.   *16*
Fee, Gordon D.   *173*
Fitzmyer, Joseph A.   *118–20, 122–23*
France, R. T.   *52*
Freed, Edwin D.   *90*
Friberg, Barbara   *23*
Friberg, Timothy   *23*

Gabel, Wesley J.   *74, 77*
Garland, David   *62–63, 137–38*
Gilbert, Greg   *108*
Gill, David W. J.   *137*
Gingrich, F. W.   *23*
Glasscock, Ed   *187*
Green, Gene L.   *173, 180*
Green, Joel B.   *77*
Griffin, Hayne P., Jr.   *187, 197*
Grubbs, Norris   *200*
Grudem, Wayne   *137*
Guthrie, G. H.   *202*

Hägerland, Tobias   *104*
Hagner, Donald A.   *95*
Hamblin, James   *xv*
Harris, W. Hall, III   *221*
Head, Peter M.   *51–52, 137*
Hendriksen, William   *200*
Hengel, Martin   *113*
Henry, Matthew   *62*
Hock, Ronald F.   *112–15*
Hodges, Zane   *105*
Hoehner, H. W.   *28, 30–31*
Hoover, R. W.   *158–59, 161*
Hosmer, Floyd E.   *74, 77*
Houdmann, S. Michael   *65*

Hurley, James B.   *137*

Isaac, E.   *51*

Jobes, Karen H.   *215*
Johnson, Eric   *226*
Jones, David W.   *186, 188–89*

Kaiser, Walter C., Jr.   *65*
Keener, Craig   *184, 240*
Kelly, Russell E.   *204*
Kistemaker, Simon J.   *200*
Knight, George W., III   *200*
Köstenberger, Andreas J.   *27–28, 31, 47, 83, 89, 186, 188, 192, 204*
Kruse, Colin G.   *219, 221*
Kvalbein, Hans   *95*

Landau, Brent   *10*
Lea, Thomas D.   *187, 197*
Levine, Lee I.   *136, 138*
Liddell, Henry G.   *23*
Long, George   *23*
Louw, Johannes P.   *22–23, 38, 75, 149, 171, 191, 196–97, 199, 208, 229*
Luz, Ulrich   *26, 95*

Maalouf, Tony T.   *14*
MacArthur, John   *60, 141, 220*
Maclear, G. F.   *62*
MacPhail, Bryn   *8*
Maier, Paul L.   *31*
Marshall, I. Howard   *108–9*
Martin, Michael   *229, 232*
McKee, J. K.   *115*
McKinley, Mike   *236*
Michaelis, W.   *115*
Mikkelson, Barbara   *xv*
Miller, Neva F.   *23*
Montonini, Matthew   *16*
Moo, Douglas J.   *40, 52, 170*
Morris, Leon   *29, 40, 62, 64, 90, 128, 133, 140–41*
Moule, C. F. D.   *120, 161*
Mounce, Bill   *47, 128, 150, 240*

Mounce, William D.   *166, 187*
Murphy-O'Connor, Jerome   *113*
Myers, Allen C.   *12*

Nida, Eugene A.   *22–23, 38, 75, 149,
    171, 191, 196–97, 199, 208, 229*
Nowell, Irene   *104*

O'Brien, Peter T.   *156, 165–66, 177,
    210*
Oladipo, Caleb O.   *90*
Osborne, Grant R.   *232, 234–35, 237*
Owens, Mark D.   *187*

Packer, James I.   *23, 179*
Patton, C. Michael   *71–72*
Payne, Philip B.   *136–37*
Pedersen, Sigfred   *133*
Pendergast, Mark   *xv*
Percer, Leo   *62*
Perriman, Andrew   *52*
Pink, Arthur W.   *104*
Piper, John   *156, 210*
Polhill, John B.   *106, 122, 226*
Porter, Stanley E.   *120, 122–23, 232*

Quarles, Charles L.   *180*

Rapske, Brian   *115*
Ray, Jerry C.   *77*
Roberts, Mark D.   *120, 123*
Rochford, James   *215*
Rogers, Cleon   *95*
Rojas, Juan M.   *156*
Ross, Thomas   *133*
Rudwick, M. J. S.   *232*

Safrai, Shmuel   *136, 138*

Sanders, Seth   *118, 123–24*
Schreiner, Thomas R.   *128, 133*
Schürer, Emil   *135–36, 240*
Scott, Robert   *vii, 23*
Scott, Shane   *90*
Sherwin-White, A. N.   *83*
Silva, Moisés   *159, 161*
Sprinkle, Preston   *8, 26, 52–53*
Sproul, R. C.   *108*
Stafford, Tom   *88*
Steele, Mary   *47*
Stein, Robert H.   *16, 75, 81*
Still, Todd D.   *113–14*
Stott, John R. W.   *38, 40–41, 197*
Strack, Herman L.   *16*
Strauss, Mark   *20, 81*
Szesnat, H.   *112–13, 115*

Tannehill, Robert C.   *101*
Taylor, Justin   *200*
Thayer, Joseph H.   *22–23*
Thielman, Frank   *235, 237*
Thielman, Frank   *235, 237*
Trudinger, P.   *47*
Turner, David L.   *38, 62, 69–71*

Utley, Robert J.   *16*

Wallace, Daniel B.   *95, 150, 153, 173,
    191, 218, 234–35, 237*
Warren, Mitchell H., Jr.   *41*
Wax, Trevin   *108, 237*
Westcott, B. F.   *208*
Wilkins, Michael J.   *52*
Witherington, Ben, III   *13–14, 165–66*
Wright, N. T.   *52, 158–61*

Zahn, Theodor   *112*

Subject Index

Aramaic *118–19, 121–22*
Aristotle *16–17*
Armenian Infancy Gospel *10*
assurance *131, 236*

Babylonian Talmud *17, 64*
beauty *212*

centrality of the cross *46–47*
church *206, 232*
church attendance *209–10*
church discipline *68–71*
Chrysostom *112*
Coca-Cola *xiv–xv*
confess(ion) *130–31, 219*
confessionism *217, 220*
contentment *165*

David Kimhi *50*
discernment *171*
discipleship *94, 132*
divorce *186*
dynamite, history *126*

evangelism *132*

Excerpta Latina Barbari *10*

faithfulness *185–186*
false teaching *171–73, 223, 225*
feeding trough *5, 7*
first-century house *5–7*
flogging *80–81*

Gehenna *49–51*
giving *35–36, 191–92, 204*
God
    attributes *179*
    omnipotence *127*
    omnipresent *179*
gospel *108, 126–27, 131–32, 234, 236*
grace *141–43*
Great Commission, defined *94*
guest room *6*

hell *179*
    misconceptions *176*
hospitality *4, 7*
hyperbole *34*

idiom *184–85*

inn   *3*

Jesus
  age   *28–29*
  birth year   *28*
  carpenter   *22, 25*
  character   *160*
  deity   *157*
  King   *12–13*
  Shepherd   *18–19*
Josephus   *17, 24, 28*
judge, defined   *38–39*

kingdom of God   *63*

Latin   *121*
Latin Vulgate   *22*
leadership   *196, 199*
leatherworker   *113*
love, *agapaē*   *87–88*
love, *phileō*   *87*

Magi. *See* wise men
manger. *See* feeding trough
Melchizedek's priesthood   *202–3*
mercy   *141–142*
Mishnah   *17*
misleading legend   *xv, 25, 241*
mistaken legend   *xv, 140, 240*

Origen   *112*
ostentatiousness   *212*

perseverance   *208*
Philo   *16–17, 24*
polyandry   *184*
polygamy   *184–85*
prophecy   *169*
Prosperity Gospel   *189*

Protoevangelium of James*   3*

remarriage   *184–85*
repentance   *89*
  definition   *57, 100–103*
  in John's Gospel   *58*
  source   *102*
restoration   *88*
Revelation of the Magi   *10*

salvation   *127, 130–31, 143, 236*
Scripture, inerrant   *74*
Scripture, reliable   *30, 76, 83*
Septuagint   *87–88, 118*
sin   *140–41*
Sinner's Prayer   *131–32*
sovereignty   *148*
stewardship   *190–92*
support of ministers   *114, 224*
synagogue   *136, 138*

Tartarus   *51*
tentmaker   *112–13*
tithing   *203*
  Abraham   *203*
  defined   *201–2*
Tyndale New Testament   *22, 177*

urban legend, defined   *xiii*

wealthy   *63–64, 189*
Wessex Gospels   *22*
wise men   *9*
  defined   *11*
  number   *10–11*
  origin   *11–12*
word study fallacy   *126*
worship   *12*

Scripture Index

Genesis
2 *137*
2:20–23 *137–38*
3:16 *137*
13 *18*
14:18–20 *201*
18–19 *4*
41:46 *30*
49:24 *18*

Exodus
3:1 *18*
23:9 *4*
35:30–35 *24*

Leviticus
10:2 *207*
19:33–34 *4*
21 *181*

Numbers
4:3 *30*
12:7 *159*
21:4–9 *46*
24:17 *12*
31:27–29 *203*

Deuteronomy
10:19 *4*
17:6 *69*
19:15 *69*
25:1–3 *83*
28:1–14 *63*
30:14 *130*

Joshua
15:8 *50*

Judges
11 *5*
11:31 *6*

1 Samuel
17 *18*
28:24 *5*

2 Samuel
5:4 *30*
13 *87*

2 Kings
23:8–10 *50*

1 Chronicles
13:10–11   *207*

2 Chronicles
28:3   *50*
33:6   *50*

Ezra
4:18   *118*
7:26–38   *51*

Nehemiah
3:8   *24*
3:31   *24*
8:8   *118*
13:23–24   *118*

Psalms
23:1   *18*
23:4   *43*
27   *50*
80:1   *18*
110:4   *202*
139:7–8   *179*

Proverbs
3:12   *234*

Ecclesiastes
5:10   *191*

Isaiah
2   *178*
2:10   *177–78*
6:9–10   *59*
6:10   *59*
58:6–10   *4*
59:20   *59*
66   *50*
66:24   *50–51, 53*

Jeremiah
4:26   *177*
7:30–34   *50*
15:7   *59*
29:11   *43–44*

Ezekiel
1:1   *30*
16:49   *4*
34:12   *18*

Daniel
2   *11*
2:2   *11*
2:4–7:28   *118*
2:10   *11*

Jonah
3:5   *101*

Micah
5:2   *4*

Zechariah
9:9   *13*

Malachi
3:8   *204*

Matthew
1:6   *13*
2   *9, 11–13*
2:1   *9–10, 28*
2:2   *12*
2:6   *4, 18*
2:8   *93*
2:16   *12*
3   *76*
3:2   *104*
3:7–9   *101*
3:16   *75*
4:15   *120*
5–7   *37*
5:15   *6*
5:29–30   *35*
6   *34*
6:1   *34*
6:1–18   *34, 36*
6:2–4   *35*
6:3   *33*
6:19–21   *36*
6:24   *189*
7:1   *37–41*
7:3–5   *38*

7:6 *38*
7:15 *38, 223*
7:26 *128*
8:5–13 *122*
8:12 *179*
8–20 *26*
9:13 *93*
11:4 *92*
12:41 *101*
13 *22*
13:55 *22*
14–28 *95*
16:13–20 *122*
16:19 *68*
17:27 *93*
18 *69*
18:5 *67–68*
18:15–17 *68, 71*
18:15–20 *38–39*
18:16 *69*
18:18–20 *68*
18:19 *69–70*
18:20 *67–69, 72*
19:24 *62–63*
21:3 *69*
21:5 *13*
21–28 *95*
24:5 *68*
26:31 *18*
27 *80*
27:11 *122*
27:11–14 *122*
27:21 *82*
27:22–24 *82*
27:24 *80*
27:25 *82*
27:26 *79–80, 83*
27:46 *122*
28:7 *93*
28:17 *12*
28:19 *68, 91–93, 95*
28:20 *70*

Mark
1:15 *53*
5:41 *122*
6 *22*
6:3 *21–22, 25*
6:25 *235*

7:25–30 *122*
7:34 *122*
9:47 *49–50, 53*
9:47–48 *53*
10:22 *63*
10:23–27 *63*
10:25 *61–64*
10:32 *63*
10:45 *159*
15:15 *80*
15:34 *122*
15:43 *235*

Luke
1:1–9:50 *19, 30*
1:5 *28*
1:28 *235*
1:39–40 *4*
2 *8, 17, 19*
2:1 *28*
2:1–7 *3*
2:2 *28*
2:6 *4*
2:7 *5–6, 8*
2:8 *16–17, 20*
2:8–12 *15*
2:12 *7*
2:18 *18–19*
2:20 *7*
3:1–3 *28*
3:23 *27–28, 30*
4:17–20 *123*
8:15 *171–72*
9:1–6 *224*
9:14 *28*
9:51–24:53 *77*
10:34 *6*
18:11 *75*
18:25 *63*
22 *75*
22:11 *6*
22:20 *44*
22:29–30 *147*
22:39–46 *77*
22:43–44 *74–75, 77*
22:44 *73–76*
22:59 *28*
23 *81*
23:4 *80*

23:7   *80*
23:14–15   *80*
23:16   *80–82*
23:18   *82*
23:22   *82*
23:23   *82*
23:24   *82*
23:44   *28*

John

1:12   *45*
1:14   *45*
1:15   *28*
1:18   *45*
1:20   *219*
1:30   *28*
1:35–51   *27*
1:43   *89*
2   *29*
2:6   *30*
2:19–20   *28*
2:20   *29*
2:23   *45*
3   *45–46, 122*
3:1–21   *47*
3:14–15   *46*
3:15   *45*
3:16   *37, 43–47, 55, 57, 147, 150*
3:16–21   *44–45*
3:18   *45*
3:19–21   *45, 57, 59*
3:20   *220*
3:21   *45, 220*
3:35   *87*
4:4–26   *123*
5:1   *27*
5:2   *117*
5:14   *57–59*
5:20   *87, 234*
6:5–15   *27*
7:22–23   *39*
7:23   *39*
7:24   *38*
9:22   *219*
9:41   *218*
10   *19*
10:11   *19*
11:3   *234*
11:36   *234*

11:55   *27*
12:1   *27*
12:38   *59*
12:39–40   *58*
12:40   *55, 59*
12:42   *219*
13   *159*
13:1   *27*
13:36   *89*
14:13   *67*
14:14   *67*
15:4   *88*
15:9   *88*
15:10   *88*
15:16   *67*
15:22   *218*
15:24   *218*
16:23–24   *67*
16:26   *67*
16:27   *234*
18:18   *88*
18:33–38   *122*
18:38   *81*
18:40   *82*
19:1   *79, 81–82*
19:2–15   *82*
19:4   *82*
19:6   *82*
19:11   *218*
19:12   *82*
19:13   *117, 121*
19:16   *82*
19:17   *117, 121*
19:20   *117, 121*
19:26   *86–87*
20:2   *87, 234*
20:16   *117*
21   *86–87, 89*
21:9   *88*
21:15–17   *90*
21:15–19   *85, 88*
21:17   *88*

Acts

1:15   *28*
1:19   *121*
2:3   *76*
2:38   *57, 99, 102*
2:41   *28*

3:19 *102, 177*
3:20 *177*
5 *102*
5:31 *102*
5:41 *177*
6:1 *119*
7:45 *177*
9:43 *113*
10:1–48 *107*
10:3 *235*
11:1 *107*
11:3 *107, 235*
11:4 *107*
11:5–16 *107*
11:18 *102*
15:7–9 *107*
15:33 *176*
16:12–40 *106*
16:16–22 *106*
16:30 *105*
16:31 *105–7*
16:31–32 *108*
16:40 *235*
17:2 *235*
18:3 *111, 113*
19:7 *28*
20:28 *19*
20:34 *111*
21:40 *117*
22:2 *117*
22:3 *112*
26:14 *117, 121*
26:20 *102*
28:8 *235*

Romans

1:16 *125–27*
2:4 *102*
3:10–18 *141*
5:12 *140*
5:14 *140*
10 *131*
10:1–13 *133*
10:6–7 *130*
10:8–10 *129*
10:9 *130*
10:9–10 *129–30, 133, 219*
10:13 *133*
14:1 *40*

14:3–4 *40*
15:3 *159*
16:17–18 *223*

1 Corinthians

1:15 *68*
4:12 *111*
5:1–13 *39*
5:5 *69*
6 *176*
6:1 *69*
6:14 *127*
6:19 *176*
8 *114*
9 *114, 224*
9:6 *114*
11 *137*
11:5 *137*
12–14 *137–38*
13:1 *241*
14 *169*
14:3 *169*
14:31 *137*
14:33 *135*
14:34–35 *135–36, 139*

2 Corinthians

8:2–3 *36*
8:5 *36*
8:8–9 *35, 36*
8:9 *159*
9:6 *36*
9:8 *36*
9:12 *36*
11:23–26 *166*
13:5 *149, 237*

Galatians

1:8 *223*
1:8–9 *39*
4:6 *236*
6:6 *224*

Ephesians

1:20 *127*
2 *140–42, 149*
2:1 *140–41*
2:1–2 *149*

2:1–10   *149*
2:2   *149*
2:4   *141*
2:5–6   *149*
2:7   *143*
2:8   *139–40*
2:9   *143*
2:10   *145–50*
3   *235*
3:14–17   *235*
3:17   *234–35*
4   *153–54, 156*
4:7   *153*
4:11   *153*
4:11–12   *151*
4:12   *151–56*
4:15   *153, 241*
4:16   *153*
5:25   *88*

Philippians
1:27   *160*
2   *160–61*
2:1–2   *158*
2:1–5   *158*
2:3   *158*
2:5–11   *158, 161*
2:6   *158–59*
2:6–7   *157–58, 160*
2:6–11   *157*
3:2   *39*
4:13   *43, 163–66*

Colossians
3:15   *234*

1 Thessalonians
2:9   *111*
5   *169*
5:21   *170*
5:22   *167–68, 173*

2 Thessalonians
1:9   *175–78, 180*
2:8   *178*

1 Timothy
2   *137*

2:9   *211*
2:11   *137*
2:13   *137*
3   *182, 195, 199*
3:1–7   *187*
3:2   *181, 183–85, 187*
3:3   *184*
3:4   *198–99*
3:4–5   *196*
3:11   *198*
5:9   *184–86*
5:14   *184*
6   *198*
6:2   *198*
6:10   *64, 189–90*
6:17–19   *189*

2 Timothy
2:10   *147*
2:15   *xi, xiv*
2:25   *102*

Titus
1   *199*
1:6   *198, 200*
3:5   *199*
3:13   *224*

Hebrews
3:13   *209*
6   *207*
6:19   *207*
7   *202–4*
7:1–10   *201–4*
7:2   *201*
7:8   *203*
10   *207*
10:19   *206*
10:19–25   *210*
10:24   *153, 207*
10:25   *205–6, 210*
13:5   *191*
13:20   *19*

James
2   *149*

1 Peter

2:25   *19*
3:1–2   *213*
3:3   *211–12, 217*
3:4   *212*
3:7   *220*
5:2   *19*
5:4   *19*

1 John

1:5–2:2   *221*
1:6   *45*
1:8   *219*
1:9   *217–21*
2:19   *219*
2:23   *219*
3:23   *219*
4:1   *39*
4:9   *45*

5:1   *219*
5:13   *45*

2 John

7   *219*
10   *39, 223–24*

Revelation

3   *64, 228, 230, 235*
3:5   *219*
3:14   *234*
3:14–19   *227*
3:15–18   *232*
3:16   *227*
3:20   *233–35*
6:6   *177*
9:11   *117*
22:19   *75*